Navigating the Cultures of
Health Care and Health Insurance

CULTURE AND HEALTH

Series Editors
A. David Napier and Anna-Maria Volkmann

Culture and Health explores a wide range of subjects that cross disciplinary borders, exploring the contexts – social, cultural, psychological, environmental and political – in which health and wellbeing are created and sustained. Focusing on new and emerging challenges in health-related fields, the series is an engaging and reliable resource for researchers, policymakers and general readers committed to understanding the complex drivers of health and illness.

A. David Napier is Professor of Medical Anthropology, UCL, and Director of UCL's Science, Medicine and Society Network.

Anna-Maria Volkmann is a medical anthropologist and health psychologist, and the UCL Research Lead for the Cities Changing Diabetes programme.

Navigating the Cultures of Health Care and Health Insurance

Highly skilled migrants in the US

Nina Zeldes

First published in 2023 by
UCL Press
University College London
Gower Street
London WC1E 6BT

Available to download free: www.uclpress.co.uk

Text © Author, 2023
Images © Copyright holders named in captions, 2023

The author has asserted her rights under the Copyright, Designs and Patents Act 1988 to be identified as the author of this work.

A CIP catalogue record for this book is available from The British Library.

Any third-party material in this book is not covered by the book's Creative Commons licence. Details of the copyright ownership and permitted use of third-party material is given in the image (or extract) credit lines. If you would like to reuse any third-party material not covered by the book's Creative Commons licence, you will need to obtain permission directly from the copyright owner.

This book is published under a Creative Commons Attribution-Non-Commercial 4.0 International licence (CC BY-NC 4.0), https://creativecommons.org/licenses/by-nc/4.0/. This licence allows you to share and adapt the work for non-commercial use providing attribution is made to the author and publisher (but not in any way that suggests that they endorse you or your use of the work) and any changes are indicated. Attribution should include the following information:

Zeldes, N. 2023. *Navigating the Cultures of Health Care and Health Insurance: Highly skilled migrants in the US*. London: UCL Press. https://doi.org/10.14324/111.9781800083646

Further details about Creative Commons licences are available at https://creativecommons.org/licenses/

ISBN: 978-1-80008-366-0 (Hbk.)
ISBN: 978-1-80008-365-3 (Pbk.)
ISBN: 978-1-80008-364-6 (PDF)
ISBN: 978-1-80008-367-7 (epub)
DOI: https://doi.org/10.14324/111.9781800083646

This book is dedicated to Amir, Lia and Clara. Thank you for being in my life and for all those wonderful big and little moments together.

Contents

List of figures and tables ix
Acknowledgements xi

1 Introduction 1

2 Context and methodology 10

3 'I really dislike insurance . . . I don't know how the concept works': the culture of health insurance 40

4 'I saw an army of doctors walk in . . .': highly skilled migrants' experiences with health care and biomedical diversity in the United States 77

5 'Here I do think before I go to the doctor': highly skilled migrants' barriers to accessing and utilizing health care in the United States 119

6 'Take a vacation, go back to India and get a treatment there': transnational health care practices and strategies navigating US health care and health insurance culture 148

7 Conclusion and outlook 177

References 189
Index 201

List of figures and tables

Figures

3.1 The occurrence of the term 'health insurance', including related terms such as sickness fund, compulsory health insurance in the Corpus of Historical American English (COHA). Source: author.   71

Tables

2.1 Interview length and number of tokens per interview group   23
2.2 Overview of my informants' sociodemographic data across all three groups   24
2.3 Visa categories held by my interlocutors at the time of the interview   25
2.4 Demographic information from my health provider informants   27
2.5 Comparison of actual word mentions and frequency per 10,000 of the category 'alternative medicine' in the narrative corpus   36
3.1 Comparison of key differences in health insurance and health costs between the US, Germany and Japan   52
3.2 Word frequency in narratives per 10,000 for selected terms   63
4.1 Comparison of key differences in health systems between the US, Germany and Japan   80
4.2 Average rating on a scale of 1 to 5 given by my interview partners for health care quality in the US vs average health care quality at home   82
4.3 Differences in attitudes towards health care in physicians in the US as reported by my informants   84
4.4 How often do patients refer to hospital or hospitals in narratives per 10,000 words?   85

4.5	Differences in the health care system mentioned by my informants during the interviews	87
4.6	How often do patients refer to access and primary care in narratives per 10,000 words?	88
4.7	How often do patient informants refer to MRI, CT, scans or test(s), x-ray(s) or ultrasound in narratives per 10,000 words?	92
4.8	Comparison of key differences in pharmaceutical spending, vaccination and pharmacies between the US, Germany and Japan	99
4.9	Answers of interviewed physicians regarding perceived foreign patient behaviours	100
4.10	Differences in medications and treatments available in the US as reported by my informants	101
4.11	Frequency per 10,000 words for selected terms	101
4.12	Use of alternative medicine in home country and the US as reported by my informants	106
4.13	Frequency per 10,000 words of homeopathy, Ayurveda and Kampo as mentioned by my informants	106
4.14	Alternative medicines and treatments used by my informants in their home country and in the US	107
4.15	Number of physicians who received cultural competence training during their medical education	110
5.1	Responses to the interview question: 'Did you have linguistic or cultural misunderstandings at a doctor's visit?'	124
5.2	Key barriers for highly skilled migrants as perceived by their US physicians	140
5.3	Recurring themes of what physicians think their patients need to know	144
6.1	Closed question results of questionnaire: differences in language and culture, opinion of US health care quality, length of stay in the US and first time living abroad	152
6.2	List of most commonly given types of advice for a fellow immigrant to the US health care system	168

Acknowledgements

I am deeply grateful to my supervisor Prof. Dr Hansjörg Dilger, who has been very supportive of this research project from the very beginning and has encouraged me throughout the process. He also provided me with thoughtful feedback on all aspects of this project, from which this work benefitted substantially. All remaining errors in this book are, of course, my own. I also owe a great deal of thanks to Prof. James Giordano, who was kind enough to act as my mentor during my time as a visiting researcher at Georgetown University and also offered me invaluable support during my field research in the United States. Additionally, I would like to thank my secondary supervisor, Prof. Dr Thomas Stodulka, for his interest in my research and his helpful suggestions.

The research that forms the basis for this book, which grew out of my dissertation work, could not have been completed without the support of the German Academic Exchange Service (DAAD), which generously funded my field research with two grants, in 2015/16 (57044996) and in 2016/17 (57210526). I am very grateful for the opportunity the DAAD has offered me. I am also deeply indebted to the Pellegrino Center for Clinical Bioethics and the Kennedy Institute of Ethics. They made it possible for me to be a visiting researcher at Georgetown University, and not only provided me with a space to work in but also connected me with a very helpful and supportive network of fellow researchers. I would especially like to thank Prof. Kevin FitzGerald, Dr David Miller and Marti Patchell at the Pellegrino Center, and Prof. Laura Bishop at the Kennedy Institute of Ethics, for all their help.

This work has also greatly benefitted from the many people who have given me feedback on my research questions, helped me throughout my field research and offered support along the way. In particular, I would like to thank Prof. Heidi Hamilton and the members of the Health Discourse research group for allowing me to present my work in its different stages and to get valuable feedback. I am also grateful to the reviewers of this book for their thoughtful comments and suggestions and the editors at UCL Press for their support and careful review of this book.

Needless to say, this project has only been possible because so many highly skilled migrants and their spouses and physicians were willing to talk and share their experiences with health care and migration with me. For their time, trust and interest in my research I am deeply grateful.

I also want to thank my friends and colleagues for being there for me and encouraging me. I am also thankful to my parents and family for their constant support, and especially to Amir, Lia and Clara, who never lost patience with me on this research project journey and never stopped believing in me. I am deeply grateful for their support throughout my field work, my dissertation and writing this book; without them the project would not have been possible.

1
Introduction

Highly skilled migrants do not commonly find themselves in the medical anthropological gaze and have arguably remained invisible in much of literature and policy, probably because host countries view them as politically, socially and economically acceptable and culturally neutral. The assumption that highly skilled migrants adapt easily to their host society also holds true for the health care setting: an inability to utilize health care successfully due to cultural or structural factors is usually only assigned to patients with cultural and socioeconomic backgrounds that strongly differ from the expected norm.

    This book aims to challenge this assumption by analysing the experiences and expectations of foreign-born skilled professionals with the US health care and health insurance systems, focusing on structural and functional discrepancies within health care and health insurance. In the framework of an ethnographic study based in Washington, DC, a highly modern, international metropolitan area with a large population of foreign professionals, three groups of migrants and their assimilation into US health care and insurance are compared and contrasted: German nationals, who are migrating from one Western industrial country to another; Japanese nationals, who represent migrants from a non-Western but industrial country; and Indian nationals, who come from the so-called 'developing world'. The results of this ethnographic study set out to show that the experiences of these groups should not be viewed in opposition to those of other immigrant groups, but rather act as indicators of remaining barriers for all immigrant groups and other newcomers to the US health care and health insurance systems.

    For this study I have drawn on three main bodies of scholarship. First and foremost, my research builds on medical anthropological scholarship on differences in global and local biomedical practices, as well as the growing interest in the value systems in transnational health culture – that is, the 'need to understand the relation between culture and health, especially the cultural factors that affect health improving behaviours' (Napier et al. 2014: 1; Hahn and Kleinman 1983; Good 1995; Lock and Nguyen 2010; Dilger et al. 2012). Second, this book draws on the growing body of migration studies on transnationalism, transnational elites and highly skilled migrants, which have offered valuable alternatives to understanding immigration simply as a process of assimilation and incorporation, especially for those groups that do not intend to settle in the host society, as is the case for many highly skilled migrants (e.g. Glick Schiller, Basch and Blanc-Szanton 1992; Basch, Glick Schiller and Szanton Blanc 1995; Findlay et al. 1996; Portes, Guarnizo and Landolt 1999; Shore and Nugent 2002; Beaverstock 2005; Favell, Feldblum and Smith 2007; Findlay and Cranston 2015). And finally, this research informs and is informed by the cross-cultural studies in public health and health policy research on attitudes towards health care and health insurance and how they differ worldwide, offering insights into how the particular setup of health care systems can shape patients' expectations, when and how they access care and their satisfaction with health services (e.g. Blendon et al. 1995; Schoen et al. 2005; Schoen et al. 2010; Horton et al. 2014; Dao and Mulligan 2016). The position of this project at the intersection of these different bodies of research will allow me to make substantive contributions to each of them, particularly since – to my knowledge – no research has been undertaken to date regarding the experiences of highly skilled migrants specifically with health care and health insurance in the United States and how these compare to home systems, which can be crucially different, as well as partially similar.

The US is a particularly interesting place to examine these aspects, since its health care system has frequently been called very difficult to navigate and rather complex (Reid 2009; Wetzel 2011), despite the fact that the Unites States is one of the world's most affluent and advanced countries.[1] This is true for citizens grappling with the system (cf. Levitt 2015), and even more so for newcomers, such as immigrants (cf. Calvo, Jablonska-Bayro and Waters 2017). In fact, according to HSBC's Expat Explorer Survey in 2017,[2] the United States was ranked as the 27th best country out of 46 for expats, taking into account aspects such as job security, work/life balance, politics, finance, integration and quality of life. However, when only comparing expats' opinions on health care,[3] the United States dropped in ranking to the second to last country, 45th, followed only by Egypt, which was also ranked last overall. Putting US health care into a global perspective will, as Horton et al. (2014) argue, reveal its peculiarities and open them up for debate, and help address immigrants' barriers to successfully utilizing and accessing health care. Additionally, focusing on the experiences of transnationals that come from one medical setting to another – whether they are physicians or patients – allows researchers a nuanced insight into how differences in health care are experienced, as transnationals are bound to compare and contrast differences in how medicine is practised and how care is accessed (cf. Dilger et al. 2012; Schühle 2018).

In fact, 'Americanness' regarding health care and health insurances (Fox 2005) has been shown to be an area where frictions between local US staff and foreign patients frequently arise. However, previous studies have focused almost exclusively on what Favell, Feldblum and Smith describe as 'ethnic' migrants, for example refugees or low-skilled manual labourers and others that stand in 'the clichéd opposition of "elite"', such as highly skilled migrants (2007: 25; cf. Ong 1995; Fadiman 1997; Clark 2008; Fechter and Walsh 2010). And as multiple studies on cultural competence show, the same seems to be true for research on physicians' views on their migrant patients, whose status is assumed to be low-skilled or uneducated (cf. Paez et al. 2009). In fact, highly skilled migrants have arguably remained invisible in much of literature and policy, because host countries view them as politically, socially and economically acceptable, and as such they are expected to adapt easily to their new environments (cf. Beaverstock 2005) and integrate smoothly into the US health care system. This group is indeed more often than not covered by health insurance and thus nominally able to access health care services in the United States. Also, since they are perceived as 'culturally neutral' and often bring high levels of human and social capital (cf. Shim 2010; Grineski 2011), the physician–patient interaction is assumed to be free of miscommunications and other barriers. Yet this group encompasses a very heterogeneous population with very diverse (biomedical) backgrounds and expectations. Therefore, in this book, I intend to analyse the particular 'cost and constraints' (Favell, Feldblum and Smith 2007: 20) of highly skilled migrants in the United States in order to add to our understanding of the persisting barriers to health care for *all* newcomers to the US health care system and the health care needs of immigrants in particular.

Additionally, the needs and expectations of those who do not plan to permanently integrate into the host society and its medical system but intend to stay for only a short duration, as is the case for many highly skilled migrants, differ from those of other groups of immigrants. They remain understudied and their experiences warrant a closer examination. For this research project, I have thus chosen to examine a group of predominantly temporary, nonimmigrant individuals that have come to the United States as highly skilled workers for a particular job or assignment, including diplomats, visiting researchers and staff of international organizations such as the World Bank, International Monetary Fund and so on. As such, the people in this group enjoy employer-provided health insurance coverage which makes them eligible for accessing health care services in the United States. In particular I will analyse and compare the experiences of three groups entering US medical care: migrants from Western[4] industrial countries – exemplified by German nationals; migrants from a non-Western industrial country – exemplified by Japanese nationals; and migrants from the so-called 'developing world' – exemplified in this study by Indian nationals.

Like the United States, Germany and Japan are both classified as high-income countries; their gross domestic product (GDP) per capita is roughly comparable and they have similar levels of industrialization. Not only are these three nations considered to be part of the Global North, they are also among the seven major developed economies (G7) in the world.[5] Despite these similarities, the attitudes towards health care systems and the ways in which health insurance and health care are set up in these countries will likely influence the experiences of their emigrants to the US in different ways. For example, while Germany is, like the United States, a Western industrialized high-income country, it is also home to the oldest social health insurance in the world that covers nearly all its citizens (cf. Swami 2002). This likely shapes not only Germans' attitudes towards this concept, but also their expectations of what health insurance coverage should entail and the types of health care services that they expect to be available. I will further investigate whether and to what extent their experiences differ from Japanese highly skilled migrants, who come to the United States from a non-Western industrialized country. Japan also has a very long history of providing health insurance to its citizens through a system that was in fact largely modelled on the German system and was also the first non-Western country to achieve full insurance coverage for its population (Reich et al. 2011). India, on the other hand, stands out in many respects. India sends by far the most highly skilled workers to the United States. For speciality occupation visas such as the H-1B visa, for example, in the 10 years leading up to 2017, Indians filed 2,183,112 million petitions, more than seven times as many as China, who ranked second in H-1B petitions.[6] However, it is neither an industrialized nor high-income country, but is classified as a lower middle-income country with a developing economy.[7] India, a part of the Global South, also has a much lower GDP per capita compared to the other three countries in question,[8] and its health care spending is a fraction of those of the other countries. Unlike Germany and Japan, India's health care system is also much more fragmented and large parts of the population are not covered by health insurance at all. It thus stands to reason that their experiences and expectations would differ substantially from the other two groups in question. Thus, I argue that an analysis of the different experiences and expectations towards health care and health insurance of highly skilled professionals from Germany, India and Japan, and how they interact with their access and integration into the US health care system, is a fruitful undertaking that will provide valuable insights into immigrants' health care needs and the role of culture[9] in health care utilization patterns.

Throughout this book, the cultural and structural differences my informants mentioned pertain predominantly to everyday health concerns, rather than those in clinical medicine, although, as Payer (1996) points out, there are differences in both which will likely have an impact on foreign-born patients in a new country. However, variations in the treatments of everyday health concerns tend to be much more palpable for immigrants, including differences in brand names for drugs, which drugs are available over the counter, suggested treatments for minor ailments such as a common cold or skin rashes, when to visit a physician and how long to wait for an appointment, as well as the interaction with one's health insurance. Furthermore, many highly skilled migrants, such as my informants, might be less familiar with the highly scientific medicine in their home country (including emergency procedures, surgeries or chronic diseases), since having the kinds of conditions that could lead to this knowledge might make them less likely to pursue a career abroad in the first place (cf. Dean and Wilson 2009). The study at hand will therefore focus less on differences in emergency treatments and more on everyday medical encounters, insurance coverage and overall satisfaction with health care and health insurance as a whole.

Research questions

The overarching goal of this book is to provide an insight into the specific conditions highly skilled immigrants face when they are navigating the US health care system and to analyse what the persisting barriers are that may ultimately also highlight broader issues affecting all groups of transmigrants within the United States. I will do so by examining the specific structural, functional and cultural differences in health care and health insurance German, Indian and Japanese immigrants are confronted with in the US and how these may inform their decisions and impact their health care seeking. Some of the questions I will address within this framework include:

How does a lack of understanding of the US health insurance system impact foreign patients' satisfaction with health care and their health-seeking behaviours?

What is 'good health care' considered to consist of for US medical staff and their foreign-born patients, and how do unexpected requests for services, treatments and medications impact the transnational physician–patient encounter?

To what extent does a more privileged group of immigrants face cultural and structural barriers, not only when accessing health care but for the entire transnational medical encounter, and how do these experiences shape immigrants' experiences?

Why and to what extent do highly skilled migrants use health care services in the United States, and when do they seek transnational health care, despite being entitled to and able to afford health care services in the US?

Overview of chapters

Throughout the field research and the analysis of the data, I was struck by how intertwined the concepts of health care and health insurance and any barriers associated with them were for my informants. For example, many of them told me about their experiences or voiced their frustration with health care in the United States, when really the issue they had concerns about was one of health insurance coverage or vice versa. While I have attempted to disentangle these issues brought up in the narratives in order to discuss health insurance, health care and barriers associated with these aspects in separate chapters, for many of my informants these were all part of their experience. I will thus refer to all of these concepts to some degree throughout the following chapters.

First, Chapter 2 will familiarize the reader with the context of this study, highlighting in particular the importance of health research in the field of immigration, and will provide an overview of highly skilled migration and reasons why this group warrants a closer examination. Furthermore, the Washington, DC area as a field site will be introduced in some detail, as well as the different groups of informants I spoke with for this research. My own positionality as well as the limitations of my data are also briefly discussed before I introduce the methodology used for the analysis of ethnographic as well as corpus data.

Based on my informants' narratives, Chapter 3 argues that commonsense assumptions of local health insurance not only impede the integration of immigrants into the host country's health insurance system but also influence how immigrants utilize health insurance services. Towards this end, the concept of health insurance and its different structural, functional and social aspects are put in an anthropological perspective and a brief overview of US health insurance is juxtaposed with health insurance realities in Germany, India and Japan.

The fourth chapter will examine what is considered to be part of a 'good' care regime by transnational patients as well as US medical staff and how these views differ. I will also analyse how immigrants access health care in the United States and their experiences with the services, i.e. treatments and medications that are typically prescribed in the US. For this, an overview of the US health care system itself, as well as the biomedical and alternative treatment standards, will be provided, before comparing and contrasting with the health care systems in Germany, India and Japan. In this context I will also consider whether or not physicians view the cultural competence training they received as relevant for addressing any arising dissonances when treating highly skilled migrants, or if their assumed privileged status deems any special treatment unnecessary.

As previous research has frequently treated highly skilled migrants as largely unaffected by barriers to health care, Chapter 5 offers insights into the remaining barriers identified by my informants that persist even if patients have health insurance coverage and are eligible for health care services in the United States. I will furthermore address how we can account for diversity in health culture for those unfamiliar with the system – such as local first-time users and immigrants – and how physicians view their transnational patients' health care experiences. Since barriers to health care have also been identified as impacting immigrants' sense of belonging in the host society, I argue that their study is important to integrating immigrants into the host health care system. Finding ways to also include those who do not intend to stay in the United States in the long term, including high- and low-skilled migrants, is arguably of particular importance in such research, as they tend to be more prone to stay outside of the host society's health care system for as long as possible, for example by delaying health care seeking, which can cause adverse health outcomes.

Chapter 6 focuses on why immigrants often choose not to utilize health care services in the host country, even though they might be covered by their health care plan, but prefer to seek alternatives to the available health care services in the United States in order to access their preferred style of care. While such transnational health care seeking has been discussed previously for other groups of immigrants, here I will demonstrate that highly skilled migrants make similar health care choices and discuss their motivations for employing these options. I will also demonstrate that an understanding of how transnationals engage in health care seeking will not only be able to improve health outcomes, but would also be beneficial for the overall satisfaction in the physician–patient encounter.

In conclusion, Chapter 7 will provide a summary of the key findings of this book and lay out some remaining open questions for future research.

Notes

1. http://www.oecd.org/about/membersandpartners (accessed 6 December 2021).
2. The Expat Explorer, commissioned by HSBC, is an independent consumer research study and aims to provide 'authoritative insights into expats' attitudes, behaviours and opinions on the financial and social aspects of the countries they live in'. The findings are based on the results of a global survey by YouGov in 2017. The 2017 report can be accessed here: https://www.hsbc.com/-/files/hsbc/media/media-release/2017/expat-explorer-global-report-2017.pdf. The most current version of the survey, which is updated periodically with new data, can be accessed here: https://www.expatexplorer.hsbc.com/survey/. Both accessed 6 December 2021.
3. This was achieved by selecting only 'Healthcare' in the section 'Experience/Setting up' of the survey menu on the Expat Explorer Survey website, as above in note 2.
4. In this book, I will use the terms 'Western and non-Western countries' (with 'Western countries' referring to industrialized countries in Europe, North America and Australasia and those outside these regions as 'non-Western countries'), 'Global North' (referring to so-called 'first world' or developed nations) and 'Global South' (referring to developing regions or 'Second and Third World' countries) as a useful albeit crude distinction between these regions, as is common in migration studies (see Leung 2017; Bailey and Mulder 2017; Horton 2013). However, I agree with Dilger and Mattes, who argue that the 'increasing collapse of simplified, postcolonial dichotomies' (2018: 267) such as the distinction of the Global North and Global South, or 'the West and the rest', needs to be re-examined (see also Dilger, Huschke and Mattes 2015).
5. http://www.un.org/en/development/desa/policy/wesp/wesp_current/2014wesp_country_classification.pdf (accessed 6 December 2021).
6. China, as the second biggest group of petitioners, had only filed 296,313 petitions in the same time span, while Japan had filed 21,497 and Germany 18,966 petitions between 2007 and 2017: https://www.uscis.gov/sites/default/files/document/data/h-1b-2007-2017-trend-tables.pdf (accessed 6 December 2021).
7. http://www.un.org/en/development/desa/policy/wesp/wesp_current/2014wesp_country_classification.pdf (accessed 6 December 2021).
8. https://www.cia.gov/the-world-factbook/field/real-gdp-per-capita/country-comparison (accessed 6 December 2021). The United States (#17 out of 229 with a GDP of $60,200),

Germany (#26 with a GDP of $50,900) and Japan (#41, with a GDP of $41,400) all rank in the top 50 countries regarding their GDP per capita, whereas India only ranks at #163, with a GDP of $6,100. See also https://data.worldbank.org/indicator/NY.GDP.PCAP.CD (accessed 6 December 2021).

9   While culture is often thought of in oversimplified terms, including as a nationality, ethnic identity or language (cf. Kleinman and Benson 2006), when I refer to 'culture' in this book I follow Napier et al., who propose a broader definition of culture as something which 'can be thought of as a set of practices and behaviours defined by customs, habits, language, and geography that groups of individuals share' (2014: 3). In their discussion on the importance of culture in health and medical settings, Napier et al. also highlight that '[C]ulture is made up of . . . behaviours and practices . . . that are covert and taken for granted' (Napier et al. 2014: 3), a point of particular relevance in the study of transnational health care, as I will discuss in detail throughout this book.

2
Context and methodology

The overarching goal of this book is to examine the differences between the health cultures of Germany, India, Japan and the United States, and the implications they have for highly skilled migrants from these countries integrating into the US health care system. Yet, in order to answer Hirsch's apt question 'What else, other than culture, shapes immigrant health?' (2003: 243) in this research, I will focus in particular on structural and functional discrepancies in health insurance and health care at the intersection of culture, economics and politics. I also aim to follow Good's suggestion that 'cultural studies of contemporary biomedicine should focus on the dynamics, tensions and exchanges between . . . local and global worlds of knowledge, technology and practice' (1995: 461). This remains an important area of research, particularly since local knowledge can also be translated into power, as Escobar (2001) points out. In the transnational context this means that local knowledge (for example knowing where and what services are available), technologies (awareness of common medical interventions) and practices (how to best approach and speak to physicians, what medications or treatments are commonly prescribed, etc.) in the host society might be unfamiliar to immigrants; this can put them in a position of disadvantage or even leave them feeling powerless. At the same time, '[m]uch of the tension in the clinical encounter, however, does not derive from the existence of diverse health subcultures, nor is it due to a failure in medical education to instil an appreciation of folk models of health and illness; rather, it is a reproduction of larger class, racial, and gender conflicts in the broader society' (Singer 1995: 85). This poses several important questions: for one, if newcomers to the US health care system, such as immigrants, fail to understand the local forms of medical practice, how does this then affect medical practice and immigrant health? Also, if tensions arising from differences in health culture are magnified by class, race and gender, as Singer suggests, does this mean highly skilled migrants and their spouses experience fewer (or any) tensions in their clinical encounters?

In order to address these questions, this research needs to be placed in context. I will thus first provide an overview of transnationalism and the categorization of immigrants and highly skilled migration to the United States, and discuss the reasons why this group warrants a closer examination. I will also demonstrate the importance of health issues for any research on immigrants, by discussing the impact migration can have on individuals on the move. I will then introduce my research participants as well as Washington, DC, where this research was conducted, and the possible impact of my own positionality as a highly skilled expat myself, before describing the qualitative and quantitative analysis tools employed in this book in detail.

Transnationalism, mobility and the categorization of immigrants

Until the 1990s much research viewed migration as 'a single, one-way process' in which immigrants were regarded as uprooted individuals, leaving behind everything they know to come to a new country, where they will subsequently acculturate (Tsianos and Karakayali 2010: 376). The term migration, therefore, as some scholars have argued, might best fit the nineteenth and twentieth centuries (Castles 2000; Smith 2005), while transnationalism as a concept has since been put forth. Transnationalism, Nina Glick Schiller, Linda Basch and Cristina Szanton Blanc maintain, has been fuelled on the one hand by 'the demise of the nation-state and the growth of world cities' (1995: 49), and on the other by cheaper modes of transportation and telecommunications[1] (cf. Vertovec 1999; Castles 2000; cf. Smith 2005; Conradson and Latham 2005b; Portes, Guarnizo and Landolt 1999). The concept has also given rise to 'transmigrants', a new category of immigrants 'whose daily lives depend on multiple and constant interconnections across international borders and whose public identities are configured in relationship to more than one nation-state' (Glick Schiller et al. 1995: 48). In the years since, studies of transnationalism have mainly dealt with either 'transnational elites' or 'developing-world' migrants, and most of the research has focused on the movements of transmigrants from Central America to North America and 'has to some extent become a de facto descriptor of just these patterns of mobility' (Conradson and Latham 2005b: 229; but see also *Journal of Ethnic and Migration Studies* 2005 on transmigrants in Europe, Australia, New Zealand and China).

And while class still remains a determining factor for which individuals can move and how and where they move (Leung 2017), the degree of individuals' 'transnationality' changes over the course of immigrants' lives and should be seen as a 'marker of heterogeneity' rather than a fixed category (Faist et al. 2015: 195). Additionally, while some forms of mobility, such as highly skilled migration, have been actively encouraged and normalized, others, such as seeking asylum, have been discouraged and criminalized, meaning mobility does not benefit individuals equally (cf. Glick Schiller and Salazar 2013; Salazar and Smart 2011).

However, choosing a category or label is a very difficult (and problematic) undertaking, as any classification depends on a multitude of factors, including the individual's motivation to leave their home, the planned length of stay, their ability to work and their presumed willingness to integrate into the host society (Castles 2000; Ku 2009). In fact, the labels that are assigned to individuals or groups – such as expatriate, tourist, traveller, immigrant, migrant, refugee, asylum seeker, displaced or trafficked person – form a kind of hierarchical spectrum, where the worth of transmigrants is valued based on, among other things, their country of origin, destination, ethnicity, religion and socioeconomic background (Crosby 2007).[2] Labels can also have severe consequences in that they serve to 'distinguish, divide and discriminate' (Crawley and Skleparis 2018: 48). This is particularly true in the context of health care, where the assigned category can, for example, determine the eligibility of individuals for health services such as Medicaid in the United States[3] (cf. Horton 2004). In this way, labels can also generate 'a politics to movement' (Crosby 2006: 3) by allowing only certain groups of individuals to move freely and with impunity (for example in order to receive health care services).

Despite the potentially wide-ranging implications of these labels, there are only official definitions for some of these categories (such as 'migrant' and 'immigrant'). Other labels that might be particularly relevant for the research at hand (such as 'highly skilled migrant' or 'expat') do not even have an accepted definition, and many scholars use these terms interchangeably (cf. Cranston 2017; see also Koser and Salt 1997; Jones 2000; Kunz 2016). Moreover, many of these labels of course describe individuals – including the group under investigation in this book – who are from highly diverse backgrounds and, as Bailey and Mulder observe, 'depending on their gender, social positioning and reception in the host society they may face varying degrees of inequalities' (2017: 2698; cf. Hercog 2017). It is therefore important that scholars use an intersectional approach to evaluate the experiences of transnational migrants and recognize the 'interconnectedness of different identities and hierarchical structures' (Anthias 2012: 102; cf. Yuval-Davis, Anthias and Kofman 2005), in particular in the context of class, gender and ethnicity.

Yet to date, much scholarship on immigration has predominantly focused more on the hierarchically and socioeconomically 'lower' end of the migration category spectrum, such as immigrants without a legal status or low-skilled workers (cf. Fadiman 1997; Ong 1995; Clark 2008), driven by an interest in inequality and the mechanisms of 'globalization from below' (Favell, Feldblum and Smith 2007: 16). However, as Favell et al. point out, the 'prototypical avatars of globalization in the skilled, educated, or professional categories' (2007: 15) have largely been absent from recent scholarship, in terms of both ethnographic research and structural analysis, with the discussion on Brain Gain, Brain Drain and Brain Circulation being the only notable exception. It is the experience of just these individuals, however, who appear to have more choice about their mobility, face fewer barriers and be at lower risk of exploitation, that will highlight persisting shortfalls for migrants even under near-ideal conditions.

However, equating being a highly skilled migrant with being privileged is too simplistic.[4] Instead, it is important to acknowledge that mobility – regardless of socioeconomic position – has its costs (cf. Favell, Feldblum and Smith 2007). For many mobility is not necessarily a choice, and for many highly skilled careers, mobility has even become a de facto requirement. A relocation, Butcher writes, can for better or for worse also instigate 'a process of identity re-evaluation' (2010: 24). This may lead to transmigrants feeling insecure or far removed from their cultural comfort zone.[5] Furthermore, living and sustaining a transnational lifestyle also requires – sometimes unwanted – high levels of organization and resources, for example in organizing the international move, getting used to a new place and the new culture and dealing with the loss of one's network of friends and family (Dean and Wilson 2009; Conradson and Latham 2005a). While a relocation can bring financial advantages, denoting upward mobility, it can at the same time cause a decrease in social status or downward mobility (Leung 2017; Faist et al. 2015; Rutten and Verstappen 2014). Many transnationals also report that leading an 'expatriate lifestyle' can be very expensive and have other serious drawbacks, such as the inability to gain insider information on issues of everyday life like housing and schooling, as well as navigating health insurance (Chapter 3) and health care (Chapter 4). I therefore agree with Cangia, who argues that many of the issues highly skilled migrants face raise 'important questions about the meaning of global mobility and "freedom" of movement for those who have long been viewed as "privileged" travelers' (2018: 9).

In fact, more recent research on transnational migrants builds on this new understanding of skilled, educated and professional migrants neither being a global elite nor desolately poor, but something in the middle, fitting a category that could be better described as 'professional, middle-class migrants' (Voigt-Graf 2005: 367), or, as Conradson and Latham suggested, 'middling' transnationals (2005b: 229). As such, these individuals are engaged much like other groups of transmigrants in 'the panoply of mundane efforts – the phone calls, trips to the travel agent, internet usage and grocery shopping – that such mobility is dependent upon' (Conradson and Latham 2005b: 228; cf. Smith 2005). 'Middling transnationals' thus could be a good way to describe all those that do not fit the definition of global elite, including those that work in occupations below their skill level in their host society despite their qualifications, or whose motivations are not based on economic gains, such as participants in GAP programmes or people on overseas sabbaticals or migrating to experience living abroad or hone their language skills or 'self-development' (Parutis 2011). For these reasons, my interlocutors are probably also best described as (middling) highly skilled migrants,[6] although for the sake of simplicity in the following chapters I will refer to my informants simply as highly skilled migrants or transnationals. This categorization, as with all attempts to classify different groups of immigrants, is of course problematic on many accounts; however, I agree with Kunz, who insists that '[I]nstead of developing new typologies, we might want to spend more time critically examining and dissecting existing ones' (Kunz 2016: 96).

And while there are ongoing debates on how to classify different groups of immigrants (cf. Salazar and Smart 2011), the politics of mobility (cf. Vertovec 2007) and an increasing awareness of the consequences of the inherent power relations of such a classification, much less research has focused on how transmigrants view their mobility and how categorization shapes their experiences (for exceptions to this trend, see Koskela 2013; Cranston 2017). In fact, as I will discuss throughout this book, these labels also create certain assumptions, which in turn can influence how individuals see themselves and their chances for successful integration into the medical system and the host society in general (Anthias 2012: 103; cf. Crawley and Skleparis 2018). And even if an individual's assigned category does not directly impact their eligibility for health care services, the way an immigrant is classified by their attending physicians can, nevertheless, shape the physician–patient encounter. For example, many physicians who took part in this research did not feel that their highly skilled patients needed any special consideration in the medical encounter. For example, Dr Silva, an oncologist I spoke with about her experiences with highly skilled migrants, explained to me that 'highly skilled [migrants] maneuver as well [as] or better than the . . . general American population'.[7] Not only did most physicians think highly skilled migrants were in a more privileged position than other patients, several also told me about the additional resources this group of migrants had access to, which as I will demonstrate in the following chapters is not how my informants experienced the US health care and health insurance system. However, if physicians assume that the better education and insurance of their transnational patients 'would be an advantage',[8] this raises the question of how this impacts the experiences this group of highly skilled migrants had in their medical encounters, especially since most of my informants reported some barriers to accessing health care, as discussed in detail over the following chapters.

Why study highly skilled migrants in the United States?

Throughout its history, the US has been one of the biggest receiving countries for immigrants, and it remains so today. In fact, immigration is generally accepted to have served the United States very well and has been an integral part of its economic and political standing (Papademetriou and Yale-Loehr 1996). However, the history of immigration in the US is also, as Batalova describes it, 'a story of increasing regulation and restriction of immigration flows' (2006: 9). Immigration into the United States is most often associated with the so-called 'Age of Mass Migration' between the late nineteenth and early twentieth centuries, which only began to slow down following the two World Wars, the Great Depression and the immigration restrictions that followed these events, during which the only notable exception to the stagnating immigration overall was the politically motivated forced movement of professionals, mainly scientists (Iredale 2001). Immigration to the United States only picked up again during the so-called 'Computer Revolution' in the late twentieth and early twenty-first centuries, when immigration policy started to strongly favour highly skilled migrants over low-skilled labourers, resulting in an influx of immigrants, mainly from Asian countries, notably India and China

(Chiswick and Hatton 2003; Chiswick 2005; Batalova 2006). As of 2018, the United States was still the preferred destination for highly skilled migrants, and their inflow benefits the country, something which is exemplified among other factors by the high numbers of immigrant inventors and Nobel laureates.[9] However, the Trump administration attempted to reduce the number of highly skilled migrants: while on the one hand it called for more merit-based immigration (i.e. favouring skilled migrants over others), on the other it tightened access to highly skilled visa categories, for example through the executive order 'Buy American, Hire American'.[10] Additionally, the Trump administration was 'also weighing additional changes to H-1B [an employment-based visa for specialized occupations] visa requirements, including redefining the "specialty" occupations that qualify for a visa' (see 'My interview partners' below for more on the different visa categories).[11] While the full impact of these policies is yet to be determined, at the end of 2017 applications for the H-1B visa, one of the most common visa types for highly skilled migrants, were already being denied about 10 per cent more often compared to the year before.

Generally speaking, however, highly skilled migrants as a group have received preferential treatment ever since the first restrictive immigration legislation, the Chinese Exclusion Act of 1882[12] (Batalova 2006). The first direct attempt to select immigrants based on skill was the Immigration and Nationality Act of 1952 (INA), which is still the basis for today's US immigration policy. The INA introduced a preference system for certain categories of immigrants – a group including individuals who were in education, had technical training or were in another way seen to be beneficial to the United States – which were given priority over others, and caps on their respective numbers were put in place. The Immigration Acts of 1965, 1970 and 1990 saw the creation of different visa categories for (temporary) skilled workers, while quotas on national origins were lifted and rights of skilled visa holders expanded,[13] which eventually led to the creation of the 'alphabet soup' of visa categories (Favell, Feldblum and Smith 2007: 18) that still marks US immigration policy today.

Of the roughly 232 million international migrants worldwide, about 35 per cent hold a tertiary degree. The United States is home to the largest number of immigrants of any country, with 20 per cent of total immigrants worldwide, of which about 29 per cent are college educated[14] (OECD-UNDESA 2013; Findlay and Cranston 2015; Batalova 2006; Lowell 2007). Highly skilled migrants are thus a substantial group within the overall discussion on international migration, which warrants a closer examination.

The experiences of highly skilled migrants probably stand in stark contrast to other groups of immigrants, since they have more choice about their mobility, experience fewer barriers and are less likely to be exploited and could therefore be described as 'less disadvantaged' (Favell, Feldblum and Smith 2007: 16). However, highly skilled migrants are by no means a homogeneous group, and Favell and colleagues argue convincingly for the importance of resisting this 'clichéd opposition of "elite" and "ethnic" migrants' and urge us to remember that '[b]ehind the image of global elites lie other socially differentiated realities' (2006: 2). And although Favell et al. have set forth a research agenda arguing for the need for a 'whole new range of empirical studies' (2007: 25), very little research has been conducted on this group and their experiences in general, and on the social and cultural aspects of this group of migrants in particular.[15] Additionally, when highly skilled migrants are the main emphasis of research, more often than not the focus lies on the flow from the Global South to the Global North,[16] leaving out the experiences of a large subset of highly skilled migrants (cf. Kunz 2016). Generally, the invisibility of this group within the literature is problematic on many counts:

(1) Treating highly skilled migrants in opposition to other immigrants does not take the heterogeneity within this group and the associated consequences of these differences into account, as this group is far from consisting of only 'highly mobile individual careerists' (Yeoh and Willis 2005: 270), but also includes nurses, students and various mid-level employees. Also, individuals who cross the border as nominally unskilled migrants because they are unable to transfer their skills to the new country can or should arguably be classified as highly skilled. The same goes for highly skilled asylum seekers or refugees (cf. Sandoz 2016).[17]

(2) Immigration for purposes other than economic betterment or political refuge but as a lifestyle choice is no longer seen as reserved for the 'global elite' (Beaverstock 2005; Findlay 1996; Iredale 2001; Koser and Salt 1997) and has become a much more 'normal and almost taken-for-granted part of the lifecycle' (Conradson and Latham 2005a: 288; cf. Cranston 2017; Salazar and Smart 2011). In fact, as globalization has opened up migration opportunities for the middle class, treating those that migrate categorically as 'elites' has become unwarranted. On the contrary, those who have opted for an international move often did not have as ample opportunities as the 'true' elite might have at home. Highly skilled individuals who

opt for migration might thus be those who see a need to improve their social standing.[18]

(3) When low-skilled transmigrants are described in direct juxtaposition to their highly skilled counterparts as 'more permanent, stable, often historically rooted' (Yeoh and Willis 2005: 270), this leaves the impression that highly skilled migrants show no interest in their host society or in their society of origin and are not 'embodied bearers of culture, ethnicity, class or gender' (Yeoh and Willis 2005). Looking at transnational communities, Smith argues that it is important not to see them as 'timeless cultural wholes' and warns against seeing these communities as 'celebratory' or 'romantic' (2005: 238). Moreover, this view implies that on the merit of being a highly skilled migrant alone, these individuals have a smoother migration experience and face less discrimination or exclusion than low-skilled migrants and can effortlessly integrate into their host societies. It is thus important to employ an intersectional approach that includes race, ethnicity, class, gender and age for the analysis of highly skilled migrants' experiences, too (cf. Kofman 2014).

(4) As discussed above, the classification of immigrant categories is mainly a political decision, and in the case of highly skilled migrants represents an 'interplay of three broad conceptual bases, centered on the migrant, the state and the employer' (Koser and Salt 1997: 287). However, how valuable a 'skill' is, is highly context-dependent and is determined not only by the time, place and gender but also by the specific requirements of employers (Hercog 2017). Additionally, highly skilled migrants are not immune to being subject to more reserved feelings, as many US-born workers would prefer fellow US natives to be employed in the kinds of jobs that highly skilled migrants are employed in (Regets 2001). This is particularly noteworthy since, as Iredale (2001) points out, increasing numbers of temporary immigrants may also have a negative impact on the treatment of permanent migrants. Also, since immigration status is dependent on employment status in the United States (e.g. the H-1B visa), foreign-born professionals are sometimes underpaid or otherwise exploited by their employers, for example when they are asked to work additional (unpaid) hours in order not to get laid off. Discrimination based on ethnicity, cultural nonconformity or even being outspoken about not wanting to settle permanently in the host country can affect this group of transmigrants.[19]

Thus, treating highly skilled migrants as an elite group seriously underplays the fact that their mobility has 'its own costs and constraints' (Favell, Feldblum and Smith 2007: 20) and highlights the need for a deeper analysis of the assumptions made about their smooth and barrier-free movement, as well as the level of choice they and their families experience. Also, as Fechter and Walsh point out, '[i]t is important, however, not only to "add privileged migrants and stir" (to borrow a phrase from feminist critiques), but to ask how the study of mobile professionals may contribute to reconceptualising mainstream migration studies and methods' (2010: 1198). In the context of transnational health care, I argue, research on highly skilled migrants will bring to light the limitations that even this overall privileged group of individuals encounters, despite being 'endowed with the kinds of levels of human and social capital most likely to facilitate the real construction of global lives' (Favell, Feldblum and Smith 2006: 5). This study aims to add to this research.

The impact of migration on health

Health and health outcomes tend to be different for immigrants and US-born individuals. For example, in his study, Ku analysed the medical costs of insured immigrants and discovered that 'immigrants as a group consume a disproportionately small share of medical care in the US ... even after controlling for level of health insurance and other confounding factors' (2009: 1324, 1326). Immigrants are also treated for chronic conditions less often and are less likely to report poor health, although Shetterly et al. argue in their 1996 study that what constitutes good health strongly depends on cultural differences as well as ethnic variations. Self-rated health may therefore not give an accurate answer to questions about health status. Despite this, most research points to the fact that immigrants, especially recent immigrants, have better health outcomes than US citizens and lower mortality rates (cf. Viruell-Fuentes (2007), who points to studies showing lower mortality rates and more positive outcomes regarding certain risk factors such as cardiovascular conditions).

There are several possible explanations for what has been called the 'healthy immigrant effect'[20] (McDonald and Kennedy 2004; Malmusi, Borrell and Benach 2010). For example, through what Dean and Wilson call a 'self-selection process', only the healthiest individuals can afford to move for both physical and financial reasons (2009: 200). Additionally, some countries might have medical screenings in place that filter out any individuals that may 'pose a threat to public health or overburden the health care system' (Dean and Wilson 2009: 200). However, any health advantage the healthy immigrant effect bestows on recent immigrants usually deteriorates quickly – and in spite of potential improvements in their socioeconomic status. This is often blamed on the process of acculturation where 'behaviors, attitudes and values prevalent within American society' are assimilated by the newcomers (Lopez-Class, Castro and Ramirez 2011: 1558) and any 'culture-related protective factors' are lost (Viruell-Fuentes 2007: 1524).[21] However, evoking culture as a main explanation for health differences is problematic, as it tends to blame patients rather than their circumstances. Viruell-Fuentes, Miranda and Abdulrahim argue, for example, that 'employing acculturation as the central concept in the examination of immigrant health outcomes in the United States ignores the sociohistorical contexts of migration, the racialization of contemporary immigrants, and the role these factors play in the differential social integration of immigrants' (2012: 2100). Additionally, as Malmusi and colleagues write, these should be seen as 'the late-effect of cumulative inequality . . . in the place of destination, with chronic exposure to work hazards, poor living conditions, hardship and discrimination' (2010: 1611). Furthermore, the loss of one's social network, such as family and friends, as well as changes to one's social status also play a part in this.

At the same time, most research on the impact of migration on health has been done on racial and ethnic minorities and on low-income and undocumented immigrants (cf. Ku and Matani 2001). And this is often for good reason, since immigrants with a low socioeconomic status tend to have less access to health care, are more often uninsured and thus more often suffer from undiagnosed conditions and experience more serious repercussions from barriers in health care than other groups of immigrants (cf. Ku and Matani 2001; Malmusi, Borrell and Benach 2010). Since health practices are often also intimately linked with migration experiences and how well one has integrated into the host society (Dyck and Dossa 2007), or whether or not individuals experienced 'othering' (Viruell-Fuentes 2007), low-income immigrants tend to be more affected. Highly skilled migrants, on the other hand,[22] are not always looking to integrate into the host society due to short-term work assignments, have better access to insurance and are generally less likely to experience discrimination (see also Chapter 5). From this perspective it seems obvious that highly skilled migrants are less affected by negative migration-related health effects.

This was generally also how the physicians I spoke with saw their highly skilled transnational patients, as they 'tend to follow health advice and be healthier in general, exercise and eat healthily and take medications when they need it'.[23] Dr Costas, a paediatric resident in his late twenties who had come from Southern Europe in 2013 to complete his medical training in the United States in a large hospital, explained to me in detail why highly skilled migrants tended to be healthier:

> A highly skilled migrant, even if something not that important is going on, they gonna seek help, because they have the ability to afford that and their insurance might also cover that. But even if it doesn't because of their background, they gonna seek for help. If you have immigrants in from another type of like category they really might postpone going to seek care until it's like too late sometimes.
> (Dr Costas, Paediatrics)

However, since unemployment has also been linked to adverse effects on immigrants' health and mental health, being highly skilled does not make them 'bullet-proof'. In fact, in a study of highly skilled migrants in Canada, Dean and Wilson (2009) found that many individuals were not able to find work in their profession and thus suffered from or feared what has been termed 'deskilling', which describes the loss of skills related to one's profession.[24] Dean and Wilson even argue that 'employment is particularly important for skilled immigrants who have their personal identity and social status tied to a number of facets of employment' (2009: 194). Furthermore, not being able to find work on one's skill or income level can also make life very difficult in areas where highly skilled migrants choose to settle (so-called 'expat bubbles') and can lead to a loss of social status. And since men are much more likely to be the leading migrant and women tend to give up their careers and become 'trailing spouses', there is also an inherent gender inequality even among highly skilled migrants (cf. Gideon 2011; Baldassar 2014), which can also impact women's health.

Thus, although it is probably fair to say that highly skilled migrants are in a better position to maintain their health after migrating to the United States than other groups of migrants, the impact of their mobility on their ability to maintain their health warrants a more detailed examination. Over the next chapters I will therefore explore how German, Indian and Japanese highly skilled migrants in the United States integrate into the US health insurance and health care system and which barriers they face, despite their overall more privileged socioeconomic background.

Research design and methodology

While this book first and foremost draws on the analysis of narratives from in-depth interviews, I have employed both qualitative and quantitative research methods to analyse my data, which includes 65 interviews and extensive notetaking, as well as several corpora: both constructed from the narratives in these interviews and openly accessible ones. This study and its research methods have been approved by the Institutional Review Board (IRB) of Georgetown University (ID: 2015-0684).[25]

My interview partners

For this research study I conducted a total of 65 interviews. Of these, 48 interviews were with highly skilled migrants (n=36) and their spouses (n=12) from Germany, India and Japan living in the Washington Metropolitan Area, and the remaining 17 were with physicians and dentists practising in the area. Among the highly skilled migrants and their spouses, 15 of my informants were Germans, 18 were Indians and 15 were Japanese. To protect the confidentiality of my informants, all names used in this book are pseudonyms and, in most cases, the place of work of my informants will not be disclosed (with the exception of embassy staff, as (1) their work situation is so different that it seems necessary, and (2) since, for example, being German is not a distinguishing factor among diplomatic staff at the German embassy, this did not compromise my informants' confidentiality).

Almost all interviews were conducted in a face-to-face meeting in a place of the informants' choosing in Washington, DC or the surrounding suburbs, usually their office, a coffee shop nearby or in a few instances their home or my home.[26] Additionally, three interviews were conducted via Skype (one Indian and two Japanese informants) and one via phone (one medical provider). Except two German interviews, all interviews were conducted in English. The interviews conducted in German were translated by the author and were included in English translation in the keyword analysis (see 'Quantitative analysis' below).[27] All but two interviews were audio-taped and transcribed verbatim. One (German) informant asked not to be audio-taped and I took extensive notes during the interview, and one (Indian) informant preferred to fill out the questionnaire in writing.

As Table 2.1 shows, since I spoke to 18 Indian transnationals, the total length of their interviews unsurprisingly lasted the longest and also

Table 2.1 Interview length and number of tokens per interview group

	No. of interviews	No. of words/tokens	Interview length
German	15	46,249	8 h 30 min
Indian	18	73,704	11 h 15 min
Japanese	15	38,760	10 h
Physicians/Dentists	17	55,496	9 h 50 min
TOTAL	65	214,209	39 h

included the largest number of words. Yet, while both the German and Japanese groups included 15 informants, the Japanese corpus is much smaller, despite the fact that the interviews lasted a comparatively long time (around 10 hours in total, compared to only 8.30 hours for the German interviews and 11.25 hours for Indians). This might also be indicative of the lower levels of confidence in English of my Japanese informants and the high levels of confidence in the same among Indians, as discussed in more detail in the next section below.

The highly skilled migrants

The German, Indian and Japanese informants I spoke with were working for (or had spouses working for), among others, the World Bank, the National Institutes of Health, the Inter-American Development Bank, the International Monetary Fund, Georgetown University, the *Washington Post*, the German Embassy, a German retail company, a German car company and one German print medium, all of which had offices in the DC area. The majority of my informants were female (about 60%),[28] in a domestic relationship (80%), and slightly less than half of my informants had children (48%).[29] My informants were on average 40 years old, had been in the United States for 7.6 years and had fairly high self-rated English language confidence (4.3, on a scale of 1 to 5). The vast majority were very highly educated and held either a master's degree (40%) or a PhD (45%), although the distribution varied substantially across the three groups (see Table 2.2).

My informants also rated their overall health (on a scale of 1 to 5) as fairly high, with Germans rating their health on average the highest (4.7), followed by the Japanese (4.5) and Indian interviewees (4.4).

Table 2.2 Overview of my informants' sociodemographic data across all three groups

	German	Indian	Japanese
Male	4 (27%)	9 (50%)	6 (40%)
Female	11 (73%)	9 (50%)	9 (60%)
In a domestic partnership	12 (80%)	17 (94%)	9 (60%)
Children	10 (66%)	8 (44%)	5 (33%)
Age, average[1]	37.6 [32–50]	37.6 [32–52]	42.5 [29–66]
Average of self-reported health on a scale of 1 to 5	4.7 [4–5]	4.4 [3–5]	4.5 [3–5]
Average length of residency	4.13 [1–14]	10 [1–23]	5.2 [2–16]
Average English confidence on a scale of 1 to 5	4.2 [1.5–5]	4.9 [4–5]	3.8 [2.5–5]
Holds a PhD	5 (33%)	9 (50%)	8 (53%)
Holds a master's degree as highest degree	6 (40%)	8 (44%)	5 (33%)
Holds a bachelor's degree as highest degree	0	1 (0.05%)	1 (0.06%)
Other	4 (27%)	0	1 (0.06%)

[1] Five informants did not give their age (1 German, 2 Indians and 2 Japanese).

The vast majority (38 out of 48) of my transnational informants also reported no change in their overall health since coming to the United States, while 6 thought their overall health had improved and only 4 experienced a deterioration in their health (largely consistent with the findings discussed in 'Impact of migration on health' above). Across the sample of 48, this group of highly skilled migrants also covered a wide range of visa categories, where over 10 different non-immigrant and immigrant visa categories as well as 2 non-visa categories were represented (see Table 2.3 below).[30]

The medical service providers

The physicians and dentists I spoke with mainly worked in individual offices in Washington, DC itself as well as the surrounding suburbs, but I also spoke to physicians from the Georgetown University Medical Center

Table 2.3 Visa categories held by my interlocutors at the time of the interview[1]

			German	Indian	Japanese
Non-immigrant visa categories					
Temporary worker	H-1B	Person in specialty occupation		3	1
	H4	Family members of the H-1B worker		1	
	L2	Intra-company transferee	1		
Exchange visitor	J1	Exchange visitor, e.g. professor, scholar, etc.	1	3	4
	J2	Spouses and dependants of J-1 exchange visitors		1	
Employees of international organizations	G4	Appointment at a designated international organization … and their immediate family members	3	4	3
	G2	Representatives of a recognized government … and their immediate family members		1	
Diplomats and foreign government officials	A1	Diplomat or foreign government official	3		
Students	F1	University or college student	2		2
Immigrant visa categories					
Employer-sponsored – employment	E1	Treaty trader	1		
Non-visa categories					
		Green Card & AOS [Adjustment of Status, i.e. those waiting on their Green Cards]: permanent residents	4	4	3
		US citizens		2	1

[1] https://travel.state.gov/content/travel/en/us-visas/visa-information-resources/all-visa-categories.html (accessed 20 January 2022).

and Sibley Memorial Hospital, both in the District of Columbia. Most of my medical informants were in Paediatrics[31] (n=5) and Family Medicine (n=3), followed by Internal Medicine (n=2), Oncology (n=2) and Psychiatry (n=1). I also chose to speak with several dentists (n=4), as dental issues had been frequently brought up by the highly skilled migrants during the interviews.

Among the medical providers I spoke with, 5 were born in the United States and 2, who had been born in Russia and China respectively, had come to the US before the age of three (which I included in Table 2.4 in the category 'Grew up in the US'). The others had immigrated from Germany, Israel, Greece, Thailand, Portugal and Colombia and had resided in the United States at the time of the interview for an average of 15.5 years. And while many of them mentioned to me that they had agreed to participate in the study because their own migration background made them acutely aware of immigrants' health care needs, interestingly none of them referred to themselves as highly skilled migrants.[32] The average years of working experience among my medical informants was 16.2 years, and while about half of my informants had only received medical training in the United States, the other half had also received medical training in their country of origin. Due to the very international nature of my sample, it is also unsurprising that the majority of my informants spoke two to three languages besides English with some degree of confidence, as Table 2.4 below shows.

Washington, DC as a field site

The field research for this project was conducted in the Washington Metropolitan Area between 2015 and 2017. This area, sometimes also referred to as DMV (District, Maryland, Virginia), comprises the city of Washington in the District of Columbia (hereafter Washington, DC or simply DC), the so-called 'Inner Core', with the neighbourhoods immediately bordering the city, and the 'Inner Suburbs' in the neighbouring states of Maryland (or MD), to the north and east, and Virginia (or VA) to the south-west. The term DMV also sometimes includes 'Outer Suburbs' and 'Far Suburbs' (cf. Singer, Wilson and DeRenzis 2009); however, all interviews were conducted in DC itself, the 'Inner Core' and the 'Inner Suburbs', a roughly 20-mile radius around DC.

Washington, DC is a relatively small city housing over 700,000 residents, of whom about 12 per cent (around 85,000) are foreign-born.[33] The DMV is not only one of the fastest-growing metropolitan areas in the United States, with much of this growth resulting from incoming

Table 2.4 Demographic information from my health provider informants

Male	8
Female	9
Average age	44 (ranging from 29 to 68)
Years of professional experience	16.2 (ranging from 1 to 43)
Grew up in the US[1]	7
Average stay of those born abroad[2]	15.5 (ranging from 4 years to 30)
Native English speakers	9
Speaks only English	3
Speaks two languages with confidence[3]	8
Speaks three languages with confidence	2
Speaks four languages with confidence	4

[1] This includes two of my physician informants that were born in China and Russia respectively but immigrated to the United States before the age of three.
[2] Excluding the two informants that had immigrated as toddlers.
[3] Self-rated language confidence has been included here only if they rated their confidence speaking as higher than 2 (on a scale from 1 to 5).

foreign-born residents, but it also has one of the country's largest immigrant populations (rank 7 according to the 2000 census) (Price et al. 2005). The area is home to immigrants from over 190 countries and territories, and according to Singer et al. it is known 'as a cosmopolitan place that prides itself on racial and ethnic diversity, a thriving knowledge-based economy, and relative affluence' (2009: 3). While in other US cities one immigrant group tends to dominate, in DC 'no single national group dominates' (Price et al. 2005: 68), although the bulk of immigration to DC is from Latin America (45.1%), particularly El Salvador (including both low- and high-skilled migrants). Regarding immigrants from Germany, India and Japan residing in DC, Indians represent the largest group, with 3,366 (about 3.9%), followed by 2,065 Germans (2.4%) and 420 Japanese residents (0.5%), the smallest group.[34]

Since the concentration of highly skilled workers is generally higher in educational or industrial centres, it is not surprising that skilled workers make up one third of the labour force in Washington, compared to most other US states, where the rate is well under 20 per cent. In fact, the city has seen a steep increase in 'high-tech and well-paying jobs' (Price et al. 2005: 66), for example in the biomedical and information technology industries.[35] The importance of highly skilled workers is also reflected in the percentage of foreign-born workers among the highly skilled (Batalova 2006) and according to the American Immigration Council the foreign-born residents in DC play an important role in the skilled labour force.[36] And with 57.3 per cent of immigrants holding at least a college degree, immigrants are even slightly better educated than residents born in the United States (56.6%). Immigrants also made up 17.9 per cent of the labour force, with the largest group being employed by professional, scientific and technical services. In fact, in DC immigrants are more likely to work in the sciences (44.2%) than in cleaning and maintenance (42.6%), production (36.0%) or food preparation and service (22.6%) (American Immigration Council 2017). Additionally, there are roughly 10,000 foreign students in DC (American Immigration Council 2015). The immigration flow in the DMV area is also markedly shaped by the fact that there are over 175 embassies and ambassadors' residences staffed with international workers living in the area, making DC a very culturally diverse place.[37]

Price et al. thus argue that DC seems to be an untypical example of what immigration areas in the United States look like, making the city a possible 'prototype of a new postindustrial immigrant gateway' (2005: 62). Indeed, my informants, and especially those that had worked abroad before, mentioned that it was the cosmopolitan and culturally diverse feel that made DC a special place for them. In fact, several of my informants felt they could belong more in DC than in other places, where they would stand out more. Jonas, a German embassy worker in his early thirties who had been stationed in several countries before being posted to DC, for example, explained to me that being an expat in DC was nothing special, especially compared to other places:

> But here that doesn't mean anything. Well, I mean, if you say in [name of country] or where we were before, that you are from the embassy, all doors open. Well, in [name of city] just where we were before, if you say you are from the consulate general, they were flabbergasted. I mean, in that city they have 1.5 million inhabitants, maybe 300 expats, that is something different than having 1 million inhabitants and half a million expats. Well, here, here you are nothing special as a diplomat and you just have to accept that.[38]
>
> (Jonas, German male, A1 visa, in the United States since 2014)

Washington, DC – at least the more affluent areas where most transnationals live – 'seems at least in this square mile, in this bubble that we live in'[39] to be an unusual place in that it was characterized by several of my informants as particularly international and open-minded. One example appeared when I discussed immigration status with Britta, who at the time of our interview was a 42-year-old German Green Card holder who had come to the United States in 2004 on an A2 diplomatic visa. Britta, who was married to a US citizen, explained to me that being in DC, 'a place where there are so many people with so many different backgrounds, who ended up here for one reason or another',[40] made it very easy for her not to stand out or feel like an outsider.

The cosmopolitan 'feel' of DC also made a difference when it came to health care seeking, because many physicians themselves were immigrants or had at least attended to many immigrant patients,[41] which made many of my informants feel that being a foreigner there had no impact on how they were treated in the medical setting. The 46-year-old Takeshi, for example, who had come to DC from Japan in 2013 to work for a large international company, felt that it was his capacity to pay rather than his ethnicity that shaped his health care experiences in Washington, DC.

Given this research location, then, we need to keep in mind that both the kind of immigrants living there and the opportunities they enjoy and the experiences they make likely differ substantially from those who live in other cities in other US states and those who live in more rural settings. The same is certainly true for the physicians working in DC. As such, this book is deeply shaped, as Viruell-Fuentes put it, 'by time, place and context' (2007: 1530).

Positionality and limitations of data

While the goal of this research project is to examine the experiences and expectations of highly skilled migrants within US health care and health insurance, their opinions on the quality of health care in the US and their country of origin and so on are not meant to be interpreted as factual statements and should not be seen as an attempt to assess differences in health care delivery or biomedical standards (cf. Schühle 2018 on immigrant physicians' assessments of biomedical differences). Instead, my informants' narratives are meant to highlight the importance of their expectations and previous experiences with health care at home and in the host society for their assessment of the services they access and barriers they experience when attempting to do so.

Additionally, the fact that I am a highly skilled migrant from Germany myself,[42] and as such nominally fit the prerequisites for one of the groups of informants I recruited for this study, certainly influenced my data collection process in many ways. For example, in the conversations leading up to the interview, my interlocutors and I often discovered that our experiences were quite similar, and we frequently discussed common experiences pertaining both to the research area and other areas of life. This often included our reasons for coming to the United States, potential plans for leaving and what we felt were the advantages and disadvantages of living in the US. Also, since 46 per cent of my informants held a PhD degree, many took an active interest in my research or reminisced about their student lives. My status as a German doctoral student may have also influenced the providers I spoke with in how they reported their experiences or phrased their answers when I asked them to speak about the German, Indian and Japanese highly skilled migrants they had been seeing as patients.

My status thus probably affected the 'distance' between myself and informants, for better or worse (cf. Mays and Pope 2000). For example, I was probably more prone to bringing my own 'perspectives and concerns' (Charmaz 1996: 34) to the analysis process and might thus have failed to accurately describe my informants' opinions, by making assumptions based on my own experiences and expectations with US health care. On the other hand, the similar backgrounds of my informants and I might have enhanced rapport and encouraged informants to share their experiences with me. Cranston writes that due to the similarity of herself and her informants, she felt as if she 'embodied [her] research subjects' (2017: 5), which at times feels like a good description of the connection I experienced with some of my informants; however, like Cranston, I also cannot be sure 'what effect my race, or gender had upon my respondents' (2017: 5). For example, while, like me, most of my informants have brought medications from visits home or visited a physician, I might have made assumptions about understanding their reasons for doing so based on my own, failing to take differences such as gender, race and socioeconomic backgrounds into consideration. Thus, while I tried to approach the data without 'personal and intersectional biases', all data needs to be seen as influenced by my 'prior assumptions and experience' (Mays and Pope 2000: 51).

Another pitfall of the research at hand may be what Wilding calls the anthropologist's tendency to 'fetishize' migration. She rightfully asks, 'When a group of individuals have their work and identities so completely dependent on reproducing and benefiting from conditions of migrancy and transnationalism, is it possible that their theoretical and research perspectives on transnationalism might be considerably influenced by this personal experience?' (2007: 338). This might be particularly the case in this research, since I share a cultural background with one group of informants, although this is not altogether unusual in transnational research, as shown by the examples of Cangia (2018), who, as a trailing spouse herself, worked with fellow trailing spouses in Switzerland, and Cranston (2017), a British expat in Singapore who conducted research among fellow Brits there.

Although I have attempted to address these issues by using an intersectional approach (cf. Anthias 2012) while analysing the data, they will most likely have shaped my interpretation, at least to some degree. As Charmaz points out, 'any observer's worldview, disciplinary assumptions, theoretical proclivities and research interests will influence his or her observations and emerging categories' (1996: 32) in the process of data analysis. Also, my results of course are limited, as Messias writes, '[d]ue to the methodological approach . . . in the sense that they are informed by the specific social, cultural, class, occupational, health, and migration experiences' (2002: 199).

Qualitative analysis

Due to the explorative nature of the research questions at hand, I followed a grounded theory approach for the analysis of the transcribed narratives (cf. Strauss and Corbin 2008). After listening to and transcribing the audio-taped interviews, I conducted the analysis of the data in two stages and developed all codes and categories from the data itself (cf. Charmaz 1996). While some of the key themes of this research project – each of which will be discussed in the following chapters – were in large part preconceived and included in how the questionnaire was set up – that is, questions regarding informants' experiences with immigration, health insurance, health care, biomedical diversity and barriers to accessing health care – several additional sub-categories and concepts soon emerged. Since I had begun analysing the narratives during the data collection period, I was able to include some targeted probing during the interviews on some of these themes that had emerged early on in the research phase.

During the first-stage analysis, I carefully read and re-read all verbatim transcripts and started coding the data using both open and axial coding approaches (Strauss and Corbin 2008), identifying significant narrative themes that occurred across interviews, such as 'health care costs', 'access to services' and 'insurance', each of which included several sub-categories. As I had more than two data sources (i.e. interviews with German, Indian and Japanese highly skilled migrants as well as physicians) and also data from different data collection methods (i.e. narratives as well as results from the keyword and collocation analysis, see below), in a second analysis stage I also compared the data across sources to 'look for patterns of convergence to develop or corroborate an overall interpretation' (Mays and Pope 2000: 51). I will elaborate this point below.

Quantitative analysis

For the quantitative research, I conducted frequency and collocation analysis on a number of corpora. The corpora included here are the narrative data from the interviews, historical data from print publications and contemporary data from US newspapers and web data from US domains. These corpora are searchable by frequency, collocation and concordance, which proved to be a very useful analysis, not only in confirming hypotheses, but also in highlighting some of the differences across the groups under investigation here. Although these research methods only had a supplemental character in this book and are to the best of my knowledge not widespread in anthropology, they provided useful insights and were a fruitful addition to the qualitative analysis of narrative data. As this type of analysis is based in the field of linguistics, specifically corpus linguistics but also critical discourse analysis (cf. Baker et al. 2008), I will first introduce some of the key terminology, before introducing the analysis process I applied:

(1) Tokens are the smallest unit in a corpus (i.e. a large body of text) by which the size of the corpus is specified. Tokens are often the equivalent of a word form; however, punctuation marks, numbers and so on are also tokens.
(2) Collocation analysis is the analysis of words that appear together more frequently than expected based on the frequency of each word by itself. This can be used, for example, to expose certain biases, for example the frequent pairing of 'Obamacare' and 'repeal'.
(3) Concordance analysis is the analysis of the contexts in which words or parts of speech appear – that is, which words precede or follow the word in question in specific instances. For the study at hand, this was used to eliminate ambiguous words from the frequency analysis, for example to eliminate the use of the word 'test' when the context was an academic rather than a medical one.

(4) Frequency analysis is the analysis of how frequently tokens or collocations occur in a corpus. For this study I have given the frequency per 10,000 tokens (hereafter per 10,000 words) to enable better comparisons across the different corpora.

The narrative corpus

For the analysis of this corpus, I have mainly employed concordance and frequency analysis. While the corpus of all the narratives transcribed includes a total of 214,209 tokens, I have only included the narratives of the transnationals for the frequency analysis in order to better compare the three patient groups and their attitudes. This patient corpus includes in total 158,713 tokens. Since the length of the interviews as well as the number of interviews varied across all three groups, the Indian corpus is by far the largest (73,704 tokens), followed by the German corpus (46,249 tokens). The Japanese corpus, with 38,760 tokens, is the smallest.

While the entire corpus includes 5,829 word types, for the frequency analysis I have focused only on those words that occurred more than five times across all groups, a total of 1,642 word types (5+ words). This means, for example, that a word such as 'technologized',[43] which only occurred once in the entire corpus, was not included in the frequency analysis. I then manually went through all 5+ words, excluded function words such as 'and', 'or', 'was', 'have' and so on, and then proceeded to label the remaining content words. For example, I labelled words such as 'alternative', 'Ayurveda', 'homeopathy', 'homeopathic', 'herbal' and 'Kampo' under 'Alternative Medicine'.

Since the corpora differed substantially in size, the important criterion for analysis is not how often a certain word was said during the interviews; instead, I gave the frequency of that word per 10,000 words for that particular corpus. So, for example, the word 'herbal' was mentioned twice during the German interviews and four times during the Indian interviews. However, since the Indian corpus is much larger than the German one, the word's frequency in the Indian corpus (0.53 per 10,000 words) was not double that of the German one (0.43 per 10,000 words).[44] However, words used for the frequency analysis can often take on several meanings; for instance, the word 'alternative' can stand for 'alternative medicine', but of course 'alternative' is also used in the narratives in different contexts.[45] Thus, for each frequency analysis I manually checked the concordances for ambiguous words such as 'alternative', 'test' (i.e. medical test or academic test, etc.) to ensure that only those words relevant for the analysis were included. Similarly, as two of the interviews were conducted in German and subsequently translated by me, I manually cross-checked ambiguous words that I had used for frequency analysis in the German original to account for possible differences in translation.

The historical and contemporary news corpora

For the analysis of contemporary news, I used the COCA, or *Corpus of Contemporary American English* (Davies 2008–).[46] This is one of the largest freely available English language corpora and contains more than 560 million tokens across different sections, including spoken broadcasts, popular magazines, academic texts and newspapers. However, for my frequency analysis, I used only the newspaper section of the COCA, as I was interested in how certain words (such as insurance) were portrayed in the news. This section contains 114 million tokens [114,341,164] and is taken from 10 US newspapers such as *USA Today* and *The New York Times*. Additionally, I used the General Web section in the corpus GloWbE (*Corpus of Web-based Global English*, Davies 2013),[47] a web-based corpus containing about 1.9 billion words, to analyse contemporary online news coverage. For the analysis of historical data, I used the historical corpus COHA (*Corpus of Historical American English*, Davies 2010).[48] COHA represents the largest structured corpus of historical English constructed to date, containing balanced data from each decade ranging from 1810 to 2009, extracted from contemporary newspapers, magazines, works of fiction and other print materials (with a total of 448,200,483 tokens).

For the analysis of these corpora, I used both collocation and frequency analysis, based largely on techniques from critical discourse analysis. According to Baker and McEnery, critical discourse analysis is a form of critical social research that 'can be applied to a range of texts' in order to 'achieve a better understanding of how societies work' (2005: 197). Pearce also argues that corpus analytic tools are useful to 'derive social and cultural information' (2008: 1). A collocation query, for example, will allow the researcher to understand 'the themes and associations that are embedded in words due to their continual pairing with other words' (Baker and McEnery 2005: 223; Pearce 2008). Queries were run using the CQPweb (Hardie 2012) interface at Georgetown University (https://gucorpling.org/cqp), a search interface allowing researchers to find occurrences of targeted keywords and collocated terms that appear with them more often than expected by chance.

Although such collocated terms 'are not valid descriptions of people's "beliefs" or "opinions", and they cannot be taken as representing an inner, essential aspect of identity such as personality or attitude' (Baker and McEnery 2005: 198), they offer important insights into how public discourse is shaped at a certain point in time. Since public discourse in the media, as reflected in the language of popular newspapers, might also influence how my interlocutors think about their immigration status or health care experiences, I argue that this is a useful addition to the analysis at hand. Additionally, a frequency analysis may help corroborate whether or not themes mentioned frequently by my interlocutors were specific to their group or also frequently mentioned in contemporary or historical news.

Comparative analysis and triangulation

As discussed above, for this research project, I compared themes that recurred not only across the narratives of my different groups of informants (i.e. German, Indian and Japanese transnationals and physicians) but also across historical and contemporary news corpora. This mixed methods approach, where the narrative analysis stands at the centre and is supplemented by the quantitative methods outlined above, has proved to be a very fruitful tool to arrive at a more nuanced understanding of the differences between my informants.

For example, while coding my data, the importance of health care costs had become clear, and its importance was clearly mirrored in the narrative corpus when I labelled and categorized the 5+ words. However, the frequency analysis of the words within this category also showed how marked the differences were across the three groups for some of the words, such as 'bankrupt' and 'reimbursement', both of which were almost exclusively used only by Indians and Germans respectively (see full discussion in Chapter 3). This triangulation (cf. Mays and Pope 2000) alerted me to key differences in how health care costs were experienced and dealt with by the three groups that might otherwise have gone unnoticed. Additionally, themes that I had identified as being of particular importance for one group during coding could also be supplemented through a frequency analysis in order to demonstrate how marked the differences between the groups were. For example, it was much more common for my Indian interlocutors to mention alternative medicines in the interviews (e.g. taking alternative medicines, bringing them from home, missing physicians who are tolerant of them, etc.) than it was for any of the other groups. And the frequency analysis of the category

Table 2.5 Comparison of actual word mentions and frequency per 10,000 of the category 'alternative medicine' in the narrative corpus

	German corpus	Indian corpus	Japanese corpus
Number of times the words of the category 'alternative medicines' are mentioned	17	83	3
Frequency of these words per 10,000 words	3.66	11.26	0.77

'Alternative Medicine' including the words 'alternative', 'homeopathic', 'homeopathy', 'Ayurveda' and 'herbal' supported by narrative analysis indicates that Indians indeed were by far more likely to speak about this category, as Table 2.5 above shows.

The analysis of the individual words in this category also allowed for comparing the use of individual therapies, for example homeopathy, across all three groups. The usefulness of such a combined approach has been previously acknowledged; for example, the corpus linguist Partington writes: 'By enabling quantitative and qualitative research methodology to be used in tandem, corpus-assisted approaches have considerably deepened our understanding of the character of political language, both from the linguistic and political scientific perspectives' (2013: 6). Thus, just as other researchers have supplemented corpus analysis with other forms of analysis 'in order to offer possible explanations for the patterns of difference uncovered' (Pearce 2008: 1), I have used these methods to complement my narrative analysis.

Notes

1. Advances in communication have also led to different types of international labour migration, such as 'virtual migration', where labour is provided online (Aneesh 2000).
2. The scope of this book does not allow me to provide a detailed discussion on the various labels for people on the move. For a discussion on labels that may describe the group of individuals who are part of this study, such as the labels 'migrant' and 'immigrant', please see Agustin 2003; Conradson and Latham 2005a; Agustin 2006; Crosby 2007. For a discussion on the label 'expatriate', see Kunz 2016: 92; cf. Castells 2000; Sklair 2002; Morley, Heraty and Collings 2006; Beaverstock 2005; Van Bochove and Engbersen 2015; Koutonin 2015; Cranston 2017; and for the label 'highly skilled', see Iredale 2001; Voigt-Graf 2005; Conradson and Latham 2005b; Smith 2005; Bailey and Mulder 2017; Hercog 2017.
3. https://www.healthcare.gov/immigrants/lawfully-present-immigrants (accessed 9 December 2021).

4 Of course, we need to keep in mind that these individuals still tend to enjoy more privileges than many other socially less privileged transnationals, in that, for example, they can afford to travel more freely, e.g. on frequent visits home, or are able to relocate their entire household rather than start from scratch in the new host society (Butcher 2010).
5 And not all highly skilled migrants come of their own accord. Many leave their home to secure better opportunities for the family members remaining in the country of origin, either through the status their families enjoy through having a relative living abroad (cf. Rutten and Verstappen 2014) or through remittances (cf. Ryan et al. 2009; Bailey and Mulder 2017).
6 While there is no official definition for 'highly skilled migrants', my informants fit the most commonly proposed definition approaches, namely the education-based (cf. Batalova 2006; Batalova and Lowell 2006) and occupation-based approaches (cf. Koser and Salt 1997; Mahroum 2001), as they either have a tertiary degree (45 informants), are in high-skill professions (1 informant) or are spouses of those who are (2 informants). It is also important to note that mobility is much more likely to negatively affect women, even among more privileged groups of transnationals. In fact, much of the literature on immigration and many immigration policies treat men as the 'lead migrants' and view women as 'trailing spouses', 'tied migrants' or 'co-movers'. Many of my female informants had indeed entered the United States as 'tied movers' or on a dependent visa and frequently mentioned that this was causing difficulties for them (they were often unable to find work either because they did not have a work visa or their partner's job required frequent relocations, not giving them enough time to establish a career themselves). While the scope of this chapter does not allow for full discussion on 'trailing spouses', the experiences of the 'trailing spouses' I spoke with did not seem to impact their experiences and expectations regarding health insurance and health care. For the purposes of this research project, I have included them in the proposed category of (middling) highly skilled migrant. For a full discussion on this topic, please see Kofman 2000; Willis and Yeoh 2002; Iredale 2005; Cooke 2008; Anthias 2012; Siddiqui and Tejada 2014; Kunz 2016; Bailey and Mulder 2017; Kou and Bailey 2017; Cangia 2018.
7 (Dr Silva, Oncologist).
8 (Dr Banik, Psychiatrist).
9 https://www.washingtonpost.com/news/wonk/wp/2018/06/20/how-the-u-s-cornered-the-market-for-skilled-immigrants/?utm_term=.4cc0787fa527 (accessed 7 December 2021).
10 https://www.migrationpolicy.org/article/even-congress-remains-sidelines-trump-administration-slows-legal-immigration (accessed 7 December 2021). Although, of course, other forms of immigration have been affected by this administration's policies to a much greater extent, including the proposal of a travel ban for majority-Muslim countries, restrictions for refugees and substantial changes for undocumented immigrants (cf. https://www.migrationpolicy.org/research/immigration-under-trump-review-policy-shifts (accessed 7 December 2021). See Mayda and Peri 2017 for the economic impact of the Trump administration immigration policies.
11 https://www.migrationpolicy.org/article/top-10-2017-issue-1-under-trump-administration-united-states-takes-steps-narrow-legal (accessed 7 December 2021).
12 The Chinese Exclusion Act denied Chinese-born workers in the United States the right to become citizens and denied new Chinese labourers access to the US altogether. However, the Chinese-born upper class, for example students and teachers, were not affected by this law. Other examples of preferential treatment for highly skilled migrants are evident in the Contract Labor Law of 1885, a literacy test introduced in 1917 and a total cap on immigration from the Eastern hemisphere in 1921. Although highly skilled or better-off foreigners usually received preferential treatment, there are also examples of when they did not, e.g. in 1907, when an executive order issued by President Roosevelt denied Japanese and Korean immigrants access, even if they were highly skilled (Batalova 2006).
13 These rights included: being allowed to work in positions described as permanent, stay in the United States for longer and more easily become a permanent resident.
14 https://www.migrationpolicy.org/article/college-educated-immigrants-united-states (accessed 8 December 2021).
15 With a notable exception in the *Special Issue of the Journal of Ethnic and Migration Studies: Highly Skilled Migration Between the Global North and South: Gender, Life Courses and Institutions* (Bailey and Mulder 2017).
16 Although the transfer of medical knowledge or medicine is more likely to be associated with the flow from the Global North to the Global South, which is more often than not 'branded as

the needy receiver' (Lidola and Borges 2017: 1), there are also multiple examples of South–South cooperation, such as the Cuban medical missions in Latin America and Africa. See also Dilger and Mattes 2018 for a criticism of such a distinction.
17 Asylum seekers and refugees might additionally have to deal with the fact that much of the support available is not adjusted to the needs of highly skilled individuals (cf. Hercog 2017).
18 Indeed, for many highly skilled migrants, their mobility does have a positive effect on their standard of living and social position; however, this is often only seen once they return home (Siddiqui and Tejada 2014).
19 Discrimination has also repeatedly been shown to lead to health disparities and a feeling of bias in health care among racial and ethnic minorities (Johnson et al. 2004; cf. Betancourt et al. 2003). However, discrimination was not mentioned by any of my informants as a major concern, with several mentioning that this may be in part due to the fact that DC is a large, international city (see also Chapters 4 and 5).
20 However, as Constant et al. (2015) argue, the healthy immigrant effect is also strongly dependent on immigration policies and thus does not hold for all countries, as their study on immigration into Israel demonstrated. Another study by Kibele, Scholz and Shkolnikov (2008) points out that immigrant mortality as an indicator for health inequalities is often underestimated.
21 See Lopez-Class, Castro and Ramirez 2011 and Viruell-Fuentes, Miranda and Abdulrahim 2012 for a critical analysis of the concept of 'acculturation'.
22 While some migrants – who are nominally highly skilled – enter the United States as refugees or through forced migration, the vast majority do not have traumatic migration experiences.
23 (Dr Stein, Family Medicine).
24 There is, however, also a debate on whether employment leads to better health or if healthier individuals are more likely to be employed. Regarding the immigrants in Dean and Wilson's research (2009), they had to be healthy in order to be eligible for Canada's Skilled Worker Program; thus, in this case, unemployment was a contributing factor that caused immigrants to become unhealthy.
25 All guidelines regarding confidentiality and storing data sets by the IRB were followed and a signed informed consent form was obtained from all participants. All participants in this research were ensured that their involvement was voluntary and that they were free to leave the study at any point, resulting in no negative consequences. They were also informed that no remuneration would be offered as compensation for participating in this research.
26 This was the case when the informant and I had met prior to the interview and had already established a relationship or when the informant was referred to me by a trusted acquaintance, thus ensuring my safety during field work. Whenever possible, I allowed informants to choose the environment in which they felt most comfortable to be interviewed.
27 As one of the key characteristics of highly skilled migrants is their supposedly good command of English (see Chapter 5 for more on this discussion), I chose to conduct all interviews in English to get a sense of my informants' ability to communicate. While none of my Indian informants felt uneasy speaking English, a few Japanese and German informants mentioned that they were inhibited by their low confidence in speaking English. However, only two informants chose to conduct the interview in German – undoubtedly because this opportunity arose, since I am a German native myself.
28 Throughout this book I use gender terms, as well as pronouns such as 'she' or 'her', in accordance with my informants' self-identification. While many of the findings in this research may generalize beyond gender categories, reference to these can be pertinent because of how gender may shape the experiences of patients (cf. Bailey and Mulder 2017; Kofman 2014; Anthias 2012; and others).
29 Although men still outnumber women in highly skilled migration, which in general tends to be associated more with young, single, male immigrants (cf. Batalova 2006), the exclusive focus on highly skilled male migrants has previously been questioned (cf. Van Bochove and Engbersen 2015; Bailey and Mulder 2017).The higher percentage of females among my informants can be explained by the fact that I spoke not only with highly skilled migrants (n=36) but also their spouses, or 'trailing spouses', the overwhelming majority of whom are women, as was the case among my informants too (n=12). A possible higher response rate bias among women also cannot be ruled out, including as a result of my own gender.
30 This wide range of visa categories (such as student visas or work visas) is not surprising, given the fact that my informants had moved to the United States for very different reasons. For

example, while none of my German informants mentioned education was the reason for having moved to the US, 55 per cent of Indians did. For my Japanese interview partners, education was the second most important reason for coming the United States; however, they were the most likely to mention job opportunities as the main driver for their move (46%).
31 One of the paediatricians I spoke with was also a geneticist.
32 While I did not discuss their own immigration category with non-US-born physicians, it seems likely that their situation was rather distinct from the patient groups in this study, in the first instance since this study's focus is on temporary, non-immigrant visa holders (such as diplomats or visiting researchers) and in the second instance because as practising physicians in the United States, their knowledge of the local health care system would be very detailed.
33 As of 2019: https://www.census.gov/quickfacts/fact/table/dc/PST045217 (accessed 7 December 2021). https://www.migrationpolicy.org/data/state-profiles/state/demographics/DC (accessed 9 December 2021). See Price et al. 2005 for a discussion on the problems arising from accounting for the inflow and number of immigrants.
34 https://www.migrationpolicy.org/data/state-profiles/state/demographics/DC (accessed 9 December 2021). See Price et al. 2005 for the distribution of immigrants in the inner city and suburbs.
35 Although at the same time there has also been an increase in the demand for lower-skilled workers (cf. Price et al. 2005).
36 https://www.americanimmigrationcouncil.org/sites/default/files/research/immigrants_in_the_district_of_columbia.pdf (accessed 9 December 2021).
37 https://washington.org/visit-dc/international-embassies-in-washington-dc (accessed 9 December 2021).
38 Jonas described his English proficiency as conversational, but asked to be interviewed in German. Translation of the original German by the author: 'Das ist hier aber auch . . . das hat hier aber auch nix zu bedeuten, ja. Ich mein, wenn Du in [name of country] sagst, oder da wo wir vorher waren, sagst, du bist von der Botschaft, da gehen alle Türen auf. Also grad da wo wir waren, [name of foreign city], wenn man da gesagt hat, man ist vom Generalkonsulat, da waren die immer baff. Ich mein, da gibt's dann halt in der Stadt 1.5 Millionen Einwohner, vielleicht 300 Expats, da ist es was anderes als wie, wie ne Million Einwohner und ne halbe Million Expats, ja. Also hier, hier ist man nichts besonderes, als Diplomat, das muss man halt auch einfach akzeptieren.'
39 (Chetan, Indian male, G4 visa, in the US since 2013).
40 (Britta, German female, Green Card holder, in the US since 2004).
41 Although in the interviews the physicians I spoke with did not identify with the group of highly skilled migrants that was the focus of this research (see above), they did often mention that their international background or their experience with international patients informed how they interacted with their foreign patients.
42 Depending on how the term 'highly skilled migrant' is defined, I would qualify for this category on multiple accounts: (1) as someone holding a tertiary degree (an MSc at the time when the interviews were conducted), (2) as an international student (a doctoral student and visiting researcher in my case) and (3) as a spouse to a highly skilled migrant (in my case my partner, who had come to the US on an H-1B visa).
43 As mentioned by one of my German interlocutors, Julia, during our interview: 'So that is the one thing I think that the medicine is more technologized. So that the physicians think if there is a new technique available then we should definitely use it . . .' (Julia, German female, A1 visa, in the US since 2012).
44 Most of the individual words I analysed did not occur that frequently throughout the corpora. For comparison, one of the most frequently used words, 'I', occurred 417.5 times per 10,000 words in the German corpus, 404.02/10,000 times in the Japanese and 381.79/10,000 times in the Indian corpus.
45 For example, Varun, one of my Indian informants, told me that physicians in India need to be available 24 hours a day for their patients. His sister and her husband, for example, who run a hospital, 'are just awake for two days, because they have to run it'. He then mentioned that '[t]here is no like alternative to that' (Varun, Indian male, J1 visa, in the US since 2017).
46 https://corpus.byu.edu/COCA (accessed 3 February 2022).
47 https://corpus.byu.edu/glowbe (accessed 25 January 2022).
48 https://corpus.byu.edu/coha (accessed 25 January 2022).

3
'I really dislike insurance . . . I don't know how the concept works': the culture of health insurance

> I think it says a lot about the health care system here, that they say you have to shop for an insurance . . . I think the biggest difference for me is, I experience, I experience . . . the US health care to be a privilege where in Germany it is a right, it is a human right. And I think that shows, that shows in the system, and also it shows in the way language is used, like shopping for insurances, and also shows in the price.
>
> (Christine, German female, Green Card holder, in the US since 2015)

Introduction

Health insurance in the United States is characterized by a very diverse and difficult to navigate range of insurance plans, yet insurance is one of the key prerequisites for accessing health care services there.[1] For a large number of immigrants, a lack of coverage or underinsurance represents one of the biggest obstacles to accessing health care. Unsurprisingly, this is also the context in which insurance is most frequently discussed in previous research on immigrants to the United States. This chapter, however, argues that this is a limited view which tends to leave out the important role that health insurance culture plays. I will also discuss the different structural, functional and economic barriers highly skilled migrants encounter in the US health insurance system, regardless of their more privileged position.

Sarah Horton and Louise Lamphere have argued in their *Call to an Anthropology of Health Policy* that '[f]ar too often our discipline has prioritized studies of quaint "health beliefs" over documenting the tangible effects of such policies, allowing the views of health economists to prevail' (2006: 36). Views held by health economists, such as health maximization being a universal and rational economic goal, have in fact been criticized as ethno- and Eurocentric. In this view, patients not only seem to display a 'universal model of sick behavior' (Horton and Lamphere 2006: 33), but they will also, given the chance, 'consume' more services than necessary, 'up to the point at which the cost of the good is greater than its value to the individual' (Horton and Lamphere 2006: 33). These discussions on health policies are thus shaped mainly by suggestions of how to efficiently discourage the consumption of health care as a 'commodity' while at the same time disregarding the realities of those who feel the consequences of health policy changes the most, namely the very sick or poor. This suggests that we should keep in mind that '[t]he model of the rational, autonomous care-seeker . . . serves best when used to study middle-class Americans who have health insurance and are seeking care for relatively minor problems' (Good 1994: 43).

Unlike other immigrant groups, highly skilled migrants in particular cannot – as discussed in Chapter 2 – be described as very sick or poor health care seekers, and as such are not overly impacted by the consequences of health policy changes. In fact, from a purely health economics point of view, this group could be described as the 'rational, autonomous care-seeker' described by Good (1994). And yet, the experiences of this very diverse group of transmigrants probably do not mirror those of middle-class or well-off US Americans. In the following discussion I will argue that one of the roots for this dissonance stems from differences in health insurance cultures between transnationals' home societies and the host country, which provides a fruitful field for anthropological analysis (for more on 'quaint health beliefs', see Chapter 4).

To this end, I will first provide some historical background to health insurance in the United States as a host country as well as Germany, India and Japan, as the sending nations in this study, and discuss the contemporary health insurance reality for highly skilled migrants in the US. In this context I will draw on anthropological and health policy literature to analyse how differences in insurance cultures may shape experiences and expectations in a transnational context as well as examining some of the difficulties of transferring insurance concepts from one context to another.

The differences in health insurances are so vast, not only across nations but also within countries and different groups of the insured, that it is problematic to think of health insurance as a distinct 'insurance system'. Rather, it is made up of insurance policies and ideologies that shape individuals' experiences and expectations. However, narratives of transnational patients as well as a narrative keyword analysis can provide a more in-depth anthropological insight into the experiences of German, Indian and Japanese highly skilled migrants in the United States and how their experiences may differ. Furthermore, I will analyse how insurance is discussed in media and public discourse through a keyword search of both contemporary news and web corpora, as well as a historical corpus, revealing changes in the time frame from 1810 through to contemporary times.

Health insurance: an anthropological perspective

While health insurance is usually discussed in terms of health policy, health financing, services and coverage of population (cf. WHO 2010), the social and cultural aspects of health insurance and health insurance coverage have not been fully explored. Yet it is important for medical anthropologists to do so, since 'insurance provides the scaffolding on which health systems are constructed' (Dao and Mulligan 2016: 6) and coverage or lack thereof has very real implications for those who are in need of medical treatment.

Insurance policies, including health insurance, are also always a product of different political, economic and social factors and shaped by the role and regulatory power of state and federal governments (cf. Ahlin, Nichter and Pillai 2016). This means that not only do the setup and scope of health insurances differ across countries, regions and the various groups of insurance policy holders, but also the benefits that are available to those insured differ vastly in terms of both access and cost – across nations, regions and different plans. What, then, determines satisfaction with health care and health insurance? Which cultural factors contribute to or reinforce how health insurance policies are set up and accepted? And what does health insurance mean for those insured or those lacking insurance?

Universal health coverage has been declared a fundamental human right by the 1948 constitution of the World Health Organization (WHO).

This right, as defined by the WHO, 'means that all people have access to the health services they need, when and where they need them, without financial hardship'.[2] By this definition, the introduction of universal health insurance coverage should (easily) translate into giving all individuals access to health care and thus contribute to reducing social inequality. Yet, counterintuitively, the introduction of health insurance is by no means a magic bullet or cure-all, and can even be a means to intensify social injustice, as I will discuss in more detail below (cf. Bump 2015). Also, the term 'universal' health insurance suggests that something like a 'one size fits all' health insurance exists and can simply be established in those places that have no insurance or insufficient coverage, given the financial means to do so. However, how health insurance policies might look, and what would be most suitable, differs from country to country and within different regions, often leading to substantial diversity within a single society. The local differences in health care and health insurance are due to both local conditions, such as economic factors, and the role and setup of governments. Certain aspects make it more difficult or nearly impossible for some types of health financing to be adapted to local conditions. These include, for example, the absence of a formal work sector allowing for employment or tax-based contribution schemes. To a large degree, historical experiences and cultural expectations also play a considerable role in which setups are going to work and which are not.[3]

The basic determinants of health insurance are: who is supposed to be covered, how many services are covered and how much of the cost will be covered (cf. WHO 2010). Yet, which emphasis is chosen will depend not only on economic but also social, cultural and historical aspects. This may substantially impact what and whom health insurance covers, as seen, for example, in the discussions on health insurance disparities in the United States in the aftermath of the introduction of the Affordable Care Act (Fletcher 2016; see also 'Health insurance in the United States' below); the significant role prescriptions drugs take on in India (cf. Ahlin, Nichter and Pillai 2016; Reddy et al. 2011); and locations where there is a reluctance to join health insurances at all, for example Senegal (Wolf 2012). The take-away lesson, then, seems to be that health insurance policies cannot be copied or imported from one country to the next; in order for health insurance plans and health care programmes to work, local conditions need to be ascertained through local research and analysis of policies and taken into account.

Generally speaking, opinions on health insurance differ across societies as well as within societies, ranging from distrust on one end of the scale to feelings of entitlement on the other (Ahlin, Nichter and Pillai

2016). A common issue for many newly insured people seems to be unrealistic expectations and a lack of information on details. This is true for those in previously uninsured subsections of the population, specific regions, or even entire countries when introduced to health insurance for the first time (cf. Virk and Atun 2015; Cheng 2003).[4] This may understandably lead to individuals feeling cheated out of services that they think they are entitled to. And having insurance does not necessarily mean gaining access to better-quality health care services or paying less money for them. In fact, the introduction of health insurance may even decrease the quality of care available, leave patients feeling that they have less access or only access to a lower-quality service, as discussed by Dao and Nichter (2016) regarding the introduction of health insurance coverage in Vietnam and Ghana, and similarly by Ahlin and colleagues (2016) in relation to India and Fletcher (2016) on the introduction of the Affordable Care Act in the United States. At the same time, costly services often seem to be associated with high quality, and if patients believe that good health care has to have its price, they may continue to prefer out-of-pocket payments over health insurance plans for this reason (Ahlin, Nichter and Pillai 2016). Furthermore, the reasons why people agree or disagree to pay for health insurance are complex and strongly context-dependent. For example, Wolf (2012) shows that in Senegal, many did not want to contribute monetarily to a (newly established) insurance scheme, but rather continued to organize themselves into saving associations or *tontines*.

The differences in the importance of and the meaning assigned to insurance also became evident during my field research. For example, while the concept of health insurance itself was not questioned by any of my German and Japanese informants, all of whom had insurance in their respective countries of origin, some of my Indian interlocutors – many of whom had not held any insurance plan or coverage prior to their stay in the United States – voiced reservations towards it. Salman, a 34-year-old software engineer, for example, was very opinionated about US health care and had thought a lot about this topic, since he had to explain how the system worked to his wife, whom he had married in India and who had recently joined him in the United States. He had, however, struggled to understand the concept of health insurance and explained to me during our interview that he initially did not think of it as something he really needed or wanted:

> Back in India, where I was working, we were given a like a kind of health insurance, but I remember the first day they offered me, I was

really confused, like 'Why do I need this?' And you know, the basic question was: 'Why do I even need to pay, you know, take money out of my pay check, to pay for something I don't really need.'

(Salman, Indian male, H-1B visa, in the US since 2007)

While he felt similarly about health insurance in the United States, he mentioned that an integration course offered by his employer proved helpful in understanding 'why I even need to have health insurance. Because without that I would have questioned why do I need that insurance.' Priya, a 40-year-old adjunct professor who had originally come to the US from India to 'go get educated and then come back and marry' had decided to stay in the United States to escape a traditional family's plans for her future and to work in academia. She had similar misgivings about the concept of insurance and was even more explicit in her negative opinion than Salman:

Priya: I really dislike insurance. I just like paying and just, I don't like dealing with what I dislike. I don't know how the concept works.
Nina: How come you dislike health insurance?
Priya: They always have rules and hidden things . . . I mean, for my laparoscopic appendectomy . . . when I saw the bills, I thought it was ridiculous. What they charged the insurance company was like insane. And then we had to pay the doctor separately and the hospital separately and then we had a huge deductible, oh my, fuck it, it was – even with insurance – absurd.

(Priya, Indian female, G2 visa, in the US since 1995)

My Indian informants' opinions are also in line with many of Ahlin and colleagues' informants in India, who mentioned that they did not trust their health insurance plans, preferred to continue paying out of pocket for health care and often viewed insurance companies as cheats that tried to avoid paying for legitimate claims. On the other hand, Indian women from lower-income groups have accepted health insurance payments as a preferable form of future investment for their family, with monthly instalments that their husbands then cannot spend otherwise.[5] And for the Indian middle class, health insurance may have become a means to show their care and responsibility for the household (Dao and Nichter 2016: 130).

A clear understanding of cultural expectations is therefore just as instrumental in establishing a trusted health insurance system as adaptation to local conditions determined by local government regulations and policies and financial options. This makes the introduction of health insurance plans or the increase of coverage a complex issue socially, structurally, politically and economically. Yet a closer examination of health insurance culture is also important on another level. Many of my conversations with highly skilled migrants showed that issues regarding health care and health insurance were often conflated. Alia, a former research assistant in her early thirties from India who had followed her partner and was at the time of our interview unable to work in the United States due to her visa status, put it bluntly:

> I think I just realized when I was talking to you that I, whenever we speak about health care I keep switching to insurance. And I don't know if that needs to be as synonymous, I don't know if it has to be that way . . . Because you need to start looking into who fits into your insurance policy and . . . And then they have all of these things they are okay, not okay that they will accept and not accept. Yeah, it is a lot of homework to do for something that should be more accessible.
>
> (Alia, Indian female, J2 visa, in the US since 2016)

Although knowledge of cultural insurance norms is also critical in understanding how easily (highly skilled) migrants can integrate into the US health insurance system and how effortlessly they can navigate it, any discussion on health care satisfaction, utilization and even health outcomes needs to take both health care and health insurance culture into consideration. I will therefore briefly describe the history and current aspects of US health insurance before discussing transmigrants' experiences with health insurance (below) and health care (in Chapter 4).

Health insurance in the United States

Wetzel describes health care in the United States as a free-wheeling system that 'has grown up over the years alongside a democratic government that leans strongly toward individual freedom and choice' (2011: 383). This has led the US to be one of the only industrialized countries in the world that did not implement a national health insurance programme, at least not until the Affordable Care Act of 2010, which differs in scope and implementation from the compulsory health care programmes in other industrialized countries. There were, however, many reasons that contributed to the particular history of US health care, including 'political and economic forces, a powerful medical establishment, the dominant private insurance industry, and extensive medical liability system' (Blank 2012: 416).[6]

In the time before and around the Civil War in the 1860s, medical services in the United States were based on fee-for-service, and the US government took no steps towards making insurance compulsory, nor did it subsidize existing voluntary funds when in the 1880s the first national system of compulsory sickness insurance was established in Germany (see more below). In the 1920s, when medical costs had become a burden for many and health insurance finally became a political issue in the United States, almost all Western European countries had already established health insurance. In 1915 the American Association for Labor Legislation (AALL) drafted a bill modelled on European schemes[7] in which employers, employees and the government were to share the costs. While this proposal originally received support, it soon fell out of favour, highlighting why establishing insurance has remained a hotly debated topic in the United States until today. There were several reasons for this:

(1) Insurance companies, and with them the corporations that had invested in these insurance schemes, feared big losses on the profits they made from the successful industrial life insurance. As Starr put it, the reformers 'unwittingly brought down upon themselves the concerted opposition of big business' (1982: 252).
(2) Physicians had refused the proposal because the method of payment was suggested to be changed from fee-for-service to a capitation of salary.[8]
(3) Even the labour unions spoke out against the bill, out of fear that it would weaken the unions and that people's health would become subject to state supervision.

It was, however, argues Starr, the entry of the United States into the First World War that sealed the fate of this first attempt at a compulsory health insurance and played into the hands of the health care opponents, who denounced it as a 'Prussian menace inconsistent with American values' (1982: 253). Arguably one of the key American values is the principle of individual choice. Any discussion of universal health coverage as a way to achieve equality in health care is for this reason seen as a restriction of this individual choice. However, the principle of equal opportunity 'might serve as a carrier for the principle of equality', since it is already 'deeply rooted in American society' (Wendt and Minhas 2010: 424; cf. Blank

2012), unlike compulsory mandatory health insurance. In a discussion published in 1917 in *The New York Times* on providing compulsory health care insurance for labourers, A. Parker Nevins of the National Association of Manufacturers describes such an idea as 'beaurocratic, not democratic' (sic), and Dr Berg, speaking on behalf of New York's Real Estate Owners' Association, said: 'It is devilish in principle and foreign to American ideals . . . The backers of this bill got it straight from Germany, and you know to what such paternalism has led all of Europe' (*New York Times* 1917; see also Numbers 1978). In fact, political discontent and the political threat of socialism did help the establishment of social insurance in Europe. The United States did not experience as strong a challenge on their political stability at the same time, and from this point of view, it is not surprising that more liberal and democratic countries like the US adopted social insurance later than 'authoritarian and paternalistic regimes, like Germany' (Starr 1982: 239–341).

Given the fear of communism after the war, health insurance did not become a political issue again until the Great Depression. The resulting financial hardships led to new social reforms and the Social Security Act was passed in 1935, but with large numbers of unemployed workers, unemployment insurance had become the most pressing issue. Health insurance was excluded from the Act so as not to 'spell defeat for the entire bill'[9] (Starr 1982: 296). Rothman (1993) argues that one of the main reasons why health reform could not be passed, although opinion polls showed that Americans overall would have tolerated it, was that the middle class had been eliminated as an advocate for compulsory health insurance by being offered group health insurances (Blue Cross) as a valid alternative.[10] The loss of an invested middle class was also an important factor in the failure of the proposal of President Truman in the 1940s, the first time a US president supported a programme for compulsory health insurance. By the end of the Second World War, employees had already begun to expect employer-based private health insurance as a response to the War Labor Board that previously restricted higher wages, and employers had started to offer health insurances in order to attract workers. By now, compulsory health insurance had also become associated with charity and personal failure 'serving only the poor, not the respectable' (Rothman 1993: 277; cf. Zinner and Loughlin 2009; Horton et al. 2014; Wetzel 2011; Schulte 2013).

Unlike Europe, whose economies were devastated by the Second World War, the United States had transformed itself into a major economic force with flourishing industrial production. In the years between 1950 and 1970, medical care became one of the country's biggest industries, with expenditures on health care rising more than 50 to 100 per cent in comparison to other life necessities (Falk 1977) and a medical workforce that more than tripled (Starr 1982). This prosperity began to shatter when costs for hospital stays doubled in the 1960s and began to be a problem. As a result, Medicare, a new proposal for covering hospital costs only as part of Social Security for the aged (individuals above 65 years), was signed into law in 1965 and proved to be extremely popular, possibly because this group was perceived as particularly vulnerable, yet deserving.[11] Later, in the 1970s, one of the main themes, in both politics and public opinion, was that health care was in a crisis. It became clear that the health care expenses had become immense and that they did not necessarily translate into health improvements, especially since US medical care did not seem to compare well to Western European health programmes. In 1974, against the advice of his cabinet, President Nixon endorsed a bill for national health insurance, and as part of his 'new national health strategy', health maintenance organizations (HMOs) were to stimulate the industry to self-regulate. But when the Watergate Affair led to Nixon's resignation, President Ford subsequently withdrew the plan (Starr 1982: 419).

A reform of the health care system again seemed inevitable when Bill Clinton was voted into office in 1992. Although health care was a major aspect of his political agenda, no compromise could be agreed upon and his health care plan never went through Congress (Starr 2011).[12] The Republicans that succeeded the Clinton administration, with George W. Bush as president, also failed to pass their attempts at reshaping US health policy, although they successfully passed the Medicare Modernization Act (Medicare Part D) in 2003.[13] The affordability of health care remained a big issue for Americans, as the Kaiser Family Foundation repeatedly found in their surveys, and became the top domestic issue leading up to the elections in 2008. In what Starr (2011) calls an 'uneasy victory', President Obama signed the Affordable Care Act (ACA, or sometimes also 'Obamacare') into law in 2010. It was the first major health care reform that had been enacted in over 45 years since Medicare/Medicaid, and was passed without a single Republican vote.[14] However, for some critics the ACA does not represent a reform insomuch as it only expands the highly fragmented employer-based health care system rather than reforming it; it failed to transform national health care to be able to compete with private providers and probably will not manage to restrict the escalating health care spending (cf. Horton et al. 2014; Blank 2012). In 2010, the year of the implementation of the ACA, about 56 per cent of US residents were privately insured, the majority of whom received their insurance through their employers, and about 27 per cent were covered by public programmes like Medicare and Medicaid. The number of uninsured decreased from 44 million in 2013 before the full roll-out of ACA to about 28.9 million people in 2019.[15] Yet, despite these successes, of those with insurance about 29 million are still considered 'underinsured', i.e. at great risk of high out-of-pocket expenses (Weil 2017). To make matters worse, in late 2016 the US government announced that the premiums for health plans had seen an increase of up to 25 per cent, and in some states coverage was hampered because fewer insurance companies were offering plans.[16]

However, the ACA also meant that for the first time in US health insurance history, individuals were prompted to purchase health insurance – the so-called 'individual mandate'. Individuals who chose to opt out of health insurance were subsequently fined, unless they were otherwise exempt. Following the ACA, so-called insurance exchanges had to be established. In these, each state offers a marketplace for individuals and small businesses where policies and premiums can be compared and purchased.[17] Services that are included depend on the type of insurance but usually include physician visits, in- and outpatient care in hospitals and potentially prescription drugs. However, most insurance plans have a restricted network of in-network providers and visits to out-of-network providers are not, or only partially, covered. Private insurance companies usually also negotiate prices with providers, which can lead to rather substantial differences in prices between insurance plans (Thomson et al. 2012).

Despite its many proponents, the ACA has seen continued and mostly negative discussion in the press. For example, the search for collocations of 'Obamacare' in the English web corpus (GloWbE)[18] exposes how contentious the law and its implementation has been and continues to be, with key collocations including 'repeal' (#1), 'repealing' (#2), 'repealed' (#5) and 'replace' (#11). The rising costs of the ACA and difficulties finding a plan were also a (minor) point of interest in the interviews (6 Germans, 4 Indians, 3 Japanese), and most mentioned Obamacare/ACA only when commenting on the US health system in general, rather than pertaining to their own experiences.

Thus, since the main goals of the ACA were to make health insurance more accessible to poor Americans and to significantly lower the number of uninsured individuals, the reform did not have much of an impact on whether or not the group of highly skilled migrants under analysis here were offered insurance or what kind of insurance was available to them. Nevertheless, they were affected by (and profited from) some key changes, such as the fact that insurance plans have to provide 'essential' benefits without co-pay and have to meet minimum standards, as well as the fact that community rates are offered to all individuals of the same sex and age and do not take previous health conditions into account. While most of my informants were holding employer-sponsored health insurance in the United States, only one (German) informant, Christine, was actually insured through the ACA and thought it 'was really complicated, it was a really stressful time trying to figure out how to do this'.[19]

My German interlocutors were not only the most likely to refer to Obamacare; they were also more positive about the introduction of the ACA, many voicing the importance of the availability of health insurance. Many also could not understand the reluctance of the American public and the political discourse on the implementation of this policy, as Anja, the 35-year-old German economist, explained to me:

> That is one of the big issues that the Germans often can't understand, you know in this whole fight over Obamacare and health care, like 'Why would somebody not want health care?' . . . It's almost like an investment decision. Like, 'Oh, am I a high-risk person or low?' and it's very strange to think about your health in those terms. And you know in Germany you don't . . . it's really changed my thinking about health I think, in the sense that I, I think about it as something that I, that you, have to budget for and how much is it worth to me.
> (Anja, German female, G4 visa, in the US since 2009)

The Indian and Japanese informants were much more likely to mention Obamacare in passing, for example while discussing other aspects of US health care, and were less likely to positively remark on the implementation than my German interlocutors. Only Vihaan, the 38-year-old IT specialist from India, had a negative opinion on the ACA. While he was not directly insured through Obamacare, but rather through his employer, he felt that the implementation of the ACA[20] had also directly and negatively affected his health care costs, as his 'premiums have tripled' and his 'deductible has quadrupled'.[21]

Health insurance in Germany, India and Japan: a comparison

In the following I will first briefly outline some differences in how health insurance is set up in Germany, India and Japan in order to provide a better understanding of the expectations towards health insurance that the three different groups may bring with them, and how their experiences could influence their expectations towards US health insurance. As Table 3.1 below shows, there are some key differences and similarities in insurance and health care spending in the different countries under investigation here (although there is little to no data available for India) that likely shape both perception and utilization of services, as I will discuss in more detail below.

Health insurance in Germany

The 'quintessential feature' of health care in Germany is sickness funds (*Krankenkassen*) (Swami 2002: 335), which represent the oldest form of

Table 3.1 Comparison of key differences in health insurance and health costs between the US, Germany and Japan. As can be seen, most data were not available for India[1]

		US	Germany	Japan	India
Insurance	Compulsory health insurance introduced (year)	2010	1883	1922	
	Publicly insured	35.6%	89.2%	100%	
	Privately insured	55.3%	10.8%	0%	
	Publicly or privately insured	90.9%	100%	100%	
Costs	Health expenditure as a share of GDP	17.2%	11.3%	10.9%	4.8%
	Out-of-pocket medical spending as a share of final household consumption	2.5%	1.8%	2.6%	
	Out-of-pocket expenditure on retail pharmaceuticals	29.1%	15.7%	26.8%	

[1] Source OECD Health at a Glance 2017: insurance coverage (all numbers 2015 or closest year): https://www.oecd-ilibrary.org/sites/health_glance-2017-24-en/index.html?itemId=/content/component/health_glance-2017-24-en; health care spending (all numbers 2016 or closest year): https://www.oecd-ilibrary.org/sites/health_glance-2017-45-en/index.html?itemId=/content/component/health_glance-2017-45-en; pharmaceutical expenditure (all numbers 2015 or closest year otherwise): https://www.oecd-ilibrary.org/sites/health_glance-2017-68-en/index.html?itemId=/content/component/health_glance-2017-68-en. All accessed 18 December 2021; some numbers may have been updated in the interim.

social health insurance in the world. The idea of sickness funds originated in the Middle Ages, when different guilds of workers set up funds to support family members with costs for health care, funeral costs or pensions. These community-based insurances became increasingly important during Germany's industrialization, when many fled the countryside to come to the cities as workers. By 1854 the first compulsory health insurance was established, when mines and foundries were obligated by a Prussian law to have a sickness fund. These funds provided sick pay and money for medication and rehabilitation. In the years that followed, several reforms started to lay out more and more regulations for these funds and slowly made membership more obligatory. However, only in 1883, with Bismarck's reform of the health care system, did membership become compulsory for all labourers. The main goal of his reform was to undermine the further politicization of workers who had become highly organized and to 'buy political support from the workers in exchange for economic protection and material benefits' (Iglehart 1991: 505; see also Bärnighausen and Sauerborn 2002; Bump 2015). To this day, the structure of the sickness funds has remained fundamentally unchanged, which is for Iglehart one of the 'most remarkable features' of the German health insurance system (1991: 504).

Germany's insurance system has achieved almost universal coverage, with 89.2 per cent being insured publicly, which is mandatory for employees who earn less than €64,350[22] yearly. Individuals whose earnings are above this income threshold are free to remain insured over the sickness funds or can opt for private insurance instead, which covers 10.8 per cent of Germans. The self-employed and *Beamte* (i.e. civil servants and some teachers) are also required to cover parts of their health insurance through private insurance.[23]

In Germany, physicians are obligated to be members of the Medical Council (*Ärztekammer*) and the Panel Physicians Associations (*Krankenärztliche Vereinigung*), in order to be able to treat patients that are members of sickness funds. All sickness funds negotiate physician fees with these panels and per diem rates with hospitals. They act as a middleman between patient and government and offer comparable benefits to their members (Bärnighausen and Sauerborn 2002; Iglehart 1991). Today there are about 103 different sickness funds in Germany[24] that guarantee comprehensive care, almost unlimited access and free choice of physician, which are based on the principle of solidarity. This means that contributions are proportional to income and rates are not differentiated according to health risks, gender or age. Family members who are not in gainful employment are insured for free, and standard medical services are provided for them (Bärnighausen and Sauerborn 2002: 1570; Wörtz and Busse 2005: 134). All sickness funds are self-governing, non-profit organizations working independently from the German government, but 'operate within a strict framework of federal and state regulation' (Iglehart 1991: 1751). However, there are different types of funds which are divided into primary funds, which are based on geography (*Gebietskrankenkasse*) or companies (*Betriebskrankenkasse*), and substitute funds (*Ersatzkassen*). While these different public sickness funds and private insurance options lead to some regional and social differences within Germany, the fact that health insurance has been compulsory in Germany since 1883 is most likely the reason why the appearance of and discourse surrounding this topic is very different from in the United States, where health insurance remains a hotly debated topic, as I shall discuss in more detail below.

Contributions to the public sickness funds are equally split between employees and employers, and while the employee contributions are solely based on income and do not factor in health risks or dependants, the costs for the unemployed are covered by the unemployment insurance and those for retirees by government pension funds. The contributions of active members (i.e. workers) are also used by the funds to subsidize the higher health care costs of the elderly (Iglehart 1991). Unlike public insurance, the premiums for private insurance in Germany are based on age-related health risks and do not offer co-insurance for family members. There are also roughly 50 private insurance companies in Germany[25] that offer both a comprehensive policy (i.e. for those above the income threshold and civil servants) and complementary policies that offer additional services to publicly insured individuals (Iglehart 1991: 507; Wörtz and Busse 2005; Bärnighausen and Sauerborn 2002: 1565; Flintrop 2003). However, remarkably few of my German informants interviewed for this study were privately insured (three had only private insurance and two had both private and public insurance). This low number is somewhat surprising, since private insurance is mandatory for civil servants, including embassy staff and their spouses. As highly skilled workers, many could potentially also qualify for the higher-income threshold, and the fact that most did not choose private insurance could again highlight that my informants are best thought of as middling transnationals rather than global elites (as discussed in Chapter 2).

There are several key features integral to German health insurance that are not found in the US health insurance system which arguably are the most likely to cause friction for German transmigrants trying to integrate into the US health care system. For example, insured patients in the United States are expected to make co-payments for physician or hospital visits and for prescription drugs, although the specifics for these cost-sharing provisions vary by insurance plan (Mossialos et al. 2016). The co-payments are either paid directly at the time of the doctor's visit or billed afterwards, which often causes some confusion or takes patients by surprise, as the informants in this study reported. Other differences include comparable insurance plans that offer similar services at the same rates that can be kept despite changing jobs, free choice of physician, deductibles and subsidized prices for prescription drugs for those insured in Germany. And indeed, these differences were frequently mentioned by my German interlocutors and were often experienced as aggravating. These differences also help to explain why several of my informants found the health insurance reality in the United States difficult to accept, as was the case when Anna, the 35-year-old consultant from Germany who was at the time of our interview working as a language instructor, was confronted with high prices for prescribed medicines:

> My daughter had a red eye . . . and she needed eye drops. I mean that's not a big deal in Germany, you get that all the time at the pharmacy, and we had the prescription from the doctor and we paid $200 for these small eye drops. I was really shocked . . . And that for example is why I do go back to Germany and get stuff like this done.
> (Anna, German female, A1 visa, in the US since 2014)

Some informants like Anna thus managed to circumnavigate several of these issues by, for example, bringing drugs with them from Germany (see Chapter 6 for a full discussion of transnational health care strategies). Other differences between the German and US insurance systems, such as billing practices, were a common source of frustration that could not be easily avoided. Markus, a German consultant in his early thirties, for example, felt that 'the whole co-pay thing is kinda confusing and makes you pay money'.[26] He was also frustrated that he 'never knew when [he] had to pay and for what' and was taken by surprise when he received three different medical bills after only one hospital visit (from the attending doctor, the hospital itself and the anaesthesiologist).

Health insurance in Japan

Japan achieved universal health insurance (*kaihoken* – 'health insurance for all') in 1961, and was the first non-Western country to do so (Reich et al. 2011). However, health care insurance was available as early as

1905 to public-sector employees through mutual aid associations, with some private worker-protection schemes already being available in the late 1800s (Iglehart 1988). In 1922, the Health Insurance Act marked the beginning of national health insurance in Japan, which was not only modelled on the German system but also had similar motives of improving productivity and preventing unrest.[27] Employers, employees and physicians were originally opposed to its enactment, since it meant higher costs for employees and employers as well as lower fees for physicians; however, 'nationalistic goals' eventually overcame all opposition (Ikegami et al. 2011: 1107). Health insurance only became mandatory in 1958 and succeeded in achieving full coverage only three years later.

Unlike in Germany and the United States, health insurance in Japan is government-run. In fact, Ikegami et al. argue, the most distinctive element of Japanese health insurance is the 'role of the national government as one, and the largest, among a group of health insurance carriers, rather than as either coordinator of insurance plans or the sole insurer' (2011: 1107). Today there are roughly 3,500 insurance plans that are either employer- or community-based. Japanese citizens are not free to choose their health care plans, but are either enrolled by their employer or by their municipality. All those that are not employed and do not receive public assistance are enrolled in a citizens' health insurance or, if they are older than 75, in the late elders' health insurance. Every citizen in Japan is covered equally and all services, which include prescription drugs, acute and long-term care, dental and some preventative care, are uniform across all plans, regardless of their ability to pay (Ikegami and Campbell 1999; Arai and Ikegami 1998). However, co-payments differ substantially: the contribution rates of the citizens' health insurance plans are three times higher than for those insured as employees of large companies, and rates also differ greatly between employee- and community-based plans. Currently, all citizens except children and the elderly have a 30 per cent co-pay rate up to a certain threshold. Individuals on public assistance are exempt from co-payments altogether. This setup of access based on need rather than the ability to pay is widely supported by the Japanese, as opinion polls have repeatedly shown (Ikegami et al. 2011; Arai and Ikegami 1998).

However, we again have to keep in mind that health insurance has been compulsory in Japan since 1958, so the discourse around insurance is likely to differ from that in the United States. Most of my informants also felt strongly that Japanese health insurance was more fair or secure and offered better coverage compared to the insurance available to them in the US. Several also felt that the insurance setup in the United States hampered their desired access to health services (see Chapter 4) or thought the US health insurance market did not make much sense, as Haruka described to me. As a 33-year-old PhD student, she holds health insurance provided to her by her university, but she thinks 'it doesn't cover much' and is so useless that 'it feels I can never use it'.[28] She was particularly upset that regular check-ups (i.e. dentists, ophthalmologists and dermatologists) were not included in her insurance coverage.

The Japanese health care system is financed out of both insurance premiums and taxes, depending on which scheme the individual belongs to. Physicians in Japan are paid via a fees-for-service method which is government-regulated according to a 'nationally uniform, itemized, and minutely defined schedule, known as the point-fee-system' (Iglehart 1988: 1168).[29] These fees stay the same regardless of the health care provider chosen or the type of insurance plan the individual has, meaning that anyone can choose either to see a physician or go to a hospital with no difference in cost.

While Japanese patients are accustomed to co-payments, which also occur in the United States, they are automatically enrolled in insurance with no free choice over which plan. Japanese transmigrants are thus probably less accustomed to choosing an insurance plan than, for example, Germans (see above). However, the key difference between the health insurance setups of Japan and the US, which Japanese in the US experience first hand, is most likely the lack of free and unlimited access to physicians and hospitals in the US. In fact, Japanese patients see their doctor 1.3 times more often than Germans and more than three times as often as Americans.[30] And in fact, this does often become a point of friction for US physicians and Japanese patients, and changes health care choices for Japanese immigrants in the United States, as Saki's story highlights (this will also be discussed in more detail in Chapters 4 and 5). I met 58-year-old Saki when she was in DC as a visiting professor on sabbatical from her university in Japan, but she had been in the United States prior to this stay in DC, both as a student and as a researcher. Her first encounter with US health care during her first visit to the US, however, was very distressing to her, not only because of the costs of her treatment ('$2,200 for two aspirins'[31]) or because she was made to feel as if her insurance coverage was more important than her health condition, but mainly because it was quite complicated and she could not be sure that her expenses would be covered dependably. These first experiences left her feeling 'scared', and as a result she mentioned that she was trying 'not to get sick' during her stay.

Health insurance in India

The situation of India as a lower middle-income country is rather different and not directly comparable to the other countries discussed in this research. The subcontinent struggles with several health care issues, including high out-of-pocket expenses, low public health spending, rising health care costs and poor services, which creates a very different backdrop to the health care and health insurance landscape. Although health insurance coverage in India is limited, in recent years it has grown dramatically. Despite the fact that the goal of establishing universal health care by 2020 has had to be postponed by two years, the rate of insured individuals has now risen to a total of about 25 per cent (Ahlin, Nichter and Pillai 2016).

Health insurance does not have a very long history in India. In fact, the Employees' State Insurance Scheme (ESIS) was the first insurance, established one year after India gained Independence in 1947. Together with the Central Government Health Scheme (CGHS, established in 1954), it provides insurance to public servants, equating to roughly 10 per cent of the population. There are also around 40 private health insurance providers operating in India, yet only about 2 per cent of the population is insured through them. Additional schemes have been launched in recent years, most of them focusing on providing coverage for the poor or those in informal employment, but are often still in an experimental stage.[32] The market for private insurance continues to grow slowly because awareness of insurances is still fairly low (Ramani and Mavalankar 2006; Ahlin, Nichter and Pillai 2016). In fact, Horton and Das argue that 'these innovations are overlaid on a system of investments in health that are deeply irrational, inimical to the needs of most Indians, and adversely influenced by the fashions of international health organizations' (2011: 182). One of these new schemes was the universal health insurance introduced in 2003, which subsidized premiums for those below the poverty line in order to protect India's poorest citizens. It proved not to be very successful and instead provided a valuable lesson that the introduction of health insurance 'should be based on local research and policy analysis, rather than trying to "copy" or "import" insurance systems from other countries' (Ahlin, Nichter and Pillai 2016: 105).

There are several reasons why health insurance uptake proves to be more difficult than anticipated in India, including not only a lack of awareness or understanding of insurance principles and a lack of trust in government and unrealistic expectations, but also reservations about the concept. These are concerns among the poor population as well as the educated middle class, as several of my Indian interlocutors confirmed (Jain et al. 2014; Ahlin, Nichter and Pillai 2016). For example, 32-year-old Varun, who had come to the United States for a post-doc position in 2017, did not have a particularly good opinion of health insurance in general. In India he felt that being insured was not only a hassle, but reimbursements were not certain, especially compared to the US, where 'you just pay $10 and then the rest is covered by the insurance company'.[33] However, while he thought that health insurance in the United States was more regulated than in India, he still did not approve of the concept, because 'in the Western countries, health care insurance system is more towards exploitation and earning money'.

Having health insurance in India may also not necessarily be experienced as very helpful. For example, some employers offer health expense reimbursements for out-of-pocket expenses; however, these are often paid from a share of the employee's income that had been set aside for medical costs. And many enrollees in the ESIS try to avoid the facilities provided to ESIS members because of their poor services, and rather opt for private treatment, usually paid out of pocket. The ESIS coverage is so unpopular that many even prefer a 'Mediclaim' policy (introduced in 1986), despite it only covering hospitalization and having rather high premiums (Kumar et al. 2011). In fact, up to 65 per cent of all medical costs in India are not covered by any insurance or reimbursement scheme and have to be paid out of pocket by patients (Ellis, Alam and Gupta 2000), and are one of the key causes of debt in rural India (Rajeev and Latif 2009).

Additionally, government spending on health care in India (3.9% of the country's GDP) remains much lower than in many other low-income and lower middle-income countries. This translates to only about 30 per cent of health care costs being covered by public financing sources, leaving over 70 per cent of health care to be financed out of pocket. However, spending levels vary rather substantially in the different states, which also use and distribute health care spending differently.[34] The key driver for health care expenditure is money spent on drugs, rather than hospital stays. To ensure health care equity in India, some even argue that health coverage should focus primarily on drugs (Ahlin, Nichter and Pillai 2016; Reddy et al. 2011). This call to offer health insurance primarily to cover the costs of prescription drugs is in itself, I would argue, an acknowledgement of culturally shaped differences in expectations towards insurance, which could possibly lead to a very different set of assumptions about health insurance.

For Indian citizens coming to the United States, probably one of the key differences is the fact that health insurance is not only required but a necessity, because of the higher costs associated with health care in the US. While all my German and Japanese informants were insured in their home countries, it is actually much less common even for the Indian middle class to be covered by insurance, and it is widely seen as unnecessary, as the experiences of Salman and Priya (discussed above) showed. In fact, more than half of my Indian interlocutors (10) did not have health insurance in India, and only 8 had had access to either the government insurance scheme or private insurance through their parents or through their employer. Many also mentioned that they did not use their insurance because it was too complicated or they did not think it was worth it, as was the case for Ayaan. The 34-year-old had come to Washington, DC in 2013 to work as an economist at a large international organization. Although he already had experience with health insurance from India, he was not happy with the way it was set up in the United States, but realized that he had no choice if he wanted to avoid bankruptcy:

> Even with very, very good insurance, there is an enormous amount of paperwork . . . You will get 20 sets of bills from various . . . from the doctor itself, first you will do a co-pay, then the insurance agency might send you a bill for something additional, the testing centre will send you something different . . . I had insurance in India, most people don't. But the cost is generally low enough that you can pay for it as you go, when you get there for something minor . . . in the US, even if you have some minor ailment, you will go bankrupt if you don't have insurance.
> (Ayaan, Indian male, G4 visa, in the US since 2013)

Experiences with US health insurance: a cross-cultural comparison

Although studies on the attitudes towards health insurance and their impact on individuals' experiences have been limited to date (this is true for the experiences of locals with health insurance and even more so for immigrants), it is an important area of research with far-reaching implications. Ahlin and colleagues, for example, argue that health insurance can have a considerable influence on 'household production of health' (2016: 116), including self-medication practices, delays in health care seeking and sales of over-the-counter medication. Differences in the way health insurances are set up can thus have a profound impact on health behaviour, such as the number of sick days commonly taken, length of stay in hospitals and the number of consultations.

Yet when it came to their transnational patients, several physicians in my study felt that whether or not these patients had insurance coverage in the United States would be the key factor in how they experienced health care. Dr Griffith, a 42-year-old family physician working at a large hospital, even felt that insured highly skilled migrants should have similar experiences to US citizens, regardless of their cultural expectations or experiences with their home country's health insurance system:

> Highly skilled immigrants, you know, again I feel like if they are insured, they do have all the same options that a US citizen has. So it is a very different experience than somebody who is not a citizen and is not insured has. So the difference becomes almost, you know, insurance versus no insurance, really more than anything . . . So, I imagine highly skilled migrants would also feel more respected through the process than other immigrants.
>
> (Dr Griffith, Family Medicine)

Some physicians, however, acknowledged that the patients' previous experiences shaped their expectations (many Indian patients, for example, appeared to be used to 'still pay[ing] for service'[35]) as well as the type of insurance coverage transnationals held, which was often determined by their employment status. Dr Gross, a 44-year-old dentist who had emigrated from Germany to the United States in 2000 and was at the time of our interview working in a very affluent suburb of Washington, DC, explained to me that her German patients were 'from embassies, from German TV . . . on temporary assignments'. As such, they would be more likely to be insured by German international insurance than through US employer-sponsored insurance, which often allowed them to afford better care than her American patients:

> Because my [German] patients here, they get a very good reimbursement, because they have a very good coverage when they are abroad . . . whereas if I have an American patient and he is with insurance and if he only gets like 50 per cent covered for that crown he is not that easily gonna go for it.
>
> (Dr Gross, Dentist)

However, not all her transnational patients seemed to be as fortunate as German embassy staff. Her Japanese patients, for example, seemed to face more restrictions through their insurance than other patients, and for that reason sometimes 'only want to have palliative treatment or emergency treatment and then they'll do the rest when they are back in Japan'.[36] It thus seems clear that the experiences of highly skilled (insured) migrants from Germany, India and Japan differ quite substantially in the United States, depending not only on their expectations, but also on the type of insurance they held or were required to hold, due to their employment status (this point will be discussed further below).

Additionally, the differences in the insurance setup and health culture can also reinforce each other,[37] and in turn impact how transmigrants access and utilize health care in the host country. For example, unmet insurance expectations (e.g. what is covered) can directly change health-seeking behaviours (see Chapter 6) or the type of insurance purchased. Nobu, the 37-year-old Japanese economist, for example, actively sought a certain insurance plan that would reflect his culturally informed expectations:

> . . . we had a plan with which we had to go to the PCP [Primary Care Physician] first and they decide. And even if I say I want to check this, they said: You are fine, you are healthy. So you don't have to do anything. But like, I wanted to check more, but 'no, no, no, you are fine'. So . . . It is, like until it happens, something severe or like . . . we cannot do anything. So that's why I changed my plan and now from this year we can go to specialist directly. Don't need a referral from the PCP.
> (Nobu, Japanese male, G4 visa, in the US since 2012)

While getting familiarized with the health insurance in the host country may be difficult for every immigrant, there may be aspects that are more of an issue for some than for others – arguably also depending on their previous health insurance experiences. Here, I argue that keyword analysis of the patient narratives is a good way to assess commonly mentioned issues and those that seem to be specific to one group or another – see Table 3.2 for some similarities and notable differences among the three different groups. These findings might also reflect how health insurance and experiences with insurance are talked about in the media or in immigrants' social networks, as I will discuss in more detail below.

Table 3.2 Word frequency in narratives per 10,000 for selected terms

	Germany	India	Japan
Money category overall[1]	82.81	62.3	100.62
Cost(s)	10.38	5.42	11.87
Expensive	8.43	5.97	7.48
Cheaper/cheap	2.59	3.66	3.61
Reimbursed	2.81	0	0.26
Bankrupt	0.22	0.95	0
Complicated	4.1	0.95	2.57
Scared/scary	0	2	3.6

[1] This category combines 37 word types such as 'dollar(s)', 'money', 'billing', 'fee', 'bucks', etc., including 'cost' and 'costs', which are also listed separately.

In the keyword analysis, two main findings stand out: the importance of costs and the emotional connotations transmigrants have regarding health care in the United States. The cost of health care, and in particular health insurance, was a key theme across all groups of my interview partners which many of my informants struggled with, but it was most often referred to by my Japanese informants. This was not necessarily because they had trouble paying for their health care bills, but because many of my informants struggled with the fact that the costs of US health care could be so expensive, as one of my Indian informants, Rahul, a visiting researcher in his early thirties, explained to me:

> I can give you an example, okay, that explains it much better. In India an MRI [Magnetic Resonance Imaging] would cost around 6,000 Rupees and a TV will cost me around 30,000–40,000 Rupees, okay? Here, a TV will cost me $400, but an MRI $1,500 . . . That's ridiculous, right? Your basic health care is more expensive than a luxury commodity. That is strange. That is very strange for me . . . I don't know what the deal is. Why there is such a disparity, just doesn't make sense to me.
> (Rahul, Indian male, J1 visa, in the US since 2016)

Generally, my Japanese and German interview partners were the most likely to mention costs, particularly compared to the Indian participants, who mentioned costs only about half as often, a highly significant difference ($p<0.0005$, $\chi^2=15.39$). There are some differences, however, in how my informants talked about costs across the three groups in terms of the United States being more 'expensive' or health care in their country being 'cheaper'. While the US system was described by all my informants as 'expensive' (and in all cases as more expensive than their home health care system), my German interview partners were slightly more likely to use the word 'expensive' (8.43 times per 10,000 words) than my Japanese interlocutors (7.48 per 10,000). For example, 39-year-old Hanna, who worked as an economist at an international organization, described to me how she struggled to come to terms with how much more expensive health insurance was in the United States, a sentiment that was shared by many of my German informants:

> Ahh, that is a huge topic. I find it is a bit of a nightmare in the US. First, when I did not have my employer-sponsored health care system, it's extremely expensive and covers very little. So, in my first years as a consultant, I purchased my own health insurance and to be very frank, I still had to pay out of pocket [for] almost everything . . . So it felt like almost as if I didn't have any health insurance . . . There is always something, there is always a struggle. It never runs smoothly. Even when you have a very expensive and good health insurance. And I never had any of those problems in Germany, none of those. It runs much smoother.
>
> (Hanna, German female, G4 visa, in the US since 2010)

Among my Indian interview partners, 'expensive' was used much less commonly, with only 5.97 mentions per 10,000 words, though the imbalance is not significant in this sample size. However, they were the most likely to use the words 'cheaper' and 'cheap' (3.66 times per 10,000), while Germans mentioned them less frequently (2.59/10,000). Additionally, unlike my German and Japanese interlocutors (3.61/10,000), who also used these words to describe some services in the United States as cheaper (in five cases), Indians exclusively referred to Indian health care as cheaper/cheap compared to its US counterpart. The reason for this difference might quite possibly be the amount of exposure the three groups had to medical costs in their home countries. My German informants, who had all been insured in Germany, were largely shielded from both paying for health care and being confronted with bills documenting the costs of health care. And since they did not pay for health care in Germany, they might be less likely to draw comparisons than other groups (i.e. saying care is cheaper in Germany), while still experiencing the costs of health care in the United States as particularly expensive. The exact opposite might be true for my Indian informants, many of whom did not have health insurance in India and were accustomed to pay for their health care and medication out of pocket; thus, having a direct comparison between the differences in health costs most often led to them referring to Indian health care as 'cheaper'. While Indians might be the most used to paying for health care and the Germans the least, the Japanese seem to fall somewhere in the middle, because unlike Indians they have been shielded from health care costs (similar to the German setup), while at the same time they are familiar with co-pays. This possibly accounts for them coming second in the keyword analysis in terms of mentions of both 'expensive' and 'cheap/cheaper'.

In the analysis of costs, two additional words stand out: 'reimbursed' and 'bankrupt', each of which is almost exclusively mentioned by one group – Germans and Indians respectively. Five of my German informants (embassy workers or their spouses and intra-company transferees) and two of my Japanese interlocutors (visiting professors) were covered not by US health insurance, but privately in their home country. However, being insured privately, which was often a requirement for embassy staff, could also come at a steep price, as two of my German informants told me. This might also be one of the reasons why the issues of medical costs and their reimbursement were an important aspect for them. Julia, a 37-year-old political consultant at the time of our interview, for example, felt 'lucky' that the type of German international insurance that she had picked at the time when her husband became a diplomat covered all their medical expenses, being fully aware that others were not as fortunate with their insurance:

> We are very lucky with our insurance but I know that this is not always the case. Cause, when my husband joined the diplomatic service in Germany he had the choice between I think only one or two private insurance companies that really are for worldwide coverage. Most of the private insurance companies exclude Switzerland and the US because of cost reasons. And I know from a colleague of my husband who has another health insurance and they came back to him and said because the costs are so high in the US we only cover, I can't remember, 60 or 80 per cent of all your expenses. And this is, we would have gone bankrupt with the medical bills that our son produced here.
> (Julia, German female, A1 visa, in the US since 2012)

Jonas, another German embassy worker who was in his early thirties at the time of our interview, explained to me that embassy staff posted in the

US are often faced with additional costs which were not compensated for by their employer. For example, he and his colleagues were required to take out German international insurance coverage, many of which 'impose surcharges . . . And not little. For some it is even 100 per cent.'[38] German international insurance, however, not only had surcharges, but it also made the policy holders appear as self-payers in the US system, so that they have to pay all or most medical costs upfront and only get reimbursed later. The word 'reimbursed' in connection to US health care was thus unsurprisingly mentioned 13 times by my German informants (2.81/10,000 words).[39]

The word 'bankrupt', on the other hand, referring to experiences with health care in the United States, was used predominantly by my Indian informants (7 times, 0.95 times per 10,000 words), and once by a German interlocutor (0.22/10,000). Most Indians referred to the risk of going bankrupt as part of stories they had heard about health care and health insurance in the US, which tends to influence how health care is talked about and experienced, as I will discuss below. For example, Vihaan, the 38-year-old IT specialist who had come as an international student from India and not through a company channel, based many of his expectations of how the US health care system worked on stories he had heard from friends and family:

> When I just landed, and it's not just me, I talked to my friends, and everyone was scared . . . to death. Because we were told horror stories, that one mistake or something bad happens to you, like you could be, you could be owing like $50,000, and you'll go bankrupt.
> (Vihaan, Indian male, waiting for Green Card approval, in the US since 2002)

More than any other group, my Indian informants had also received devastating medical bills often incurred by visiting family members with insufficient travel insurance coverage, which might have contributed to their sense of health care costs leading to bankruptcy. These bills also left several of my Indian informants worried about their parents visiting, fearful that they could accrue massive health care costs. Since none of the other groups mentioned similar issues, it is thus possible that the lack of good visitor's insurance is in part a result of the generally limited insurance options in India (see above). Salman, for example, recounted an episode when his visiting father had fallen so ill with food poisoning on the plane from India that he had to be taken straight to the emergency room (ER). And despite having had travel health insurance, the family was left with a bill of $7,000, leaving Salman, an engineer in his thirties, very disillusioned.

Luckily for him, some of his acquaintances had told him that first-time visitors to the ER in the state of Maryland can apply for a deduction of costs, which he successfully managed to secure, leaving him with only $1,500 to off pay. But even that amount was a difficult sum to pay at the time when he had just started to work in the United States, making him question how best to handle his ageing parents' visits in the future. Another of my Indian interlocutors, the 34-year-old postdoctoral student Tanvi, had similar concerns and said that her previous experiences with visitors' health insurance made her very 'hesitant'[40] to have her parents visit her again in the US, because she feared that if something happened, 'even though they buy visitors' insurance, which I don't think helps at all, because it covers nothing', they would end up with 'an outstanding bill of $25,000'.

A second area that deserves attention is some of the emotions transmigrants seem to experience regarding the US health insurance system. Again, there are some striking differences in how frequently some words are used. 'Scared' or 'scary', for example, was mainly used by my Japanese informants (3.6 times per 10,000 words) and to a lesser extent by my Indian informants (2/10,000), while none of my German informants used these words to describe their experiences.[41] This may very well result from the fact that Germans tended to experience fewer barriers to health care (see Chapter 5). Feeling scared or admitting to having scary experiences is probably also related to how my informants viewed their status and their integration into US culture. Since the majority of my German interview partners had come to the US on an assignment, for example as intra-company transferees or dispatched embassy staff, they might feel less vulnerable than those who had come of their own volition, like many of my Indian and Japanese informants had – for example to pursue further education.

Germans, on the other hand, seemed to be particularly concerned that getting health care is more complicated in the United States and mentioned 'complicated' by far the most times (4.1/10,000) compared to the Japanese (2.57/10,000) and Indians, who rarely mentioned it (0.95/10,000). A typical example of this trend is Christine's story. The 31-year-old, who at the time of our interview was a German-language instructor, struggled with setting up her insurance in the US:

> So that was really complicated. I still haven't fully figured out how my insurance really works, how to use it, how to use the website. It is a lot simpler in Germany, because everyone, almost everyone

has basic insurance, and so ahmm . . . But here I found the access really complicated. So, finding my way through the insurance, figuring out which doctors I can use with my insurance.

(Christine, German female, Green Card in the US since 2015)

This is not altogether surprising, since the insured in Germany can choose to keep their insurance company and insurance plan even if they change jobs, as discussed above. And since all sickness funds offer the same services with essentially no deductibles and co-pays, even changing plans might not be experienced as a difficult or complicated choice. In fact, seven of my German informants had changed their insurance in Germany and five had changed insurance companies in the United States. They are thus in a better position to compare this process than Indians, 11 of whom had changed insurance in the US, but none of whom had done so in India. Several also had little or no previous experience with insurance in India. The fact that the Japanese, who are also automatically enrolled in health insurance in their home country, do not describe their journey to insurance as 'complicated' may have several reasons, including a cultural preference for not talking negatively,[42] differences in visa status (most of my interview partners came to the United States either as international students and thus were covered by compulsory university health insurance or as spouses of US citizens, and had coverage through their partner's insurance) and the fact that most of the Japanese informants had not changed insurance companies in the US.[43]

The fact that differences in health insurance setups have a big impact on transnationals is also attested by the fact that the majority of my informants preferred the health insurance system they had in their own country: while none of my German or Japanese informants preferred the US health insurance system,[44] a third of my Indian informants thought that the US system was better than the Indian system, because it was better regulated and covered more people. The fact that only my Indian interlocutors were positively impressed with health insurance is probably due to the fact that health insurance in general is not common in India and that many of my Indian informants were not previously insured. Yet, the main reasons most of my informants gave for preferring their home country's insurance system were similar across all groups (despite the vast differences in insurance policies in all three countries): the extreme costs in the United States, the complicated rules and regulations of insurance coverage and the fact that the system was experienced as unfair.

In fact, several informants, predominantly from Germany, pointed out that in the US, health care was not a right but rather 'a privilege'[45] and that insurance was a 'marker of social inequality'.[46] Others also mentioned that the United States had a 'very unfair system'[47] that was 'only good for rich people'.[48] Britta, a 42-year-old project manager from Germany, for example, did not agree with the way health insurance was set up in the US compared to what she had been used to from Germany:

> That is just wrong, because it should be a right for everyone to be healthy and to be able to go the doctor if they need to. And basically I still think that. It's just not the system that I live in anymore.
> (Britta, German female, Green Card holder, in the US since 2004)

Several of my informants even mentioned that insurance was a key factor in their decision of whether to stay in the United States. For example, 32-year-old Tobias, a researcher from Germany who had come to the US as a post-doc, told me that while he was very happy to be working in the US, he 'would probably have to go back' to Germany if he had to buy health insurance himself. 'That would be a deal breaker for me.'[49]

And while issues regarding health insurance are often reduced to a lack of coverage or underinsurance, which did not affect my informants, health insurance is nevertheless an important aspect for many. While further research is needed to establish whether or not US health insurance culture and (negative) experiences transmigrants made have an impact on highly skilled migrants' decision to come to the United States, for some, health care in the US was an important factor. Aishwarya, for example, a software engineer who had come to the US as an F1 student visa holder in 2002 and who preferred not to give me her age, said that she would advise fellow Indians to reconsider immigrating to the US:

> Make sure that your insurance covers all the details that you need. And look at the fine prints please . . . you probably end up bankrupting yourself. So yes, that's what I'd advise them . . . And I will tell them, think again if you want to come to the US (laughs) for this health care issue.
> (Aishwarya, Indian female, H-1B visa, in the US since 2002)

Attitudes and beliefs: how health insurance is discussed

Since health insurance is such a broadly defined concept with a myriad of different options that vary between nations, within local regions and even within different plans offered by the same provider, it is not surprising that expectations and experiences with health insurance are also strongly influenced by shared views within one's social network of family and friends or as propagated by the media. In fact, attitudes towards health care and in particular towards health insurance have been shown to be influenced by a wide array of aspects, such as country of origin, one's health status, age, socioeconomic and sociopolitical attitudes, patients' experiences and the media portrayal of health care and health insurance (cf. Cleary et al. 1991; Schnusenberg, Loh and Nihalani 2013; Yamada et al. 2014).

Political ideology and associated public relations or ad campaigns across media platforms (including newspapers, television and, increasingly, social media) are also powerful tools in shaping public opinion and may thus play a part in how health insurance is viewed, although these correlations have not been studied sufficiently (Schnusenberg, Loh and Nihalani 2013). However, much research points to the fact that exposure to political information can influence one's personal opinion on the matters discussed, and this should hold particularly true when it comes to 'the polarized partisan messages about government health insurance requirements' (Wilson 2014: 1). Public opinion is thus not constant or unchanging, but is at least in part shaped by the role of the media in their attempts to influence it.[50] This would also partly account for the fact that discussions surrounding health care in the United States have been shown to fluctuate a lot over time (Blendon et al. 2006; Kohut and Remez 2009).

An analysis of contemporary news from the Newspaper section of *The Corpus of Contemporary American English* (COCA – Davies 2008–) shows that the issue which was key to most of my informants' experiences, namely 'costs', was also the most common issue associated with insurance in the news, as demonstrated by the common collocations of health insurance, such as 'premiums' (#3), 'buy' (#7), 'rates' (#16) (see Chapter 2 for collocation analysis methodology). Directly related to costs are also the collocations surrounding issues of 'coverage' (#5) and 'covered' (#17). Also, as discussed above, the collocations for 'Obamacare' (i.e. 'repeal'/'replace') are indicative of how health insurance is commonly discussed in US media. This more negative news coverage might have also been influenced by the fact that health insurance and related terms do not have a long history in public discourse in the United States. Due to the different historical and social setting of health insurance in the US discussed above, the term insurance or terms relating to insurance, such as sickness fund,[51]

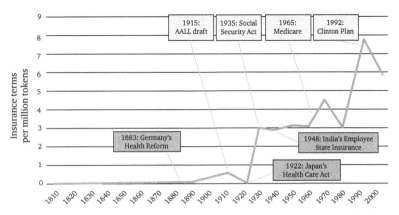

Figure 3.1 The occurrence of the term 'health insurance', including related terms such as sickness fund, compulsory health insurance in the Corpus of Historical American English (COHA). Source: author.

compulsory health insurance and so on, were historically much less present in the United States than in Germany or Japan, for example, as can be seen in Figure 3.1 above.[52] The lower social acceptance might thus be correlated with the limited and recent embeddedness of the term in society.

Figure 3.1 is based on an analysis of *The Corpus of Historical American English* (COHA – Davies 2010),[53] the largest structured corpus of historical English containing balanced data from each decade ranging from 1810 to 2009, extracted from contemporary newspapers, magazines and other print materials (with a total of 448,200,483 tokens). As can be seen, terms related to health insurance are not mentioned in the corpus in the years between 1810 and 1890. Only from then on do we get a few more hits: for example, the word combination 'compulsory' and 'health' gets mentioned for the first time once in the decade starting in 1890 and then six times in the following decade. The increase in mentions of insurance and related terms appears to correspond to several landmarks of US health insurance policy mentioned above: the first increase begins around the time when the 1915 bill by the AALL was drafted. Then a steep increase is noticeable starting in the 1920s, a decade that saw the introduction of Blue Cross in 1929 (discussed above). The decades of the 1930s and 1940s saw a slow increase in insurance being mentioned in the newspapers (the terms were mentioned 2.95 and 2.78 times per million tokens, up from 0.1, or once per 10 million, in the 1920s). During this time the Social Security Act was passed in 1935 and Blue Shield was established in 1939. The next big increase in mentions in the news occurs around the time of Nixon's 'new national health strategy' in the 1970s and Clinton's 'health reform' in the 1990s (with a total of 240 mentions).[54] Figure 3.1 also gives some landmarks of the other three countries for comparison: the establishment of Germany's compulsory health insurance in 1883, Japan's Health Care Act of 1922 and the establishment of India's first health insurance in 1948, which all happened before health insurance was frequently discussed in the United States.

While the coverage of the topic health insurance is likely shaped by policy (e.g. the passing of the Social Security Act) and how important the topic is deemed by the public at any time, Kohut and Remez (2009) argue that views on health care are not predominantly shaped by the news, but that personal experiences are the most decisive factor regarding attitudes. As I have demonstrated above, however, these personal experiences, especially those of immigrants, need to be examined against the backdrop of structural and functional differences in health insurance culture, since they too shape and reinforce health culture beliefs as well as expectations and experiences.

Conclusion

As we have seen, health insurance has far-reaching consequences for health-seeking behaviours, not only by affecting when and how often medical advice can be sought, and who can seek it, but also by influencing how long individuals delay health care seeking and their choices to self-medicate with either over-the-counter drugs or other forms of medicine (cf. Ahlin, Nichter and Pillai 2016). Yet, each country's health insurance policies are a product of a unique set of historical, social and economic factors (cf. Dao and Mulligan 2016). And since experience with and expectations towards health insurance seem in large part also to be culturally shaped, this area of research is crucial to understanding foreign patients' health care needs and their successful integration into the US health care system.

As this research shows, despite some similarities (i.e. regarding the costs of US health insurance and the importance of the right to access health care), there are some striking differences between the three groups under investigation here that are arguably affected by immigrants' previous experiences with health insurance in their country of origin as well as the type of insurance coverage they have access to in the United States. In this way, while several of my Indian informants, many of whom had no previous experience with insurance in India, thought health insurance should be unnecessary or was even a nuisance, none of my German or Japanese interlocutors felt this way. In fact, many of these informants, and especially German ones, could not understand the political debates on health insurance coverage, and all groups frequently pointed out advantages of the insurance plans of their respective home countries.

Unsurprisingly, the key reasons my informants gave for their dissatisfaction with US health care were not only based on their lack of knowledge of how insurance works, although this was a major issue many reported, but also on services or access that they had previously enjoyed and did not find during their stay in the United States, and which thus seemed to lower their satisfaction with health care delivery in the US in general. As I will discuss in further detail in the following chapters, many of these dissonances will have far-reaching consequences and shape how health care is itself experienced (next chapter), constitute a significant barrier to health care for highly skilled migrants (Chapter 5) and shape many of the choices these groups make when it comes to transnational health care seeking (Chapter 6).

Notes

1. The quotation in the chapter title is from my informant Priya (Indian female, G2 visa in the US since 1995).
2. http://www.who.int/health_financing/universal_coverage_definition/en (accessed 16 December 2021).
3. In order to do so, we need to keep in mind that the concept of health insurance should also be viewed through a postcolonial lens; see also discussion in Chapter 4.
4. The World Bank has also published a study tracking the establishment of universal health care in 24 developing countries including India (see Cotlear et al. 2015) outlining some of these issues.
5. This willingness of women to invest limited resources in health insurance may also be influenced by the fact that in India women traditionally receive less necessary (pay for service) health care than men (Dao and Nichter 2016).
6. In the scope of this book, this section cannot, and does not aim to, give a full account of the history of the US health care system. For a detailed account until the 1980s, see, e.g., Starr 1982. For a summary of health care reform between 1980 up to the Affordable Health Care Act of 2010, see, e.g., Starr 2011. For a detailed account of the public presentation of the Blue Cross, see Rothman 1991; for a detailed list of health care proposals between the years 1912 and 1976, see Falk 1977. For details on the Affordable Health Care Act, see, e.g., Fletcher 2016. For an assessment of the Trump administration on health care in the United States, see Galea 2017.
7. In particular, the British National Health Insurance of 1911 (Falk 1977).
8. While 'fee-for-service' rewards physicians for each service provided, making their income dependent on how many services they have performed, the capitation of salary rewards physicians per patient in a given time period, thereby not incentivizing an increase in services provided. Arguably, capitation of salary places the burden of financial risks on providers, especially if they have to attend to less healthy patients. See Rudmik, Wranik and Rudisill-Michaelsen 2014 for a discussion of the benefits and disadvantages of different payment methods.

9   Starr quotes Edwin Witte, the Staff Director of the Committee on Economic Security. For a detailed discussion on why health insurance was excluded from the bill in 1935, see, e.g., Rothman 1993; Starr 1982.

10   The idea of a group health plan that would be nominally nonprofit had already emerged in 1929 with the establishment of a hospitalization insurance called Blue Cross and in 1939 with Blue Shield, an insurance against medical expenses. Blue Cross specifically advertised to the middle class and 'presented itself as the best alternative to government involvement' (Rothman 1993: 275); and Blue Shield also 'was clearly aimed at preventing a government program from being adopted' (Starr 1982: 308).

11   While Medicare is a federal insurance programme that primarily serves the elderly, Medicaid is a federally and state-funded health coverage programme assisting low-income patients from all age groups. See also https://www.hhs.gov/answers/medicare-and-medicaid/what-is-the-difference-between-medicare-medicaid/index.html (accessed 18 December 2021). In order to get Medicare/Medicaid passed, reformers had always stressed that – albeit for strategic reasons – it was not a national health insurance scheme. According to Rothman, this actually reinforced the view that the middle class could take care of their medical needs on their own and that it was only the elderly and the poor who needed assistance.

12   For more information on Clinton's health care plan, see Clinton 1992, and for reasons why it fell out of favour with the public, see Blendon et al. 1995.

13   Part D mainly covers prescription drugs and can be seen as a direct result of the costs of prescription drugs that had tripled in the 10 years between 1990 and 2000 (Zinner and Loughlin 2009; for a more detailed description, see Starr 2011).

14   See Oberlander 2010 for a more detailed discussion; see also Starr 2011, esp. Chapter 7, for a detailed account of the struggle to pass reform.

15   https://www.kff.org/uninsured/fact-sheet/key-facts-about-the-uninsured-population/ (accessed 18 December 2021). It was projected in 2012 that by 2022 the ACA would have reduced the number of individuals with no insurance by 30 million (Thomson et al. 2012). However, according to a January 2017 report of the Congressional Budget Office, a repeal of the ACA would lead to an increase of 18 million uninsured in the first year and up to 32 million by 2026 (Congressional Budget Office 2017).

16   This led to a renewed discussion on the ACA and arguably also helped to set the scene for the then Republican presidential nominee Trump to call for its repeal; see https://www.nytimes.com/2016/10/25/us/some-health-plan-costs-to-increase-by-an-average-of-25-percent-us-says.html. The rise in costs also varies drastically by state; see https://www.washingtonpost.com/news/get-there/wp/2016/11/01/where-obamacare-prices-are-rising-dramatically/ as well as https://www.nytimes.com/2016/10/26/upshot/rising-obamacare-rates-what-you-need-to-know.html. In the presidential election campaign, then presidential nominee Biden vowed to protect and expand the ACA: see https://joebiden.com/healthcare/. And in 2021, the new Biden administration extended ACA enrolment in an attempt to extend coverage to those Americans who lost health insurance coverage during the COVID pandemic; see https://www.washingtonpost.com/health/biden-to-reopen-federal-aca-insurance-marketplaces-for-three-months/2021/01/27/fc54ea22-6117-11eb-afbe-9a11a127d146_story.html. All accessed 18 December 2021.

17   For a full discussion, see Blank 2012.

18   For this search I have used the General Web section of the GloWbE corpus, a web-based corpus containing about 1.9 billion words (Davies 2013; https://corpus.byu.edu/glowbe). See Chapter 2 for keyword analysis methodology.

19   (Christine, German female, Green Card holder, in the US since 2015).

20   As discussed above, the implementation of the ACA increased not only premiums but also the costs of health care in general, by covering a larger percentage of residents in the United States.

21   (Vihaan, Indian male, waiting for Green Card approval, in the US since 2002).

22   Number referring to income threshold in 2021: https://www.pkv.de/themen/krankenversicherung/so-funktioniert-die-pkv/wer-kann-sich-privat-versichern (accessed 18 December 2021).

23   https://www.pkv.de/themen/krankenversicherung/so-funktioniert-die-pkv/wer-muss-sich-privat-versichern (accessed 18 December 2021).

24   Historically, each sickness fund had covered only a small number of workers, which were assigned to their fund based on their occupation or site of residence. However, when the number of workers began to increase, funds began to merge. Merging still continues and is

regulated, e.g., by the Health Care Structure Reform Act of 1992 (*Gesundheitsstrukturgesetz*). From an original 21,238 funds that existed in 1913, only 123 existed in 2015 and 103 in 2021. See https://www.gkvspitzenverband.de/krankenversicherung/kv_grundprinzipien/alle_gesetzlichen_krankenkassen/alle_gesetzlichen_krankenkassen.jsp (accessed 19 December 2021).
25 https://www.pkv.de/verband/ueber-uns/ (accessed 19 December 2021).
26 (Markus, German male, G4 visa, in the US since 2012).
27 In the Meiji era (1868–1912), Japan aimed at modernizing the country and 'sought to replicate the institutions and practices of other countries' (Iglehart 1988: 808). During that time, the Japanese attraction to Western technology led to the adoption of biomedicine in general and German medicine in particular, 'which, at the time was considered the most advanced in Europe' (Iglehart 1988: 808) as well as German medical terminology (Grimmer-Solem 2005: 203), but also included British Navy or Prussian Army methods. See also Ikegami et al. 2011.
28 (Haruka, Japanese female, F1 visa, in the US since 2012).
29 However, the system is set up in such a way that doctors have incentives to prescribe products for which they are paid higher fees with less work, a practice that has led to an excess of prescription drugs and lab work (Arai and Ikegami 1998). A contributing factor to this practice may also be that hospitals are often run by families, and it is not unusual that a hospital or clinic has been in the hands of one family for several generations (Mayhew 2001; Iglehart 1988).
30 https://www.commonwealthfund.org/international-health-policy-center/system-stats/annual-physician-visits-per-capita (accessed 8 February 2022).
31 (Saki, Japanese female, J1 visa, in the US since 2016).
32 There are various health insurance types available in India, including private and social insurance, employer-provided insurance, community insurance and government health care spending. There are also nonprofit insurance schemes (CHIs) available that are based on the principle of solidarity. However, most of these still cover only small sections of the population (cf. Ahlin, Nichter and Pillai 2016; Ellis, Alam and Gupta 2000; Kumar et al. 2011).
33 (Varun, Indian male, J1 visa, in the US since 2017).
34 Of the money privately spent on health care, over 80 per cent is paid out of pocket by the patients, 9 per cent by employers and only 5 to 10 per cent is covered by health insurance companies. Unsurprisingly, these out-of-pocket payments are a leading cause of poverty and debt for Indian patients and have been directly 'responsible for the deepening of poverty in both rural and urban areas, pushing between 32 million and 39 million Indians into poverty every year' (Ahlin, Nichter and Pillai 2016: 103). However, it is the poorest and most desperate people in rural India or in informal employment that are burdened the most with bearing out-of-pocket costs. The Indian middle class to which my informants generally belonged usually suffer less from out-of-pocket costs.
35 (Dr Griffith, Family Medicine).
36 (Dr Gross, Dentist).
37 India's large out-of-pocket health expenditures for prescription drugs (research suggests they account for anything between 61% and 88% of all OOP expenditures) (Ahlin, Nichter and Pillai 2016: 104) could be seen as one such example of insurance-influenced health behaviours or indeed health culture that is reinforced by the insurance system. Drug expenditures are partially due to the very liberal prescription practices of physicians, the very prevalent use of over-the-counter medication and the self-medication practices of the Indian lower and middle classes. Arguably, a cultural preference for self-medication as expressed by large sales of over-the-counter medications, shapes the form of insurance planned to cater to the cultural determinants of health insurance satisfaction. Unsurprisingly, then, any plans for universal health insurance tend to focus on access to medication as a measure for equity and the system's quality (see Ahlin, Nichter and Pillai 2016).
38 (Jonas, German male, A1 visa, in the US since 2014).
39 'Reimbursed' was also mentioned once by one Japanese informant (0.26/10,000), and not at all by Indians.
40 (Tanvi, Indian female, H-1B visa, in the US since 2006).
41 For the categories scared/scary, I not only checked the word frequency analysis, but manually checked the German originals for similar words to account for differences in translation made by the author. While none of the Germans used the words 'scared' or 'scary', they would, however, use the words 'fear', 'worry' or 'afraid' to describe some of their experiences (3 times per 10,000 words), compared to Indians (2.85/10,000) and Japanese (3.6/10,000).

42 Kurata et al. also argue that in Japan physicians are seen as more authoritarian figures than in the United States, making Japanese patients possibly less likely to voice criticism, and that in Japan, dissatisfaction is often responded to with resignation (*shikata ga nai* or 'it can't be helped'). Thus, neutral responses may be 'a subtle way of expressing dissatisfaction' (1994: 1074; Elleuch 2008).
43 Of my Japanese informants, three had changed insurance companies in Japan and three in the US.
44 Although three Germans and three Japanese also remained neutral, pointed out some advantages in the US or were critical of some aspects of their home insurance.
45 (Christine, German female, Green Card holder, in the US since 2015); see full quote at the beginning of the chapter.
46 (Anja, German female, G4 visa, in the US since 2009).
47 (Christine, German female, Green Card holder, in the US since 2015).
48 (Saki, Japanese female, J1 visa, in the US since 2016).
49 (Tobias, German male, J1 visa, in the US since 2017).
50 While it is widely recognized that public opinion influences the policy process, there is little agreement on the amount of actual influence it has over it. Polls on health care also do not adequately take the complexity of the public's views into account (Blendon et al. 2006: 624, 625).
51 In fact, the term 'sickness insurance' 'fell out of favor as overly Germanic and was replaced' in the US with the term 'health insurance' during the First World War (Bump 2015: 35).
52 While the way health insurance is discussed and the type of content in these debates tend to differ from country to country, future research might show that differences are shaped depending, e.g., on what plans are available for whom and how long health insurance has been compulsory in each country, as well as the role of the media. As such, this might provide a useful tool for examining cultural norms for health insurance.
53 https://corpus.byu.edu/coha/ (accessed 21 December 2021).
54 Since the corpus data ends in 2009, the impact of the discussions of the ACA cannot be documented fully.

4
'I saw an army of doctors walk in . . .': highly skilled migrants' experiences with health care and biomedical diversity in the United States

In India, it's not to say that it's all clean and all good. But accessibility, access to medicine, access to doctors, is much better, much easier. There is a lot of human component, less procedural . . . And the major difference I feel here . . . I think they make you take test over test over test . . . Excessive force, they would prescribe stronger doses, stronger medicines and then, if it is anything slightly more, not complex, something they can't cure with pill bomb, then they test, test, test, test. And in the end it is either antibiotics or surgery. And I have seen that over and over.
(Chetan, Indian male, G4 visa, in the US since 2013)

Introduction

As discussed above, the highly skilled migrants under investigation in this research project were all covered by insurance for the duration of their stay in the United States, nominally enabling them to access and make use of the US health care system, and thus putting them in an advantaged position over many US citizens as well as different groups of immigrants lacking insurance in the US.[1] However, the United States' health care system has been repeatedly described as the most inefficient health care system in the developed world (Reid 2009), and a 'disjointed, for-profit, employer-based system' (Horton et al. 2014: 4). Wetzel even claims that the US health care system is no system at all, but rather a conglomeration of various organizations and institutions that provide health care through '"a confusing maze" of hospitals, clinics and individual physicians' (2011: 383). Thus, even after immigrants have cleared the first hurdle in accessing health care by successfully acquainting themselves with US health insurance requirements, they will subsequently need to learn how to navigate the 'Americanness' (Fox 2005) of the health care system.

Since immigrant health care-seeking behaviour has been shown to differ by country of origin and social class, among other variables (Choi 2013), this Americanness can inadvertently cause dissatisfaction and negatively impact health outcomes when transnational patients base their expectations on the kinds of services, treatments or medications available to them in their home country. However, as Papanicolas, Cylus and Smith (2013) point out, it is patients' attitudes rather than their experiences with health care that are the best predictor of health care satisfaction. Transnational experiences with health care could thus be affected by two factors: first, by different attitudes towards health care, and second, by how these influence their expectations of US health care.

Yet, it is not only the differences in health care setups that influence transnationals' experiences with services and their health care satisfaction. The diversity of biomedicine itself (Dilger et al. 2012), as well as its implicit 'separation between the "West" and the "Rest"' (Dilger and Mattes 2018: 268), also shapes transnational medical encounters, for example when differences are brushed aside by physicians either as cultural or as an indication of patients' experiences with a lower quality of health care in their home countries. Johnston and Herzig, for instance, argue 'that health care providers interpret health care in an evolutionist paradigm' (2006: 2505) that has led US physicians to interpret their Mexican patients' requests for certain medications as a lack of familiarity with the modern, advanced medicine available to them in the United States. Any 'biomedical particularities' (Schühle 2018: 299) displayed by transnational patients can therefore not only shape their own experiences with health care in the host society, but also inform how local physicians in turn interpret their health-seeking behaviour.

In this chapter I will thus (1) discuss the impact of differences in health care systems, such as the role of hospitals, access to physicians and medical devices, using the example of Japan's health care system, which displays the biggest differences in its set up compared to the United States in these key areas (cf. Table 4.1 below); (2) closely examine differences in the types of biomedical and alternative medicines[2] used by highly skilled patients from Germany, India and Japan and discuss how US physicians' views of any deviations from US-born patients' usage of these medications impact the transnational physician–patient encounter; and, finally, (3) analyse whether or not the cultural competence training physicians in the United States receive is seen as relevant for treating highly skilled migrants and the possible implications of assuming that their privileged status deems any special treatment unnecessary.

Health care system diversity

The wide variety of (relatively) well-functioning but different health care systems around the world[3] clearly shows that each health care system is a product of the country's historical and economic development, and different cultural aspects inform and interact with the structural setup of the health care system. When it comes to defining what entails a 'good' health care system, even the WHO can only offer a fairly unspecific guideline, arguing that '[A] good health system delivers quality services to all people, when and where they need them', while at the same time acknowledging that the services offered vary 'from country to country'.[4] However, many of my informants did not rate US health care as particularly 'good', despite the high quality of care that was available to them. For many, good health care was instead dependent on the provision of a level of comfort or reassurance and easily or informally accessible doctors. It can thus be seen as mainly structural rather than cultural differences that left my informants dissatisfied with US health care, although, of course, it could be argued that it is the structural differences in each country that shape the local health care culture and inform patients' expectations. In fact, the structural variations that seemed to inform my interlocutors' expectations and satisfaction the most – namely the role of the hospital, access to physicians and use of medical devices – are also among the main differences in their respective health care systems, as summed up in Table 4.1.

Satisfaction with health care systems is very difficult to measure and depends on a multitude of aspects, including the sampling frame of the population being examined (i.e. the general population or patients), sociodemographic aspects and experiences with health care delivery. Interestingly, studies have shown that the health outcomes or care provided are not as relevant for satisfaction as certain health care delivery processes, for example physician–patient relationships or free choice of provider (Papanicolas, Cylus and Smith 2013). In fact, Papanicolas and

Table 4.1 Comparison of key differences in health systems between the US, Germany and Japan. Most data were not available for India[1]

		US	Germany	Japan	India
Hospitals	Hospital beds (per 1,000 population)	2.8	8.1	13.2	0.5
	Average stay in hospital (in days)	6.1	9.0	16.5	
Access to physicians	Physician density (per 1,000 population)	2.57	4.19	2.37	0.76
	Number of doctor consultations (per person)	4.0	10.0	12.7	
Medical devices	MRI units (per million population)	39.0	33.6	51.7	
	CT scanners (per million population)	41.0	35.1	107.2	

[1] Sources OECD or WHO: hospital beds (all numbers 2015 or closest year): https://www.oecd-ilibrary.org/social-issues-migration-health/health-at-a-glance-2017/hospital-beds-per-1-000-population-2000-and-2015-or-nearest-year_health_glance-2017-graph156-en; average stay in hospital (all numbers 2015 or closest year): https://www.oecd-ilibrary.org/sites/health_glance-2017-64-en/index.html?itemId=/content/component/health_glance-2017-64-en; physicians density (all numbers 2016 or closest year): https://www.who.int/data/gho/data/indicators/indicator-details/GHO/physicians-density-(per-1000-population); number of doctor consultations per person (2015 or closest year): https://www.oecd-ilibrary.org/sites/health_glance-2017-60-en/index.html?itemId=/content/component/health_glance-2017-60-en; MRT and CT units (all numbers 2015 or closest year): https://www.oecd-ilibrary.org/social-issues-migration-health/health-at-a-glance-2017/medical-technologies_health_glance-2017-61-en. All accessed 24 January 2022; some numbers may have been updated in the interim.

colleagues argue that 'some of the keys to improving overall satisfaction with a health system may lie outside that system's direct control and are related to differences in expectations across countries and to other factors that influence perceptions, such as national political debates, reporting in the news media, and national cultures' (Papanicolas, Cylus and Smith 2013: 734).

Previous studies have also shown that attitudes of patients towards health care differ according to country. US Americans, for example, have much higher expectations of modern medicine, and a stronger belief that biomedicine can cure most of their illnesses, than citizens of other nations do (Blendon et al. 1995). Another study showed that the importance of the available health care varies across countries: when employees were offered an expat position by their employer, only 20 per cent of Americans rated access to quality treatment in the destination country as the most important criterion when considering whether to accept that offer, compared to 58 per cent of Germans who, when offered an equivalent job abroad in any number of countries, rated access to quality health care in first place (Consumer Science & Analytics 2013: 67). Despite ranking very low on overall health performance and having one of the highest levels of private health care and out-of-pocket expenditures in the world, India scores higher on confidence levels in the health care system among its own citizens than the United States, which only ranks 88 out of 120 countries (Deaton 2008; cf. Reddy et al. 2011; Patel et al. 2011). The Japanese, on the other hand, utilize their health care system more than three times as much as Americans, but tend to test as less satisfied with the health care they receive than US patients (Kurata et al. 1994).

These differences in expectations towards health care systems, unsurprisingly, become an important aspect of transnational medical encounters. For example, most of the physicians I spoke to as part of this research reported that their highly skilled transnational patients displayed substantial differences in health care behaviours and treatment expectations when compared to local patients with a similar educational background, as, for example, Dr Stein, a 50-year-old family physician who was working at a hospital department, points out:

> Americans expect things to be fixed. If there is some pain, it has got to be fixed. Whether it is through surgery or medication or something. Europeans in general, everybody else, I think they have a sense, that life means that you got to have aches and pains. There are going to be times when you are not going to feel very comfortable physically, and/or emotionally, and it doesn't mean that something needs to be fixed about that. There is more of a sense that it is going away, or you can live with it.
>
> (Dr Stein, Family Medicine)

The different expectations and experiences patients from Germany, India and Japan bring with them into their medical encounters in the United States also cause differences in how physicians interact with them. This was also an experience that 46-year-old Dr Thomas, a paediatrician at a private office who had originally immigrated from Germany in 1999, had had with her transnational patients. She described her Japanese patients, for example, as generally 'very pleasant, very respectful. Low-maintenance',[5] her Indian patients as medium maintenance, because 'they are . . . so quickly worried about everything' and her German patients as 'high-maintenance . . . because they want everything kind of explained and they want to understand'.

Yet the different health care setups did not only have an impact on how physicians interacted with their foreign patients. Several of my informants also mentioned that they were unsure about what to expect and were worried, for example, about differences in quality and availability of treatments and medicines, or were uncertain about the costs associated with health care (see Chapter 5 for a detailed discussion on barriers to access). Despite this, the vast majority of my informants acknowledged the very high standard of health care quality available in the United States, with several describing this as the best in the world.

Overall, my German informants gave health care quality in the US the highest rating on a scale of 1 to 5,[6] with an average of 4.03, and my Japanese group gave it the lowest rating (3.33). On average, my Japanese informants also rated health care quality back home much higher than the US and than informants from elsewhere rated their own home countries (Table 4.2).

Although my Indian informants gave health care services in the United States a relatively low rating (3.4), they also gave a comparably low rating to health care quality in India. They were also the only group that rated health care quality in the United States to be higher on average than in their own country – albeit only by a minute margin. This seemed to mainly be due to the fact that most informants rated Indian health care quality to be extremely diverse, ranging from very bad to excellent, although they personally did not have actual complaints about the health care they had received at home. The fact that German and Japanese informants rated their home health care quality higher was usually not due to a lack of quality in the United States, but because of issues

Table 4.2 Average rating on a scale of 1 to 5 given by my interview partners for health care quality in the US vs average health care quality at home

	Germany	India	Japan
Health care quality in US	4.03	3.40	3.33
Health care quality at home	4.43	3.36	4.60
Difference	–0.4	+0.04	–1.27

with access, overtreatment and costs. And in most cases these additional costs did not seem to translate into better health care quality. Julia, who was 37 at the time of our interview and who worked as a political consultant in DC, for example, explained to me that while 'the medical standard here is, is really high', she struggled to accept what she called the 'cost difference'.[7]

There were several reasons my interlocutors mentioned that led them to be dissatisfied with US health care. For example, almost half of my interlocutors (23 out of 48) felt that health care in the United States was mainly focused on money and that it felt more like a business transaction. Ten informants also felt that there were too many tests or stronger dosages, which several conjectured (n=4) were linked to a general fear of lawsuits against US physicians. This fear, leading to what has been called 'defence medicine', was also thought by my informants to be linked to the high level of specialization causing many unnecessary tests.[8] This style of medicine can have a direct impact not only on immigrant patients, but also immigrant physicians (cf. Schühle 2018), and was experienced by some of my informants as impacting the doctor–patient relationship, because 'it's really obvious that the doctor is trying not to take, you know, any responsibility for the treatment or surgery'.[9] Others were initially worried about the amount of personnel or resources that were common in the United States, as they took it to mean something more serious was happening. Irrfan, a 44-year-old software engineer from India, for example, was shocked to see 'an army of doctors' attending the caesarean section of his wife, thinking this meant something serious had happened:

> I saw an army of doctors walk in. And that was 'Oh, wow!' That was scary to me. I was like 'Tell me what is going on. I am not afraid, but I want to know.' And they are like: 'Oh nothing, this is just a precaution.' And then that's when I understood, that's how American you know, medical system works. They had to cover from all angles, so they had to have all kinds of specialists within the room.
> (Irrfan, Indian male, Green Card holder, in the US since 2002)

Most of my informants also felt that there was a rather different attitude towards health care in the United States, with only three of my informants reporting that they thought attitudes were the same. The most commonly mentioned differences in attitudes were that US physicians were friendlier or seemed to respect their patients' privacy or autonomy more, again closely followed by a presumed fear among physicians of litigation, causing them to force more responsibility on patients. This fear was also thought of as restricting the flow of communication between doctors and patients and at times caused distress among my informants. Jana, for example, got very frustrated when her physician appeared to refuse to give her a clear answer on whether or not she should take a certain medication. She was certain that the reason why doctors in the United States are careful with what they say to their patients was because they 'are afraid to, if something goes wrong you sue them'.[10]

Similarly, 31-year-old Jonas, who was on parental leave from his job at the German embassy at the time of our interview, felt uneasy about lab technicians not providing him with information on the tests they had run, leaving him uncertain about his health status until his next doctor's appointment. While he was aware that this was a common practice in the United States, he felt it was an unnecessary precaution to avoid possible law suits, which took him some time to get used to:

> But in those cases, this is sometimes a bit awkward for the patient when physicians focus only on their area of expertise and then say something like: 'There is something, but we can't say any more about it, you will need to see a specialist.' Although I have the feeling that they would know more. That is the same when they take sonograms. The woman or man that takes the scan is not allowed to say what they see because they aren't physicians . . . What you do then the first time you immediately get a bit unsettled, because you think, maybe there is something wrong. But the bottom line is, they simply don't have the authority.[11]
>
> (Jonas, German male, A1 visa, in the US since 2014)

Several of my Indian informants also complained that physicians in the United States were not as personable as back in India, and my Japanese informants felt that medical staff in the US tended to be less polite than in Japan, none of which seemed to be an issue with my German interlocutors; see Table 4.3 below.

Table 4.3 Differences in attitudes towards health care in physicians in the US as reported by my informants

	More respectful/ friendly	Fearful/less responsibility	Less polite	Less personable
Germany	3	2		
India	8	6		3
Japan	1	1	4	

Hospitals

As we have seen above in Table 4.1, Japan has by far the most hospital beds and longest hospital stays on average, not only compared to Germany, India and the US, but worldwide. The common practice of long hospitalization rates in Japan can also serve as a good example of how cultural preferences and health care setups are deeply intertwined. On the one hand, as Mayhew (2001) argues, long hospitalizations in Japan are incentivized by the fact that there are no upper limits on reimbursements, making it more valuable for hospitals to keep low-maintenance patients hospitalized. Additionally, acute and chronically ill patients in Japan are often lumped together in the assessment of hospitalization rates. On the other hand, long hospital stays have often been explained in the anthropological literature by invoking the concept of *ansei*, usually referring to the belief that bed rest is the best treatment (Ohnuki-Tierney 1994; Iglehart 1988; Borovoy 2005). The importance of long stays in hospitals as well as the hospital itself as a point of care for Japanese patients also becomes clear from the fact that my Japanese informants mentioned them during the interviews twice as often as my Indian and more than two and a half times as often as my German informants (Table 4.4).[12]

Prices for all health care services in Japan, including hospital stays, are restricted by a government point-fee system. The fact that hospital visits do not incur additional costs has also led in some extreme cases to hospitals taking on a social role in addition to being a medical provider. Furthermore, all fees for individual health services in Japan are the same, regardless of location or physician's expertise, making a trip to see a specialist at a hospital just as expensive as seeing a physician in a smaller clinic or doctor's office. Since many Japanese patients view and use hospitals in Japan as a first point of care, the limited access to hospitals in the United States was a major concern for many of my Japanese informants. Ichiko, for example, only realized after coming to the US that hospitals have a different place in the health care delivery system there compared to Japan. She had come to the United States to marry her US

Table 4.4 How often do patients refer to hospital or hospitals in narratives per 10,000 words?

	German	Indian	Japanese
Hospital(s) & clinic(s)	12.3	17.2	33.3
Doctor(s) & physician(s)	47.8	50.9	64.0

partner after completing two bachelor's degrees and working as trade coordinator in Japan, and did not yet have a work permit for the US at the time of our interview:

> In Japan, when you are sick, whatever happens, you just go to the hospital. Like here, hospitals just help people who are really in danger or need surgery. And if you are sick or unwell or something you need to go to the PCP [Primary Care Physician] and . . . I feel it is too long a process.
> (Ichiko, Japanese female, K1 visa, in the US since 2016)

The restricted access was also an issue for 46-year-old Takeshi, who felt that prices for hospital visits in the United States presented a 'psychological hurdle'.[13] He was also keenly aware that hospitals had a very different role within the Japanese health care system compared to the US and that hospital stays reflected different cultural values in both countries. Takeshi, who was at the time of our interview working at a large international organization, felt that physicians in the US were very efficient, because they trusted in the capacities of their patients and counted on them to take care of themselves. In Japan, he explained, patients expected to be supported through the system and used hospital visits for more than primary care. In that sense he felt that the Japanese health care system was very 'luxurious' for patients because it also coped 'with the people's anxiety not limited to the acute issues or some kind of specific disease'.

In fact, the role of hospital visits beyond acute care in Japanese society was frequently mentioned by my Japanese informants. While several missed the access and reassurance given by the possibility of frequent hospital visits, some also saw this practice as unsustainable or as something patients took advantage of. Hitoshi, a Japanese PhD student in his late twenties, for example, felt that in Japan patients sometimes 'see a doctor without any specific reason', making hospitals a 'kind of the place where some older people . . . have conversation without any disease, so it's like a cafe or something'.[14]

Access to physicians

The aforementioned fixed prices also create a strong incentive for Japanese physicians to see as many patients as possible, and Japanese patients visit their doctors more than three times as often as patients in the US (12.7 consultations per year/person versus 4.0), although the ratio of physician to patients is comparable in both countries (see Table 4.1; Ikegami et al. 2011). In contrast to that, US insurances usually limit their choice of physicians to cover only in-network providers, which differ across insurance policies (Mossialos et al. 2016). It is thus very likely that the restrictions on access in the United States were experienced as particularly problematic, since not only the Japanese, but also the German and Indian informants were able to freely choose physicians in their respective home countries.

The impact of transnationals' frustration with restrictions to access in the US should not be dismissed. Papanicolas and colleagues found that the reported levels of confidence in finding affordable and effective care as well as how the doctor visits were rated impacted patients' satisfaction with the health care system (2013). In fact, among my informants, having difficulties with making appointments was one of the key themes that were mentioned unprompted during the interviews when I asked them for differences between the US health care system and the system in their home country, as Table 4.5 below shows.

While 9 out of 15 Japanese informants mentioned difficulties with making appointments in the United States – most were used to walk-in clinics in Japan – it was my Indian informants who seemed to have the most issues with access. They generally felt that making appointments was difficult (8 out of 18), that waiting times for appointments were much longer than in India (n=8) and that physicians in the US were not as available without long waiting times or for (informal) advice as in India. Irrfan, like many of my Indian informants, explained to me that the restricted access to health care in the United States meant that he can't 'just walk in and talk to a physician anytime I want to do',[15] which made him feel that he couldn't see a doctor in the US 'unless it's an emergency'.

Table 4.5 Differences in the health care system mentioned by my informants during the interviews

	Longer wait for an appointment	Shorter wait at doctor's office	Making appointments difficult	Making appointments similar
Germany	2	3		2
India	8	1	8	
Japan	2	1	9	

Several of my Indian informants, such as 31-year-old Rahul, a visiting researcher from India, also mentioned that it wasn't only the long wait times, but also the degree of specialization prevalent in the United States (discussed in more detail below) that caused their health issues not to be handled in a timely manner:

> Actually, I didn't have much of an idea about how the system would work. I thought it would be similar like Indian system. But I didn't know how crazy it would be . . . That is a very stark contrast between the Indian system and . . . The physician just looks at you and says, okay, this might be the problem and he will send you off to a specialist. So before, and then again, another two weeks for getting an appointment with the specialist and setting up. But in India if I have problem, I can go. Maybe there is a long wait and I might have to wait for three or four hours in the physician's office, but by the end of that I have some medication or some kind of a strategy is there for me to go ahead with my treatment.
> (Rahul, Indian male, J1 visa, in the US since 2016)

For this reason, many of the Indians continued their longstanding relationships with family physicians in India. Anaya for example told me that she 'still call[s] the doctors or WhatsApp them or text them'[16] to get a medical opinion (see also Chapter 6).

In contrast to these experiences, my German interlocutors generally did not report difficulties with waiting times for appointments or with making appointments, and were more likely to focus on more positive aspects, such as shorter waiting times at doctor's offices (n=3). They were also the only group that felt that the process of making appointments was similar in both countries. Unsurprisingly, the varying degrees of issues regarding access to services and physicians my informants reported also became apparent in the narrative keyword analysis, as Table 4.6 below shows, with Indians mentioning issues relating to

Table 4.6 How often do patients refer to access and primary care in narratives per 10,000 words?[1]

	Germany	India	Japan
Access*	3.2	6.2	4.4
PCP & Primary	0	2.2	3.9

[1] The category 'Access'* combines the mentions of the words access, accessible and accessibility.

access more often than the Japanese and twice as often as my German informants.

While many informants mentioned differences in access, several thought that visits to physicians were similar to what they had expected. Other differences were frequently mentioned throughout the interviews. My Indian interlocutors in particular missed having personal relationships with their physicians (n=4) or felt that physicians did not spend as much time with them (n=3) compared to those in India. The most striking difference between the groups, however, was the fact that my Indian interview partners were much more likely to point out that US physicians showed them more respect, for example by providing them with more information or involving them in the decision process. This kind of responsibility, however, was not always appreciated by my German and particularly Japanese informants.

Another notable difference across all three groups was the importance of the concept of the family physician. The words 'PCP' (Primary Care Physician) or the word 'Primary' (standing for primary care or primary care physician) were most commonly mentioned by my Japanese informants (3.9 times per 10,000 words). However, since Japanese patients were used to seeking health care in hospitals, it is not surprising that they usually described PCPs rather negatively as gatekeepers to accessing specialists. Ayami, a 43-year-old trailing spouse from Japan who had come to the United States to live with her American husband, for example, saw PCPs simply as an annoying obstacle in the process of getting care, whereas in Japan she didn't 'need to see a family doctor first' but was instead 'able to see the doctor . . . directly'.[17]

Unlike in Japan, family doctors are very common in both Germany and India. Sonam, a 34-year-old economist who had come to the United States on a student visa and who held a G4 visa at the time of our interview, for example, saw PCPs as positive and in fact preferred seeing family physicians as a way to circumvent the specialized US medical care that she viewed as needlessly aggressive.

While PCPs were often mentioned by my Indian informants as a positive aspect, they were not brought up at all by any of my German informants. This may be because the concept of the family physician is well established in Germany and may therefore not be a noteworthy issue, or because PCPs were not seen as an obstacle to access, as was the case for the Japanese informants. However, while PCPs were not mentioned by the German group, many did describe access to physicians in general as difficult. Since the German health care system provides its members with 'comprehensive, uniform, and universal health coverage'

(Swami 2002: 349), covering a wide range of services (Mossialos et al. 2016: 70), it is not surprising that US health care could not meet their expectations. In particular, the fact that the choice of physician was regulated through one's insurance was something that several informants, such as Katja, a stay-at-home mother from Germany in her thirties, who felt that 'looking for a physician was maybe a bit more difficult than in Germany',[18] struggled to understand when they first accessed US health care.

Medical devices

Japan has not only the most hospital beds, longest hospitalization times and the most physician visits, as we have seen above, but also by far the highest number of computer tomography (CT) scanners and magnetic resonance imaging (MRI) units in the world (cf. Table 4.1). It has more than 2.6 times as many CT scanners and 1.3 times as many MRI units as the US and 3 times as many CT scanners and 1.5 times as many MRI units as in Germany, although the health care infrastructure in all three countries is roughly comparable. Again, one reason might be the particular setup of the Japanese point-fee system discussed above, together with the fact that hospitals are the first point of health care seeking. The extraordinarily large quantities of high-tech equipment prevalent in Japan may also explain why my Japanese informants expected to receive diagnostic tests and considered them an integral part of good preventative health care. In fact, most complained that they did not receive enough tests in the United States. A typical example is Ayami's experience. As part of what she thought would be a routine check-up and unaware of the possibility of incurring costs, she asked her physician for 'some tests, cancer test, cancer check or a blood check'[19] that were not covered or only partially covered through her insurance. She was unpleasantly surprised when she received a bill of over $1,000 a couple of months later.

The lack of availability of tests can also lead to a feeling of being misunderstood or not taken seriously, as Nobu, a Japanese economist in his late thirties, told me. After several serious health issues in his family, Nobu wanted to get a preventative medical check-up. But because he was healthy at the time, he felt that he did not get the medical attention that he thought he needed:

> I think at the time I went to see the doctor I had a lot of stress. So, I went to see, to check the stomach or something. And then in Japan

it is relatively easier to do, like the camera [gastroscopy]. Here I had to pay, I don't remember exactly, but $600 or $700 to do the camera . . . In Japan, I think we can like, examine bodies and find problems already at an early stage. But here it seems they don't do it . . . And my mother, she passed away a few years ago, like sudden heart issues . . . I was worried that this is family stuff and that and my grandmother, their mother, also had a stroke in the brain, yeah. So I said, I am worried! And they check blood and pressure, and 'No, you are fine.' So, I couldn't check anything further.

(Nobu, Japanese male, G4 visa, in the US since 2012)

From his experience Nobu learned that patients in the United States sometimes need to present their symptoms in a more serious way to get medical attention, as one of his friends did:

My friend, he had a headache or something. And he is my age, he had to lie to get examined. This pain is not going away, tried to make it even more serious. And then they did and found out that it was a disease. Otherwise, they would have said it is fine.

(Nobu, Japanese male, G4 visa, in the US since 2012)

For many of my Japanese informants, their issues with US health care were not only that they couldn't receive MRI or CT scans for preventative health care to the degree they had in Japan, but also the fact that they were discharged much sooner after surgery than in Japan. For Kyoko, a 41-year-old medical researcher from Japan, the willingness of physicians to perform an ambulatory surgery to treat a matter for which she had previously been 'hospitalized for five days' in Japan was a clear indication for her that the US health care system was willing to risk her health:

For the same disease. But here, it was one day. Kind of very dangerous I think. It was not a good situation for me, because you know after the systematic anesthesia, after I woke up, after two hours, I have to go home. And then my family is not here, right. My friend helped me . . . my friend said to the nurse: 'But she is still vomiting and you know she is still dizzy; so can we stay longer?' And the nurse said: 'No, you have to go! This is a common symptom. So there is nothing wrong, so you can go home.' You can go home (laughs) that is the United States! That is very different. That is what I wanted to talk to you about.

(Kyoko, Japanese female, H-1B visa, in the US since 2015)

Table 4.7 How often do patient informants refer to MRI, CT, scans or test(s), x-ray(s) or ultrasound in narratives per 10,000 words?

	German	Indian	Japanese
MRI, CT, scan, test(s) x-ray(s) & ultrasound	5.83	8.95	4.64

Although my Japanese informants were the only group that missed diagnostic tests in the United States, they were the least likely to mention these medical devices or diagnostic tests (4.64 mentions per 10,000), while my Indian informants (8.95/10,000) were nearly twice as likely to refer to them as my Japanese informants and mentioned them about 1.5 times more often than my German informants (5.83/10,000); see Table 4.7 above.

Unlike the Japanese, my Indian interlocutors usually described the amount of tests administered in the United States as an over-reliance on tests on the part of US physicians, or thought of it as 'aggressive'.[20] Sonam, for example, explained to me that for her, health care in the US on the one hand was more structured than in India but on the other involved many unnecessary tests and interventions. She described US health care as follows:

> I was running in college and I was, I had some chest pain. It was on the right side, but it was pretty sharp. So I went to our university health clinic ... he said he thought that I had heartburn but that I should go see a doctor anyway. And so I went and we did a Holter monitor test [a type of electrocardiography], we did a stress test and ... it was so much more structured and but also so much more interventionist than it would have been in India, that I was a little taken aback ... it just felt unnecessary. And expensive. I mean ... at the end of the day it was just, 'Oh, yeah, you had heartburn' ... So there is that aspect of covering their bases whenever you go to see a specialist, which I don't, I understand, but don't appreciate.
> (Sonam, Indian female, G4 visa, in the US since 2001)

One of the reasons why my Indian interlocutors did not associate good health care with tests and other interventionist practices might simply be that they are not as readily available in India and thus not part of the expected medical routine. Although India has been formally obliged to provide universal access to health services since it gained independence in 1947 (Reddy et al. 2011), in practice government health care services are either not readily available or are not seen as a viable option for better-off patients, so that many households seek private health care, often at high costs (Mossialos et al. 2016).[21] And despite the fact that India's economy is among the fastest-growing in the world, government spending on health care remains very low and is in fact among the lowest worldwide (Ramani and Mavalankar 2006: 562). Many of the medical support services available in the Global North, like ambulances, blood banks or hospital waste management, are lacking in India, especially in rural areas. This is also true for the availability of health services (i.e. health infrastructure, staff, supply of drugs). Even compared to other countries with similar levels of economic development, some of which are poorer than India, its health indicators are inadequate, lagging behind, and the system itself is 'underperforming' (Reddy et al. 2011: 762). Horton and Das argue that 'the failing health system is perhaps India's greatest predicament of all' (2011: 181). In this context it might not strike us as very surprising that there are no numbers available for the amount of MRI and CT scanners in India (cf. Table 4.1), but it is probably safe to assume there are far fewer than in the other three countries examined here.

However, it is not only the lack of medical devices, but also the sheer number of patients, as mentioned by several Indian informants, that make interventionist practices less feasible in the Indian health care context. For Nitya, a senior economist from India in her late thirties, this was not a negative aspect of Indian health care, but rather showed Indian doctors to be more skilled. In fact, she points out that she was troubled by what US interventionist health care said about physicians' expertise:

> I think the big difference I have seen in America, physicians are mostly relying on diagnostics, there are a lot of procedures that are diagnostic being done. Whereas in India it is much more low-tech, so they diagnose you more symptomatically and based on visual observation, whereas in the US you go straight to the CT [computer tomography] or MRI. The US is also a lot more specialized, so one person will order the CT and somebody else will do it. As for India, doctors tend to have a larger span of expertise. I think in India, because of the sheer volume of numbers, doctors get very good at recognizing symptoms early on . . . So a lot of the issues I had with the US health system has been over-reliance on diagnostics.
>
> (Nitya, Indian female, Green Card holder, in the US since 1998)

Some of the physicians I spoke to were also aware that some of their patients had expected different types or amounts of treatments or medications compared to what they received. For example, Dr Silva, an oncologist at a DC hospital in her late forties who had moved to the United States from Europe in 2004, got frequent feedback from her patients 'saying that the care in America is more invasive, . . . doctors order much more unnecessary tests'. She also acknowledged that frequent testing was caused by a fear of litigation (see also Schühle 2018 on the very similar views of Nigerian physicians in the United States on this issue), yet as an oncologist she also felt that there was merit in the US approach:

> The doctors commit less and won't make these decisions without ordering a huge number of tests and they also prescribe more . . . But, and this is a reflection of the American system, that really trains you not to miss things. The European system treats you, trains you to use your clinical judgement and skills and the American system puts first to not miss things. So of course it has, that is translating into how people practise.
>
> (Dr Silva, Oncologist)

While some studies have shown that Americans indeed place a lot of trust in modern medicine, for Germans, access to the latest technology appears to be less important (Blendon et al. 1995; Schoen et al. 2007). This might also be the reason why many of my German informants seemed to be the least concerned with diagnostic tests or procedures, but when they did mention tests, they were more in line with my Indian informants on the fact that these were overused in the US because they 'oversearch for something that's not relevant [and] you have a million tests going on',[22] or because 'the physicians think if there is a new technique available then we should definitely use it, while in Germany . . . they are a little bit more cautious and reluctant'.[23] Many of my German and Indian informants also saw the prevalence of diagnostics in the United States as a result of the highly specialized medical system in the US. Hanna, for example, a German economist in her late thirties who at the time of our interview was working at an international organization in DC, felt that the specialization in the US not only led to more tests, but also meant that patients 'have to deal with like five different individuals for five different parts of the process',[24] whereas in Germany a physician would be responsible for a larger part of the same health-seeking process.

In fact, many of my informants across all groups felt that US medicine was following a script where '[c]hecklist gets checked off . . . In

Germany they follow a script as well, but in the US they stick to it more obviously'[25] and that American physicians 'lack sometimes common sense' and 'are also afraid of doing something which is not in their books. It's not part of protocol.'[26] Emi, a 36-year-old medical researcher from Japan, for example, explained to me that this style of medicine felt as if '[t]hey have a mission, they take an x-ray, they take blood'[27] without taking the patient's wishes into consideration.

While these structural and cultural differences in health care system setups affect all groups of immigrants and should be taken into account when considering their integration and satisfaction with US health care, they are only some among many aspects influencing transnational medical encounters. Biomedical differences are another area where misunderstandings about treatments or diagnosis occur between patients and physicians. Although 'biomedicine' and 'biomedical treatments' are available in all the countries in question, in the following section I will explore how much the expectations of what 'biomedicine' as a specific type of medical practice entails may differ across these groups and what impact this may have on treatment choices and health care utilization.

Biomedical diversity or the culture of biomedicine

The term biomedicine and many of its epithets such as '"Western," "Cosmopolitan," "Modern," "Scientific," or "Allopathic"' (Hahn and Kleinman 1983: 305) most often refer to a practice of medicine 'based on the application of the principles of the natural sciences and especially biology and biochemistry'.[28] As such, biomedical practice is characterized by its assumption that 'the human body is, for all intents and purposes, universal and amenable to intervention through standardized approaches to medical management and care' (Lock and Nguyen 2010: 2). Biomedicine has become the predominant medical practice not only in Euro-American societies, but worldwide, and usually refers to an institutional structure as well as an epistemological and ontological system (Hahn and Kleinman 1983; Kleinman 1997). The successful dissemination of biomedicine even beyond clinics and hospitals, Lock and Nguyen argue, was in part due to applying statistics and other 'technologies of bodily governance' (2010: 24), which at the same time have created more regulatory power over populations (cf. Rabinow and Rose 2006; see also the discussion on biopower below). While I will use the term biomedicine in this book because it 'emphasizes the established institutional structure of the dominant profession of medicine in the

West, and today, worldwide' (Kleinman 1997: 25), it is of course a sociocultural system, and we may 'speak about a plurality of biomedicines that are socially and culturally situated rather than about a single unified body of knowledge and practice' (Good 1995: 462; Hahn and Kleinman 1983).

However, despite the apparent cultural differences and its internally diverse practices, practitioners of biomedicine often view it as universally applicable and based on scientific paradigms. As such, its practitioners often understand biomedicine as representative of 'real' knowledge and a 'Culture of no Culture' (Taylor 2003). This is particularly problematic in transnational health care settings, since biomedicine not only encompasses clinical practice but also extends its influence to the norms and social needs of modern society. Ong, for instance, argues that biomedicine goes 'beyond providing health care to shaping, in both intended and unintended ways, the cultural citizenship of different categories of patients' (1995: 1244, 1245). What makes biomedicine's role in shaping patients' 'cultural citizenship' particularly worrying is the perceived superiority of 'Western' biomedicine. Quirke and Gaudilliere (2008), for example, argue that biomedical practice in the US has become a key reference point for European researchers, arguably making US biomedicine the 'standard' and by extension causing it to be considered more authentic (or global) in the West (particularly in the United States but possibly by extension also in Germany and other countries) and more 'corrupted' and less authentic (or more 'local') in the East (for example in Japan and India). Expecting the US 'standard' outside of the United States can then easily lead to judging medical treatments abroad as folkloristic and unscientific, rather than a cultural choice between one of many therapeutic or diagnostic options. For example, in her book *Medicine & Culture*, the journalist Lynn Payer admits that she 'believed medicine to be a science, with a "right" and "wrong" way to treat the disease, and any deviation from the American norm to be "wrong"' (1996: 15), finally coming to the conclusion that '[t]he choice of diagnosis and treatment is *not* a science' (Payer 1996: 154; cf. Reid 2009). However, many of the biomedical variations present in different countries are based not only on the social and cultural contexts of each society, but also the history.

Arguably, the tradition of biomedicine began at the start of the nineteenth century, marking the 'birth of the clinical gaze' (Rose 2007: 4, following Foucault's (2002 [1963]) argument in *The Birth of the Clinic*). It was at that time that advancements in microbiology became more prominent in theories of disease causation, paving the way for the 'recognition of a universal human biology, enabling the means for using standardized interventions on human bodies wherever they reside' (Lock and Nguyen 2010: 146), which also led to vast changes in how medicine was taught, practised and recorded (cf. Rose 2007). The emergence of biomedicine also coincided with the increasing recognition and support of governments for clinical care and public health in the late nineteenth century, which also allowed governments and other bodies of authority to apply 'biopower', controlling and regulating populations in areas such as reproduction (Rabinow and Rose 2006; cf. Foucault 1978).[29] Yet biomedical practices seemingly became an integral aspect of modernization and stood for the ideals of progress. Marks even argues that biomedicine was 'the product of Europe's technological revolution' (1997: 208).

This led to the often unchallenged assumption that biomedicine was 'made in the "West" and then exported to the "rest"' (Lock and Nguyen 2010: 146). This export, Lock and Nguyen argue, occurred in four distinct phases: prior to 1920, in the Imperial Phase, biomedicine was used to keep soldiers and settlers healthy, while in the Colonial Phase (1920–60), biomedicine was used to guard native labourers from epidemics. During the 1960s to 1980s, it became a symbol of nationalist efforts of nation-building and modernization, but since then, NGOs have tried to improve global health through 'biomedical globalization'. Thus, unsurprisingly, biomedicine has frequently been criticized for its inherent ethnocentricity (cf. Turner 2005) and for not taking into consideration that the place biomedical practices have within health care delivery as well as in patients' understanding of their ailments and treatments differs vastly across groups, regions and countries (cf. Dilger, Kane and Langwick 2012).

This also becomes apparent when we take the different historical circumstances at the introduction of biomedicine to Germany, Japan and India into consideration. In Germany, for example, the advances of science-based medicine were formally adopted at around the same time as the country was unified under Chancellor Bismarck in 1871. The impact of the adoption, according to Maretzki and Seidler, was 'in tune with the new social and political ethos that encouraged industrialization and the national unification' (1985: 389). In Japan, biomedicine took off at around the same time. In the Meiji era, which started in 1868, the government tried to westernize and unify Japan, including the 'westernization' of their local medical traditions (see more on this below). For this purpose, those Western institutions and practices perceived to be the most advanced were copied and replicated in Japan.[30]

Unlike in Germany or Japan, where the biomedical tradition was politically embraced by the national governments, it was more forcefully introduced to India by its colonial rulers and 'has long been understood as a "tool of empire"' (Lock and Nguyen 2010: 64).[31] While it is not entirely surprising that none of my German or Japanese informants mentioned biomedicine in this context, as neither country had been a colony, none of my Indian informants referred to biomedicine in a postcolonial setting either. That said, it is quite possible that my Indian informants, who represent a very narrow group, are not representative of prevalent attitudes in Indian society.

In general, biomedicine as a concept was not discussed by my informants and none of them mentioned that they experienced the role of the biomedical tradition in the United States as different from their home society, with the possible exception of Aishwarya. The software engineer[32] seemed to reject the idea of universal and standardizable bodies, as stipulated by biomedical theory (see Lock 2013; Hamdy 2013), particularly when it came to how they would react to medications. Aishwarya explained to me that American physicians should treat her – an Indian woman – differently and prescribe different medications than for their other patients based on her Indian body type:

> I may be wrong, but every culture or every race for that matter, and by race meaning like Indians, all of them are made differently. In the sense that just because one medicine works for a certain type of people, it doesn't work for everybody. I don't think the health care providers understand this . . . So they don't understand that the way the body works, body system work in different cultures is different . . . the body type is different from American body types. So, depending on that, you have to go through medications accordingly.
>
> (Aishwarya, Indian female, H-1B visa, in the US since 2002)

However, apart from the different role biomedicine takes on in a society's medical practice and individuals' beliefs on disease causation, there can also be substantial differences in attitudes towards biomedicine, including in the usage and prevalence of biomedical drugs, and those differences are rooted in historical, social and cultural differences, as becomes apparent in the overview in Table 4.8 below.

These variations, in turn, shape not only what patients expect of their health care providers, but also how they express their medical needs.[33] Biomedical differences can also shape how patients describe their symptoms and thus impact how successfully patients and physicians interact with each other, as 40-year-old Dr Wang, a family physician

Table 4.8 Comparison of key differences in pharmaceutical spending, vaccination and pharmacies between the US, Germany and Japan. As can be seen, most data were not available for India[1]

		US	Germany	Japan	India
Medications	% of health spending on pharmaceuticals	12.2	14.3	18.8	
Medications	% of total GDP on pharmaceuticals	2.07	1.60	2.04	
Medications	Practising pharmacists per 100,000 population	92	64	170	
Vaccinations	% of vaccinated children	92	97	96	87

[1] Pharmaceutical spending (2016 or closest year): https://data.oecd.org/healthres/pharmaceutical-spending.htm; practising pharmacists (2015 or closest year): https://www.oecd-ilibrary.org/sites/health_glance-2017-69-en/index.html?itemId=/content/component/health_glance-2017-69-en; per cent of children aged one vaccinated for diphtheria, tetanus, and pertussis and measles (2015 or closest year): https://www.oecd-ilibrary.org/sites/health_glance-2017-43-en/index.html?itemId=/content/component/health_glance-2017-43-en. All accessed 24 January 2022 (newer numbers may have become available in the interim). Although there are no comparative data available for te number of surgeries performed and types of drugs prescribed in each of the countries in question, it is safe to assume that they will differ from each other based on differences in the setups of health care and health insurance discussed above.

working in a hospital setting, experienced with several of his Japanese patients:

> It's not so much that they describe their symptoms differently, but they seem to have a different, you know how patients have theories of why they develop certain symptoms and I feel that they are, and the way they describe their symptoms and their theories as to why they experience them, is different . . .
>
> (Dr Wang, Family Medicine)

While I will discuss the impact cultural differences in biomedical treatments and medicines had on my transnational informants in more detail below, it is also important to remember that the medical practitioners I spoke with felt that there were some differences among

Table 4.9 Answers of interviewed physicians regarding perceived foreign patient behaviours

	Different description of symptoms	Different medications or treatments	Different health decisions	More compliant
German patients	2	6	12	3
Indian patients	5	8	9	5
Japanese patients	9	5	10	11

their highly skilled patients from Germany, India and Japan, which can possibly be mapped onto the varying degrees of perceived differences in biomedical practices in each of the countries in question, as Table 4.9 above demonstrates.

The biggest difference the physicians reported between the groups was how their transnational patients described their symptoms: only two physicians thought their German patients described their symptoms any differently, while the majority (9 of 17) said that their Japanese patients did. This could either be caused by cultural differences or by how similar to the United States the biomedical standards in the countries of origin were perceived to be. Another likely explanation might be linguistic barriers, especially since the differences between the three groups were less pronounced when I asked whether or not their transnational patients asked for different medications or made different health decisions (i.e. asking for a certain medication might be less problematic than describing a symptom).

According to my interview partners, Japanese patients were the least likely to ask for different medications (5 of 17 physicians thought so) and Germans the most likely to make different health decisions (12 of 17). However, this might have more to do with how comfortable the different groups felt communicating their wishes to US physicians than linguistic barriers or actual preferences for medications or health care decisions. This interpretation would also be supported by the fact that the physicians thought their German highly skilled migrants were least likely to be more compliant than other patients of a similar socioeconomic background and Japanese patients were the most likely to be described as more compliant (see Table 4.9 above).

Biomedical medications and treatments

The fact that 'biomedicine' did not necessarily mean the same across the three groups was also evidenced by the fact that the majority of the highly skilled migrants I spoke to experienced substantial differences between the treatments and medications in their own countries and those in the US – usually referring to the amount prescribed or the dosages rather than active ingredients. Only seven of my informants (14%) said that they had not experienced any differences, as Table 4.10 shows.

Generally speaking, US medications were the most frequently commented-on difference between my informants' countries of origin and the US, for example regarding the prevalence of antibiotics and pain medication in the US ('most of the time the answer is either antibiotics or ibuprofen'),[34] which is also reflected in the results of the keyword analysis shown in Table 4.11.

Particularly my Indian and Japanese interlocutors mentioned differences in attitudes towards pain, which led in their opinion to a higher prescription rate of analgesics in the United States, where physicians 'immediately they give . . . some strong, strong painkillers, so I didn't feel anything'.[35] Many informants attributed this over-prescription

Table 4.10 Differences in medications and treatments available in the US as reported by my informants

	Germany	India	Japan
No difference in meds/treatments	1	5	1
Difference in prescriptions/dosage	2	4	3
Stronger meds/overprescription in US	3	1	2
Weaker meds/underprescription in US		7	
More regulation in US		4	
Less regulation in US	2		

Table 4.11 Frequency per 10,000 words for selected terms

	Germany	India	Japan
Pain & painful	2.16	5.56	4.90
Antibiotic(s)	2.38	4.21	0.77
Vaccine & vaccination(s)	4.97	0.14	2.06

of pain medication to 'the me-first attitude . . . And then, they don't tolerate even a single, one minute they [can't] tolerate the pain.'[36] Several others, such as Aishwarya, thought that the prevalence of pain medications was due to a particularly low pain threshold among Americans:

> Maybe it is because many Americans, or maybe the people over here are taught not to have any tolerance. And that's why they are getting an instant cure or instant relief. Sometimes tolerance is fine . . . That's my culture, that you are tolerant . . . My friends were really surprised that I didn't take any medication after the C-section.
> (Aishwarya, Indian female, H-1B visa, in the US since 2002)

My Indian informants were also more than five times as likely as my Japanese and almost twice as likely (1.77) as my German interlocutors to talk about antibiotics, most often mentioning that they were easier to come by in India and available in much higher dosages. My German informants, on the other hand, were the most likely to mention vaccinations, compared to the other two groups – whether because they experienced different vaccination schedules (i.e. for children), because of differences in administering them ('they gave her three different vaccinations . . . three different vaccinations in the same muscle, which to me is insane'),[37] because they felt they had less choice on whether or not to get their children vaccinated than back in Germany or because of differences in costs.

Several of my German and Japanese informants also reported that they felt that medicine was excessively used in the United States. However, only my Japanese informants described US prescription drugs as too strong or having different doses available that were not necessarily suitable for Japanese patients. Saki, a visiting professor from Japan, who was in her fifties at the time of our interview, explained to me:

> I am much smaller than average size American, and I feel that the quantities of the medication is, you know, better for the Japanese people.
> (Saki, Japanese female, J1 visa, in the US since 2016)

The reluctance of Japanese patients to take 'American dosages' was also something some of the physicians I spoke to picked up on. For example, 50-year-old Dr Brown, an internist who was working at a hospital and had 25 years' work experience, explained to me that many Japanese patients were under the impression that American drugs were too strong. Although he did not take their concerns seriously, he felt he could help them by creating the impression that he was responding to his patients' preferences (more on this in 'Cultural competence for highly skilled transnational patients?' below):

> That is a common perception in the Japanese . . . 'That is just too much for me, I have to take half of the tablet, I can't take the whole tablet.' And you are just like . . . so what you do is, you start with a higher dose, so then you take half (laughs). There are ways, we are helping them, but you are still allowing the culture, you know . . . But it is kinda one of those things where you simply have to adapt to the person to help them with what they need.
> (Dr Brown, Internal Medicine)

Unsurprisingly, many transnationals reported that they were more at ease with medicines from home because they were familiar with dosage, application and side effects, and many brought basic over-the-counter medications like painkillers or cold medications from home, which will be discussed in more detail in Chapter 6.

Interestingly, while my German and Japanese informants were more ready to complain about medications being too strong or over-prescribed in the United States, several Indian informants complained about the exact opposite. Many felt that medications were not given as often as in India or that they were not strong enough. Indians were also the only group who felt that regulations of medications in the United States were much stricter (compared to some of my German informants, who thought that regulations in the US were not strict enough). However, the lack of restrictions in India was not seen as a positive aspect by all. Sonam, for example, felt that the tighter regulation on the type of medicines and the lower frequency of prescriptions (in India 'doctors will give you antibiotics like they are candy'[38]) were a positive aspect of US health care that she had come to appreciate.

In fact, many of my Indian informants' experiences seem to be in line with what Ahlin, Nichter and Pillai call 'liberal prescription' practices in India, which have been identified as a major problem of the local health care system there (2016: 103–4). According to Khare (1996) many drug regimens prescribed in India are multi-drug therapies, where patients take three or more drugs.[39] And since medical staff often receive remuneration for prescribing and handing out drugs, there is also an incentive for over-prescription of medical treatments and drugs (Berger 2014).

In general, however, most of my informants described the biomedical differences they experienced as more structural (i.e. access, waiting times) than cultural, as the difficulties they had were not 'necessarily with medications itself or treatments, but with respect to the procedure and the access',[40] often even reaffirming that 'treatment-wise, the medicine and everything is just the same'.[41] Biomedical treatments and medicines were, however, only one aspect of my informants' health care routine, and more than half of them had used so-called traditional, alternative and complementary medical approaches in addition to biomedicine, such as homeopathy, Ayurveda or various herbal remedies, which I will discuss in more detail below.

Differences in alternative medicine

According to the World Health Organization, traditional medicine is 'the sum total of the knowledge, skill, and practices based on the theories, beliefs, and experiences indigenous to different cultures, whether explicable or not, used in the maintenance of health as well as in the prevention, diagnosis, improvement or treatment of physical and mental illness',[42] while complementary and alternative medical approaches have been defined by Debas, Laxminarayan and Straus as having 'emerged primarily in Western, industrial countries during the past two centuries as scientific or Western medicine' (2006: 1281). However, terms such as 'alternative, 'traditional', 'complementary' or 'holistic' medicine are controversial. In fact, O'Connor (1995: 3) argues that 'the very actions of naming and describing presuppose a particular point of view and often carry a moral tone'. Van der Geest also points out that this terminology is not only misleading 'because it suggests that there is a more or less homogeneous body of medical thought' but also embarrassing, because it lumps 'together everything which is not "ours"', 'treating it as if it were one type', labelling this as 'a school example of ethnocentric ignorance'. Finally, he argues the terminology is naive 'because it suggests that "our" medical system is not traditional' (van der Geest 1997: 904). Additionally, despite the fact that these different terms generally denote diverse practices, they are increasingly used interchangeably. Thus, as I will be discussing these practices mainly as additions or alternatives to biomedicine, as was the case in the conversations with all of my informants, I have decided to use 'alternative medicine' as an umbrella term, following Debas and colleagues, to describe 'practices and products that people choose as adjuncts to or as alternatives to Western medical approaches' (2006: 1281).

What is considered to be part of standard versus alternative medical treatment depends not only on the country of origin, but also on the history of biomedicine and alternative healing traditions in each society.[43] In Germany, for example, when biomedicine became more formally recognized in the nineteenth century, the region also saw the development of several alternative forms of healing, leading to an idiosyncratic German medical pluralism, including homeopathy, anthroposophical medicine and hydrotherapy. This development also meant that these therapies as well as some of the older folk traditions were organically integrated into the German biomedical practices (Maretzki and Seidler 1985: 383).[44] Today, several alternative treatments have formally been accepted and are covered by health insurance (Frank 2002; WHO 2001).

The situation in India is rather different, since biomedicine was introduced relatively late through the British colonial rule. Even as late as 1914 it had not reached beyond the large metropolitan areas and was restricted to what Khan calls 'colonial enclaves', including hospitals, prisons and the army (2006: 2788). Today India has a pluralistic medical system in which Western biomedicine coexists with Ayurveda and its regional variations (Siddha, Unani-Tibb and Yoga) as well as naturopathy and homeopathy, which are all recognized by the government (WHO 2001). There remains some resistance to biomedical (in India often referred to as allopathic) treatments, although many Indians today seem to prefer biomedical treatments wherever they are available, especially for acute conditions (Ramakrishna and Weiss 1992).

In Japan, the first official medical system, Kampo,[45] was introduced to the nation in the sixth century CE and was adapted from the Chinese medical tradition to fit the local culture (cf. Ohnuki-Tierney 1994; Watanabe et al. 2001; Yu et al. 2006). Kampo remained the main medical practice even after biomedicine was first brought to Japan by Portuguese missionaries. The attempted westernization of medical practice under Emperor Meiji in 1875 also included the prohibition of alternative healing traditions, and by 1920 only 100 physicians practising Kampo remained (WHO 2001). However, several of these practices, including Kampo, acupuncture and moxibustion, have seen a rise in popularity in recent years and enjoy a more official status, having been accepted by biomedical practitioners (WHO 2001). They are even partially covered by health insurance (Ohnuki-Tierney 1994; Borovoy and Roberto 2015; Iglehart 1988).[46] However, Lock and Nguyen argue that alternative medicine has a special role in Japan, as it exists in a 'carefully monitored, standardized form' (2010: 62).

Table 4.12 Use of alternative medicine in home country and the US as reported by my informants

	Germany	India	Japan
Used alternative medicine in home country	60%	83%	66%
Using alternative medicine in the US	40%	50%	6%

Which and how often certain alternative medicines or treatments were used among the three groups is likely influenced by the differences in the history and importance of alternative medicine in Germany, India and Japan, as discussed above. For example, although the majority of my informants had used alternative medicine in their home country,[47] there were striking differences across the groups regarding the continued use of alternative medicine in the United States, as summarized in Table 4.12.

Overall, my Indian informants were the most likely to have used alternative health care in their home country (15 out of 18) and were also the most likely to continue using alternative medicines in the United States (n=9).[48] They were also by far the most likely to refer to them in the interviews, as the frequencies of the narrative analysis indicate, whereas my Japanese informants only very infrequently mentioned alternative treatments at all (see Table 4.13).

The picture among the Japanese patients looked quite different. While two thirds of both Japanese (n=10) and German (n=9) informants used alternative medicines in their home countries, only one Japanese informant had continued with their treatments in the United States, compared with six Germans who continued using alternative treatments (see Table 4.14).

The most commonly used alternative medicines and therapies were homeopathy (used by 15), Ayurveda (used by 10) and chiropractors

Table 4.13 Frequency per 10,000 words of homeopathy, Ayurveda and Kampo as mentioned by my informants

	Germany	India	Japan
Homeopathy & homeopathic	1.08	4.07	0
Ayurveda	0	3.39	0
Kampo	0	0	0.52

Table 4.14 Alternative medicines and treatments used by my informants in their home country and in the US

	Germans/Germany	Germans/US	Indians/India	Indians/US	Japanese/Japan	Japanese/US
Homeopathy	7	2	8	1		
Ayurveda			10	3		
Chiropractor	2	1	1			
Kampo					3	
Home remedies	1		1		3	
Herbal medicine			1	1	1	
Acupuncture					2	
Osteopath	1					
Naturopathy	1					
Massage					1	
Supplements				1		
'Self-medication'		2				1

(used by 6). However, the distribution and variety of the medicines and treatments sought differed quite distinctively across the three groups. While some of the categories might overlap (for example what my informants referred to as home remedies, herbal medicine, supplements and naturopathy could refer to similar practices), the only therapy that all the groups shared was chiropractic. Homeopathy, home remedies and use of herbal medicine were mentioned by two groups; however, the majority of treatments were only mentioned by informants of one group (for example Ayurveda among my Indian informants; Kampo, acupuncture and massages by my Japanese informants; and osteopaths and naturopathy by my German informants). This also corresponded to how the physicians I spoke with experienced the preferences of their highly skilled transnational patients. When I asked them whether or not their transnational patients were more likely than US patients of a similar socioeconomic background to ask for more or different types of alternative medicines, Indians were mentioned more often and Japanese patients were noted as the least likely to ask for these treatments.

That Japanese patients in particular did not feel that continuing these treatments was a viable option for them bears further research. One explanation might be that they were much less likely to use 'material resources' (such as Ayurveda and homeopathy), which can be brought to the host country and self-administered, than 'human resources' (i.e. acupuncture, chiropractor and massage) (cf. Gonzalez-Vazquez, Pelcastre-Villafuerte and Taboada 2016: 1192). Another reason why alternative medicines might be much more accessible to Indians in the United States than to Japanese transnationals could be that a large number of physicians in the US were from India too. In fact, several interview partners said that it was easy for them to find someone who would be supportive and understanding of alternative medicine. Additionally, as pointed out by Varun, who was in his thirties at the time of our interview and had only recently come to the United States from India to work as a researcher, Ayurvedic medicines were easy to come by or make at home.

Regarding alternative human resource options, only one German informant sought out a chiropractor in the US and only one Indian informant mentioned that he used home visits specifically to continue alternative treatments or seek advice from traditional healers – however, this was probably mainly due to his sister owning an Ayurveda clinic there. Furthermore, when I asked my informants if practitioners in the United States had different attitudes towards alternative medicine, my Indian informants felt most strongly about the differences between

India and the US. My German and Japanese informants were generally more unsure, which is not that surprising, since, as we have seen, many individuals had not continued using alternative medicines in the United States. However, the majority of my informants thought that medical practitioners were more open to alternative medicine in their home countries (n=11), or that either these medicines were not offered or covered or they were difficult to find in the United States (n=9), which would also explain why many discontinued using once they arrived.

Cultural competence for highly skilled transnational patients?

As we have seen above, transnationals are confronted with an array of structural but also cultural factors that may make integration into the host country's health care system difficult and negatively impact the medical encounter. As a way to address some of these issues, cultural competence, or what has been referred to as culturally sensitive health care, has been part of the training in many medical schools in an effort to make medical staff more aware of how culture and ethnicity may shape the patients' expectations and knowledge as well as their behaviour in a medical setting (cf. Betancourt et al. 2003; Wear 2003; Kleinman and Benson 2006; see also Stülb and Adam 2009 on cultural competence training in Germany). As such, it aims to raise awareness among medical staff towards 'greater sensitivity to culture in general and a deeper understanding of particular cultural groups and their values, norms, social practices, health beliefs, and health practices' (Baker and Beagan 2014: 578).[49] Although there is no universally accepted definition of cultural competence (cf. Johnson et al. 2004), I base the following discussion on the description of the concept provided by Betancourt et al., who argue that culturally competent health care 'acknowledges and incorporates – at all levels – the importance of culture, assessment of cross-cultural relations, vigilance toward the dynamics that result from cultural differences, expansion of cultural knowledge, and adaptation of services to meet culturally unique needs' (2003: 294). While many cultural competence curriculums are 'knowledge- or skill-based' and 'revolve around the development of respectful attitudes, accurate knowledge, and appropriate behaviors in care givers toward diverse groups and cultures' (Wear 2003: 550),[50] there is, however, also no fixed notion of what constitutes cultural competence training.

Table 4.15 Number of physicians who received cultural competence training during their medical education[1]

Did you receive cultural competence training?	
No	8
In medical school	1
During residency	6
As a practising physician	2

[1] Two informants had received cultural training during the various stages of their training – in Table 4.15 they are only listed once, at the time they received cultural competence training first. Another informant did not formally receive any training and is thus listed as not having received cultural competence training, although he gained experience as a practising physician.

Both the lack of understanding of what cultural competence means and the variability in how it is taught quickly became clear during my field research, as the experiences of the physicians I spoke with differed quite substantially. Although only about half of my informants had received cultural competence training at all, of those who did, most had received their training early on in their career, and two had only encountered the concept as practising physicians, as Table 4.15 above shows.

While some felt that their training 'wasn't very helpful'[51] or were 'a bit suspicious of that, because it is all stereotypes',[52] most seemed to have had similar experiences of what this type of training entailed as Dr Griffith, a family physician in her forties. She explained to me how cultural competence training was handled at the hospital she was working at:

> So our cultural competency training tends to be anywhere like from one to four hours a year and is probably integrated like into every year of medical school, residency. We still have to do it every year. What it usually includes is some sort of broad statements about diversity . . . how to ask sort of some open-ended questions as to gain a better understanding. The worst cultural competency training that I have been to, and this has been only a couple, has been like 'Hey, in your Hispanic patient population, if you look at a baby, but don't touch them, that's *mal ojo* and that's putting a bad curse on them.' . . . I mean it is not totally useless but you can never capture everything you need to know.
>
> (Dr Griffith, Family Medicine)

However, another of my informants, Dr Ferreira, a 38-year-old oncologist who had immigrated from Europe in 2008 and worked at a hospital at the time of our interview, also spoke with me in detail about the cultural competence training she had received, but it quickly became clear during our conversation that she was referring to something quite different than I had anticipated:

> So, when I say cultural training, it was more for Americans. Not thinking about you know, 'How do you treat a Chinese immigrant.' That I did not have at all. So, what I had was as part of the training that you need to have when you come . . . they make sure that everybody that is practising knows how to treat American patients. American, regardless of the race and ethnicity, but what is considered to be appropriate in the US.
>
> (Dr Ferreira, Oncologist)

Keeping in mind that cultural competence training can mean very different things for those who are trained in it, none of my interlocutors outright critiqued cultural competence, either in general or in regard to highly skilled patients. When I asked them to rate the importance of their training (on a scale of 1 to 5), most did not rate it very highly, with the average rating being just 3.1. The majority of physicians agreed that while it was helpful to improve communication and to readjust their expectations from the medical encounter, several (5/17) felt that their experience with patients was a lot more informative to them than any training they had received.

However, as discussed in Chapter 2, the physicians that took part in this study were not only very international themselves, but were also all practising in Washington, DC, a very international city. Of the 17 physicians I spoke with, 10 were immigrants themselves[53] – most of them, however, were not recent immigrants, since the average stay in the United States was 17.2 years – and not all of them had worked in their country of origin before coming to the US. In fact, all of my informants had received their medical training in the United States, although nine of the immigrant physicians had also had previous training in their home country. Also, only five of my informants had not worked abroad before and all but four physicians spoke more than one language with confidence (eight physicians had one additional language, four spoke three languages with some degree of confidence and one spoke four languages; see also Table 2.4). That is to say, their opinions of cultural competence training and their need for cultural sensitivity in their day-to-day practice are probably different from physicians working in a rural or less international setting or those with limited international experience. Dr Kowalski, a 41-year-old dentist who worked in downtown DC and almost exclusively had patients from the nearby World Bank and other international organizations, for example, felt that he was better equipped to deal with transnational patients compared to his rural colleagues, because he has 'a lot of exposure to multiple cultures'[54] as well as frequent contact with international patients.

Most of my interlocutors found the training they received useful not in terms of being made aware of differences in culture but rather as a method to question their own behaviour and their own role in miscommunication issues. In fact, many were suspicious of the 'cultural' aspect of their training, and often thought of this as problematic. In the best-case scenario, as Dr Wang explained to me, cultural competence training could help physicians to step back and not 'immediately assume something about somebody, just because they are obviously from a certain background'.[55] Indeed, previous research has also widely critiqued the concept of cultural competency, either because it treats culture as a static entity (Kleinman and Benson 2006; Carpenter-Song, Nordquest Schwallie and Longhofer 2007; Knipper, Seeleman and Essink-Bot 2010), is 'reductionistic'[56] (Wear 2003) or quickly deteriorates into a kind of cultural beliefs checklist (Krause 2008). Even more problematic is what cultural competence training says about what 'normal' is, as more often than not the diverging '"difference" means nonwhite, non-Western, non-heterosexual, non-English-speaking' (Wear 2003: 550). Cultural competence training can thus even lead to negative health outcomes, for example when physicians are not able to see past cultural stereotypes (Betancourt et al. 2005: 501) or make their patients feel 'singled out and stigmatized' (Kleinman and Benson 2006: 1675). Dr Kildare, who had worked abroad for almost two years and had very good Spanish proficiency, was very critical of the negative aspects of cultural competence training, especially when it came to seeing patients as nothing more than typical examples of their 'culture', which she explained to me 'can be harmful' and 'then kind of perpetuates this stereotyping'.[57]

Furthermore, as Lock and Nguyen (2010) argue, cultural competence not only leads to the 'medicalization of culture', but also doesn't take into account the heterogeneity among immigrants – even among those who are from the same country – particularly in terms of gender, education and age. In fact, when analysing the experiences of transnationals in the health care context, we need to be aware that this broadly described group is, as Smith notes, 'highly differentiated by class, gender, generation, region, religion, and political and economic circumstance of migration within the same migrating "nationality", even within a single transnational city' (2005: 239; cf. Hirsch 2003). Yet, when cultural sensitivity fails to account for diversity within the different groups, miscommunications or difficulties in the treatment can be blamed 'on a patient's culture' (Carpenter-Song, Nordquest Schwallie and Longhofer 2007: 1363). This effect arguably gets amplified when the patient has a lower socioeconomic background (Betancourt et al. 2003), which raises the question of how relevant cultural competence even is for the highly skilled migrants.

Generally, however, of the nine physicians with cultural competence training, most felt it had helped them in their practice to at least some degree. The most common reason why they experienced it as useful was that it improved the way they interacted or communicated with their patients (n=5), that it made them more aware of their prejudices (n=2) or that they realized they would need to take more time with immigrant patients (n=1). Others, however, admitted that cultural sensitivity changed the way they approached their patients; for example, it made them more reserved and less 'spontaneous'[58] or it seemed to undermine the need for basic interpersonal skills. For example, Dr Gross, a dentist in her forties who worked at her private practice at the time of our interview, was very doubtful of the concept, although she had not received any training herself:

> I am not sure there is a lesson for that. I mean you really have to also get a feeling for a person. And also skills. You know, a lot comes with experience when you work.
>
> (Dr Gross, Dentist)

Most of my informants did not rule out the need for cultural competence when treating highly skilled migrants, although the majority rated its importance as fairly low. This might be because many of the misunderstandings in the medical context or dissatisfactions on the side of the patient can be traced back to structural differences, rather than cultural ones. However, structural differences might not regularly be included in cultural competence training curriculums. Additionally, since Washington, DC is an international city with a large population of transnationals, many of whom are in highly skilled professions, cultural sensitivity might simply be less important because most medical practitioners have frequent contact with patients from different cultures. Despite this, as I will discuss in the next chapter, transnational patients often do face both cultural (i.e. different communication styles) and structural (i.e. health care costs and unfamiliarity with the health care system as a whole) barriers to health care that their attending physicians should be made aware of – for example through cultural competence training courses.

Conclusion

As we have seen, transnational patients looking to successfully integrate into the US health care system are confronted by several obstacles. They will not only need to learn how to access health care, but also which services, i.e. treatments and medications, are typically prescribed in the United States and considered part of a 'good' care regime. Since both accessing care and the prescription standards of services differ from country to country (cf. Mossialos et al. 2016), transnational patients often find themselves at a disadvantage.

While some research has seen the causes of miscommunications or unmet treatment expectations as based exclusively on cultural differences, this research has shown that structural differences were just as important, if not more so, for my informants' satisfaction or dissatisfaction. For example, many of the differences that my informants pointed out to me during the interviews were based on differences in how the health care systems were set up in the countries of origin. Coming from a health care system where hospitals are the first point of access for primary care, as was the case for Japan, financial and other restrictions to health care services in US hospitals are understandably experienced as more problematic by Japanese patients, compared to the other two groups that did not harbour the same expectations. Similarly, my Indian informants, who had rarely received interventionist health services in India, regularly criticized US physicians for what they experienced as an over-reliance on diagnostic testing (e.g. through CT and MRI scans). At the same time, Japanese patients, who based their expectations on a system with the highest number of CT scanners and MRI units in the world, unsurprisingly felt that US physicians did not provide enough tests.

Furthermore, the expectations my informants had regarding medications – that is, regarding how frequently which medications were prescribed and in what strength – were in large part not due to 'cultural peculiarities', but informed by patients' previous experiences with health care in their country of origin, which have been formed by the different historical circumstances surrounding the introduction and social acceptance of biomedicine and alternative medicines. In that sense it could be argued that patients' cultural health beliefs are to a large degree informed by the structural setup of the health care systems. For example, for patients who experienced Indian prescription practices, where there were fewer regulations surrounding medicines and drugs were frequently prescribed in high dosages (cf. Ahlin, Nichter and Pillai 2016), the market in the United States in comparison will understandably look more regulated. As such, these differences impact transnationals in two ways: unusual requests of foreign patients that deviate from the US norm inform how physicians interact with them, while unmet expectations also cause transnational patients to view US health care services in a more negative light. In this context it also becomes understandable why cultural competence training as a way to address the different cultural needs of ethnic minorities and migrants was thought of by my medical interlocutors as a useful but not indispensable tool.

While previous research on transnationals' difficulties with the US health care system seems to suggest that people with a lower socioeconomic background or those 'from less familiar cultures with visible ethnicities' are the worst affected (Koskela 2013: 25), I would argue that many of the unmet treatment expectations transcend socioeconomic, cultural and gender differences, simply because they can be traced to structural and functional differences between health care systems. As such, they are likely to affect all newcomers to the US health care system – including highly skilled migrants in urban centres such as Washington, DC, who nominally have insurance coverage and access to high-quality health care. In the following chapters I will thus discuss in more detail the barriers transnational patients experience while attempting to integrate into US health care (Chapter 5) and how they navigate these difficulties by applying various transnational health care practices and strategies (Chapter 6).

Notes

1 The quotation in the chapter title is from my informant Irrfan (Indian male, Green Card holder, in the US since 2002).
2 Since alternative medicines are quite common in Germany, India and Japan, a discussion of not only differences in biomedical drugs – generally the standard when accessing US health care – but also alternative medicine is important. In fact, including an examination of the use of alternative medicines among highly skilled migrants is essential, as more than half of my informants had used alternative medicine in their home country but only very few continued using them in the United States (see Table 4.14).
3 See Mossialos et al. (2016) for an overview of 18 different health care systems around the world.
4 http://www.who.int/topics/health_systems/en/, accessed 24 April 2018; this page may have been updated in the interim.

5   (Dr Thomas, Paediatrics).
6   We need to keep in mind, however, that the majority of my informants based their experiences on visits to primary care physicians or visits to the emergency room for minor ailments. While a few of my interlocutors had mentioned that they had received surgeries for non-life-threatening conditions, none had any experience with serious illnesses or chronic conditions.
7   (Julia, German female, A1 visa, in the US since 2012).
8   For more information on the impact of litigation on US medical practice, see Blendon et al. 2006; Beider and Hagen 2004; White and Hagen 2006.
9   (Saki, Japanese female, J1 visa, in the US since 2016).
10 (Jana, German female, Green Card holder, in the US since 2014).
11 Translation of the original German interview by the author: 'Ist . . . manchmal für den Patient, irgendwie ein bisschen misslich, wenn die Ärzte sich halt nur auf ihr Spezialgebiet fokussieren, und . . . die sagen dann halt: "Da ist was, wir können aber nicht mehr dazu sagen, sie müssen zum Spezialist gehen". Obwohl ich manchmal das Gefühl hab, dass die mehr wissen. Das ist genau so, wenn Ultraschallbilder gemacht werden. Die Dame oder der Herr, die die Ultraschallbilder machen, die dürfen nicht sagen, was sie sehen, weil sie nicht die Ärzte sind . . . Wenn man das dann beim ersten Mal macht, ist man gleich so ein bisschen verunsichert, weil man denkt, vielleicht stimmt irgendwas nicht.'
12 It should be noted that hospitals in Japan underwent a rather different historical development compared to Europe, where hospitals developed out of previously existing religious institutions, which did not exist as such in Japan (Reich et al. 2011).
13 (Takeshi, Japanese male, G4 visa, in the US since 2013).
14 (Hitoshi, Japanese male, J1 visa, in the US since 2014).
15 (Irrfan, Indian male, Green Card holder, in the US since 2002).
16 (Anaya, Indian female, Green Card holder, in the US since 2006).
17 (Ayami, Japanese female, Green Card holder, in the US since 2010).
18 (Katja, German female, L2 visa, in the US since 2015).
19 (Ayami, Japanese female, Green Card holder, in the US since 2010).
20 (Priya, Indian female, G2 visa, in the US since 1995).
21 Although India has achieved some substantial public health improvements during this period, improvements to accessing universal health care have been slow (cf. Reddy et al. 2011; Patel et al. 2011). Yet the inequalities within India remain significant 'between states, rural and urban areas, socioeconomic groups, castes, and genders', leading to differences in the infant mortality rate, number of health services available and number of hospital beds and health workers per capita (Mossialos et al. 2016: 83).
22 (Stefanie, German female, G4 visa, in the US since 2012).
23 (Julia, German female, A1 visa, in the US since 2012).
24 (Hanna, German female, G4 visa, in the US since 2010).
25 (Anja, German female, G4 visa, in the US since 2009).
26 (Aishwarya, Indian female, H-1B visa, in the US since 2002).
27 (Emi, Japanese female, J1 visa, in the US since 2013).
28 Entry in the Merriam-Webster Dictionary: https://www.merriam-webster.com/dictionary/biomedicine (accessed 22 December 2021).
29 Although there is no one accepted definition of 'biopower' (Anderson 2011), the concept is based on Foucault's discussion on the 'Right of Death and Power over Life' (Foucault 1978). As such, biopower refers to medical regulations through authorities in areas such as reproduction and genomic medicine with the intent to 'intervene upon the vital characteristics of human existence' (Rabinow and Rose 2006: 196).
30 As discussed in Chapter 3, Japan chose to model its health care system on the German one, which at the time was considered to be the most advanced in Europe.
31 The space in this chapter does not allow for a full discussion on medical pluralism in India, especially in terms of how 'power, domination and hegemony' are located 'in a larger historical, social and political context' (Khan 2006: 2786; cf. Prasad 2007 for a discussion on the power relations between providers and receivers in Indian medical culture). We should keep in mind, though, as Anderson urges, that a postcolonial lens on biomedicine will allow us 'to recognise that biomedicine is constitutively colonial: that it derives from colonial practices, becomes a means of managing the colonial aftermath, and functions always in a multiply contested contact zone' (2014: 381). Frankenberg argues that biomedicine in India also takes on an

32 important role 'in the legitimation and reinforcement of capitalist state power' (1981: 115), although there has also been a political ambition to strengthen Ayurveda and homeopathy as part of a nationalist movement, which Frankenberg argues is ironic, since both biomedicine and homeopathy were introduced to India through British traditions.
32 Aishwarya was one of the few informants who did not want to give her age.
33 See, e.g., Ecks 2005 for Indian idioms for explaining symptoms of depression.
34 (Hanna, German female, G4 visa, in the US since 2010).
35 (Emi, Japanese female, J1 visa, in the US since 2013).
36 (Krish, Indian male, US citizen, in the US since 2000).
37 (Jana, German female, Green Card holder, in the US since 2014).
38 (Sonam, Indian female, G4 visa, in the US since 2001).
39 These drugs are sometimes chosen for their appearance and form (vibrant colours are preferred over white ones; capsules are preferred over tablets). Many medications are also available as injections, which are very popular and seen to be a particularly potent way of administering medication. These practices are proof, argues Khare, that the biomedical practice in India has 'influenced, and has been influenced by the Ayurvedic, Unani and Homeopathic medical systems' (1996: 839).
40 (Alia, Indian female, J2 visa, in the US since 2016).
41 (Kareena, Indian female, H4 visa, in the US since 2015).
42 https://www.who.int/health-topics/traditional-complementary-and-integrative-medicine#tab=tab_1 (accessed 22 December 2021).
43 Although these practices are often seen in opposition to biomedicine or modern medicine, their use, as Langwick, Dilger and Kane (2012: 10) point out, 'should not automatically be understood as a rejection of biomedical healing practices per se'.
44 Although alternative therapies in Germany have always been viewed critically by the (bio)-medical establishment, a law that was passed in 1869 acknowledged lay healers (i.e. not biomedically trained individuals) and guaranteed their freedom to cure (*Kurierfreiheit*). This law was modified over the years, but is arguably one of the reasons for the widespread acceptance of lay healers (*Heilpraktiker*) in Germany until today (Maretzki and Seidler 1985: 398–9). Another important aspect is that the National Socialist Party had a particular interest in the New German Medicine (*Neue Deutsche Heilkunde*) and openly supported research on natural healing like homeopathy and folk medicines (Jütte 1999: 352).
45 Kampo is the Japanese variant of Traditional Chinese Medicine, which was introduced to Japan from China and was then 'modified to meet local needs' (WHO 2001: 155). It refers mainly to herbal medicines, but the term is also at times extended to include acupuncture, massages and moxibustion (i.e. the burning of herbs on the patient's body).
46 Several alternative treatments have only recently become popular in Japan and are often associated with Western trends, with, e.g., aromatherapy being advertised as having an 'authentic British style', dietary supplements being 'very popular in the USA' and homeopathy being marketed 'with a catchphrase such as "in the German tradition"' (Yamashita 2004).
47 Of the nine German informants who had said they had previously used alternative medicines in Germany, five mentioned that they had either used alternative medicines only once, as children, or used it only reluctantly. The same was true for 4 of the 15 Indian informants included in Table 4.12.
48 Whyte (2009: 7) points out that individuals often identify with therapeutic systems. Thus 'pride in, or allegiance to, Ayurveda or African traditional medicine or Homeopathy is a kind of medicinal cultural politics that places a person by expressing loyalty to one system in opposition to another'. While this did not seem to be a motivator for any of my informants, it is possible that this might be the case for other groups of immigrants.
49 The scope of this chapter can only provide a brief overview of the many issues relevant to cultural competence and cultural sensitivity. For a critique of the concept, see Kleinman and Benson 2006 and Carpenter-Song, Nordquest Schwallie and Longhofer 2007, which will also be discussed in more detail below. Cultural competence also has a business side to it, argue Betancourt and colleagues, in that it can positively affect outcomes by making care more effective and thereby reducing costs (2005: 500).
50 See Betancourt et al. (2003) for other areas that are part of cultural competence training, as well as possible interventions to address health disparities in health care through cultural competence training.

51 (Dr Banik, Psychiatrist).
52 (Dr Wang, Family Medicine).
53 Another two were born abroad but came to the United States as toddlers and spent their entire lives in the US.
54 (Dr Kowalski, Dentist).
55 (Dr Wang, Family Medicine).
56 Some scholars even question the very premise of the concept of cultural competence training. Fox, e.g., cynically remarks that '[i]t is commendable that the authors who address these attributes think of them as professional abilities that can be taught and implemented in clinical training, rather than primarily as virtues associated with moral character' (2005: 1316).
57 (Dr Kildare, Internist).
58 (Dr Silva, Oncologist).

5
'Here I do think before I go to the doctor': highly skilled migrants' barriers to accessing and utilizing health care in the United States

> If I had a disease I probably try to overcome the disease without seeing the doctor here, if the kind of disease is kind of small, you know, like a regular flu or regular cold, then I think I will try to, you know, ahmm, lying on the bed . . . But if I were in Japan and had the same disease, I am 100 per cent certain that I would see the doctor . . . I think this is probably because of the kind of fear of the cost. And fear . . . of the communication . . . actually prevents me from you know, going to see a doctor.
>
> (Hitoshi, Japanese male, J1 visa, in the US since 2014)

Introduction

The US health care system has been identified repeatedly as very complex and difficult to navigate (Reid 2009; Wetzel 2011), leaving many of its citizens struggling to use it (cf. Levitt 2015).[1] However, these difficulties are often amplified for newcomers to the system. In fact, previous research has repeatedly shown that transmigrants face various (additional) barriers in accessing health care in the United States, impacting their levels of health care utilization as well as health outcomes (cf. Gideon 2011; Lee, Kearns and Friesen 2010; Wang and Kwak 2015; Derose, Escarce and Lurie 2007; Ku and Matani 2001). These additional barriers, due to the different styles of medical training, available technologies and so on, shape local (biomedical) characteristics, which can inform what health care services patients expect and how they engage in them (Dilger, Kane and Langwick 2012; Schühle 2018; Dilger and Mattes 2018). Patients who appear to struggle with the host society's health care setup, who encounter barriers or who otherwise seem to be 'problematic', are sometimes even treated differently by their physicians (Good et al. 2002), which can then further reinforce barriers (Scheppers et al. 2006). Several scholars have also demonstrated that access to health services takes on an important role in shaping patients' 'cultural citizenship' (Ong 1995: 1254) and their sense of 'moral worth' and 'deservingness', impacting not only health satisfaction and outcomes but ultimately also 'their incorporation into American society' (Horton 2004: 473; Holmes et al. 2021). A detailed analysis of remaining barriers to care, as well as the strategies used to circumvent these (see Chapter 6), is thus a crucial task to ensure immigrants' overall well-being.

However, most research on health care barriers to date has been focused on low-skilled and undocumented immigrants, as inequality and powerlessness are key indicators to barriers to access (cf. Langwick et al. 2012). Highly skilled transnational patients, on the other hand, are usually assumed not to face any barriers to health care, since they are thought of as not having language difficulties, having insurance coverage and not being affected by health illiteracy (cf. Shim 2010; Levitt 2015). On the contrary, they are characterized by their 'ability to embed themselves into translocalities (both home and work)' (Beaverstock 2005: 250) and are expected to just blend in – that is, they are assumed to successfully incorporate into US society. Yet, as the research at hand shows, the majority of my informants experienced one or more barriers to health care, similar to those typically described for immigrants of lower-income groups in previous research. A good example of some of the difficulties they experience is Hitoshi's story. As an international PhD student in his late twenties holding health insurance in the United States, he would probably not normally be identified as an immigrant patient who seriously struggles with health care in the US. Yet, as the quote at the beginning of the chapter showed, he was worried about many different issues, including concerns about the costs of medical care in the US health care system and his inability to communicate his health issues to the doctor, which I will discuss in more detail below. At the time of our interview, these barriers had led Hitoshi to avoid going to the doctor for his entire three years in the United States. While his case was the exception among my informants, as none of the others experienced barriers to such a degree that they refrained from accessing the system altogether, many of them still faced difficulties that shaped the way they viewed US health care quality and delivery.

Although the focus on immigrants of a low-income background and other more vulnerable groups in much of the previous research is justified simply based on the far greater repercussions of the barriers for these groups (e.g. the costs might be so prohibitive that they cannot access health care services for chronic or even life-threatening conditions), I would argue that leaving out the experiences of a substantial group of transnational patients, such as highly skilled migrants, leads to crucial gaps in our overall understanding of transnational health care needs and the causes of barriers. In turn, a better understanding of these persisting barriers to health care may also highlight some of the underlying issues which are at times overlooked in transnational health care.

In this chapter I will thus first discuss the most commonly described barriers that prevent many immigrants from accessing health care, i.e. communication and financial issues. While these can be prohibitive for vulnerable populations' access to health care, most of my informants – with the exception of Hitoshi – had accessed US health care and received treatments more or less successfully. Then, while much literature focuses on immigrants' struggles to overcome this first hurdle, I would like to focus below on barriers during the medical encounters that, I would argue, influence immigrants' satisfaction and health outcomes despite their educational and socioeconomic background. Most of my informants, for example, lacked an understanding of the US health care and health insurance system in general, preventing them from making common-sense decisions about accessing and utilizing health care to their advantage as they might have been able to in their country of origin. This lack of knowledge led many to make 'wrong', i.e. costly, health care decisions (for example seeking out-of-network physicians or visiting the emergency room (ER)). In many instances, newcomers to the US health care system also did not know how to be a 'good' – that is, successful – patient in the United States. For example, several of the physicians I spoke to explained to me that their foreign patients are not used to taking responsibility for their health care decisions and are not proactive enough to ensure that they are getting the best health care. Thus, by focusing on barriers not only to accessing health care but affecting the *entire* transnational medical encounter, I strive to provide a broader understanding of those aspects that are negatively shaping immigrants' experiences.

Common barriers to accessing health care

Migrants are a very heterogeneous group, and their need and willingness to access health care depends on their individual health needs as well as the experiences they had with health services in their home and the host country (Gideon 2011). However, there are also a multitude of barriers that individuals experience when attempting to access health care, and most research has focused on low-income, immigrant or other 'at risk' populations. Some of the barriers vulnerable populations are exposed to generally do not affect patients of higher socioeconomic backgrounds or education levels. These mainly include structural barriers such as poor access to food and healthy living conditions, difficulties with transportation to and from health services and uncertainty about eligibility to health services, as a review of 54 papers on ethnic minority patients in Western, industrialized countries such as Australia, Canada, Germany, the UK and the USA has shown (Scheppers et al. 2006). Those with an uncertain legal status often even avoid health care services completely out of fear of being deported, as Derose, Escarce and Lurie (2007) have demonstrated to be a common issue among immigrants in the United States. However, this was also the case for Polish immigrants in Scotland (Sime 2014; see also Gideon 2011 on Latin American immigrants in the UK). Generally, entitlements to health services and migrant status play a large part in health care access (Gideon 2011), but are usually not an issue for the group under investigation here.[2] The types of barriers immigrants experience as well as the extent to which they affect their health care also depend on their area of residence and the safety systems available for immigrants in each state – mainly affecting recipients of state programmes such as Medicaid in the United States (Calvo, Jablonska-Bayro and Waters 2017).

Barriers that tend to affect immigrants to at least some degree, regardless of their socioeconomic background and migrant status, are, for example, feeling uprooted or uncomfortable in the new setting and feeling distrustful of the medical system or medical providers in the host society. This was the case in a study by Lee, Kearns and Friesen (2010) that examined why many first-generation Koreans chose not to access health services in New Zealand but preferred to return to South Korea. Horton and Cole's research (2011) on Mexicans in the United States also determined that these aspects were just as important for the immigrants' decision to return home for medical care as their lack of insurance coverage. Another key barrier that previous research identifies is a lack of understanding of how the new system works, which, for example,

Bergmark, Barr and Garcia (2010) identified as one of the barriers Mexicans in the United States were confronted with. Similarly, among South Korean immigrants in Hawaii, unfamiliarity with the system in the US was one of the two most important barriers (Choi 2013). But by far the most frequently discussed barriers for immigrants are: (1) communication issues, for example among South Korean immigrants in Canada (Wang and Kwak 2015) and Polish immigrants in Scotland (Sime 2014); (2) lack of health insurance as well as costs associated with health care services, which, as Brown (2008) showed, are of great concern for Mexican immigrants in the United States (cf. Choi 2013); and (3) lack of dental insurance (Calvasina, Muntaner and Quiñonez 2015). To my knowledge, none of these have been discussed in relation to highly skilled migrants.

Communication: language confidence and feeling 'other'

One of the barriers most frequently mentioned in previous literature is a lack of language skills, sometimes leading to serious repercussions, as was the case for Latino parents in the United States who avoided visiting a physician for their unwell children (Flores et al. 1998). Poor English skills were also identified as a reason for misunderstandings between doctors and patients, resulting in misdiagnosis and noncompliance (Sime 2014). Shetterly and colleagues (1996) also found that a language barrier caused Latinos to report their health status as lower than those who had better English skills. But language is not the only aspect that made communication more difficult for immigrants. Calvo and colleagues found that access to Spanish-speaking health care providers or 'elements of a shared culture' did not necessarily improve the experiences of Spanish-speaking immigrants as long as the rules and regulations surrounding their ability to access services remained unclear (2017). Cultural differences in communication styles also affect 'information, . . . satisfaction, and trust' (Messias 2002: 192). Messias points out that the feeling of not being understood and being marginalized as 'other' often runs deeper than mere linguistic barriers. This notion of feeling 'other' or not belonging was also frequently pointed out by my informants (cf. Stodulka 2017). Several of my informants, for example, mentioned that they feel like foreigners in the United States, and my Indian and Japanese informants in particular reported that they felt (positively or negatively) stereotyped. In fact, communication difficulties, including both language and culture, were frequently mentioned. While my Japanese patients predominantly mentioned linguistic barriers in their

Table 5.1 Responses to the interview question: 'Did you have linguistic or cultural misunderstandings at a doctor's visit?'

Barriers reported	German	Indian	Japanese
Linguistic & cultural barriers	2	0	0
Cultural barrier only	4	1	0
Linguistic barrier only	4	1	13
No difficulties	5	16	1

health care seeking, Germans were more likely to also identify cultural barriers. Of my Indian interlocutors, on the other hand, only two had experienced moderate communication barriers[3] (see Table 5.1 above).

These experienced levels of difficulties appear to correspond to the level of confidence in English reported by my informants (on a scale of 1 to 5). Here, the Japanese, who overall reported the most issues in the physician–patient encounter, ranked the lowest, with an average of 3.8. Germans rank their English language skills on average at 4.2 and had reported fewer issues, particularly with language. Indians, on the other hand, had rated their English confidence at an average of 4.9, and the vast majority reported not having had any difficulty during doctor visits. Although confidently communicating in English sometimes posed a problem for highly skilled migrants and their so-called 'trailing spouses', most physicians I spoke to did not feel that language was a barrier for highly skilled individuals, with few notable exceptions, such as 46-year-old Dr Thomas, a paediatrician who was working in a paediatric practice. However, her views might have been shaped by the fact that she was a German immigrant herself, although she had come to the United States in the late 1990s and had received part of her medical training in the US:

> In a place like here where you have so many embassy people, language can actually become a barrier . . . often it is just the one highly skilled and then you have the spouse that comes along and that never learned English.
>
> (Dr Thomas, Paediatrics)

Among the linguistic barriers, most informants singled out lacking medical terminology or not being able to describe medical conditions appropriately. For example, 46-year-old Takeshi, an employee at an international organization from Japan, worried that although he felt he can easily explain some medical issues ('when I dropped off my bicycle and my hand is fractured, I can explain very easily what happened'[4]), he might not be able to explain other issues appropriately, since it would be 'more difficult to explain mental situation and also some chronic pains'.

In general, my informants reported having several miscommunication issues with their physicians, although none of them mentioned that physicians made them feel that they were expected, as highly skilled migrants, to be not only linguistically but also culturally inconspicuous in the medical encounters. While cultural communication barriers seemed not to be as frequently mentioned as language difficulties, several informants felt that 'cultural differences' were to blame for the fact that they could not get the answers they were looking for from their physicians or that the medical advice they received was not 'trustworthy'. Jana, for example, a trailing spouse from Germany in her late twenties who had followed her US American partner to DC and who was at the time of our interview enrolled at a university, did not have a linguistic barrier, but told me that her physicians refused to tell her which medications and exercises were safe for her during pregnancy. One of the key differences she described to me was that she did not always get a 'straightforward' answer, and to make matters worse, physicians in the United States made her feel like she got 'on their nerves'[5] when she asked too many questions.

In this, my informants' experiences are largely in line with previous research. Lee and colleagues noted, for instance, that although language presented a barrier for some informants, the issues surrounding communication went deeper and 'communication barriers can still exist even when language itself is mutually understood' (Lee, Kearns and Friesen 2010: 112). In their research on first-generation South Koreans, most of whom were described as skilled, they found that they often felt their physicians in New Zealand were not as knowledgeable as their doctors back home, and, because they used phrases such as 'I think', appeared to be uncertain in their diagnosis. A perceived unwillingness to commit to a diagnosis was also a common complaint among my informants. For instance, Krish, a 50-year-old Indian who had come to the United States in the year 2000 to work as a research scientist, felt forced to take responsibility about his health care decisions, a sentiment that several informants shared:

> If you are from Asia and you come here, you will want doctor to tell everything to you, you don't have any of your own opinion. But here, doctor will want that . . . the doctor has some expectation and you don't know how to interact there. Because you are coming from

a different setup . . . Because you are always told to do something [in India]. Here, he is asking you. Why is he asking me? Give me some medication to take!

(Krish, Indian male, US citizen, in the US since 2000)

Although some of my informants, like Krish, mentioned that physicians had 'some expectation' of how patients would react, these expectations did not seem to concern my informants and were not frequently mentioned. In fact, only one, Hitoshi, mentioned feeling distressed or ashamed for not knowing how to interact with US physicians.

However, much of the dissonance in the experiences of immigrants towards US physicians could be located in the different roles physicians are expected to take on, an observation that the 38-year-old oncologist, Dr Ferreira, a recent immigrant herself, could relate to as well:

Opposite to other countries in general, it's a system where the role of the doctor is to inform the patient . . . And many times the decision is on the patient. It's an informed decision, but it's on the patient . . . And it's something that Americans like, to understand that they are making the decision, is something that for other cultures is very scary . . . And from what I have heard, for instance, from Portuguese friends that are patients, sometimes they are like: 'The doctor does not want to have the responsibility and wants me to choose.' But it's not. It's a different culture, where the patients want to be the one to choose. And that's sometimes . . . it is difficult for you to change.

(Dr Ferreira, Oncologist)

Another important aspect of experiencing a communication barrier may be how different the host country's culture is seen to be. When I asked my informants how different they thought their home country's culture was from US culture on a scale of 1 to 5, Germans rated US culture to be more similar to German culture, with an average of 2.9, whereas Indians (average 4.11) and Japanese (average 4.13) both rated the cultural difference as relatively high. Interestingly, this seemed to have less of an impact on the perceived cultural communication barriers in the actual physician–patient encounter itself, which most interlocutors described as similar to what they were used to from home. Their increasing experience of feeling unfamiliar with the local (health) culture was, however, mirrored by the increasing use of transnational health-seeking strategies among these three groups, which will be discussed in Chapter 6.

Many of my informants who experienced communication barriers did not feel that this threatened or seriously impacted their health care. Several reported that they felt quite comfortable handling their linguistic issues by, for example, looking up medical terms in online dictionaries.[6] Shun, a 43-year-old from Japan who was working at an international organization in DC, for example, felt that in addition to checking medical terms online, a good way to not miss any of his physician's explanations was to ask for his diagnosis in writing so he 'could do research once I go back home'.[7]

There are likely many reasons why the consequences of communication barriers were not as dramatic for my interview partners as for other groups of immigrants mentioned above. Among them are presumably their higher socioeconomic and educational background, their access to employer-provided health care and probably also a sense of entitlement and agency that many less privileged immigrants may lack. This might also explain why Shun was comfortable asking his physician for a memo. Additionally, as several of the physicians I spoke with pointed out, their transnational patients tended to be 'more likely to have a smart phone or a computer'.[8] Indeed, several of my informants told me that they were using online dictionaries on their smart phones at the physician's office if they had trouble with medical terminology, and none of them reported feeling uncomfortable or ashamed to do so. For these reasons, it is not surprising that many physicians feel that their highly skilled patients are generally 'more empowered'[9] and much more adept at overcoming barriers. For example, Dr Wang, a 40-year-old family physician at a large hospital, felt that 'language is less of a barrier' for his highly skilled patients and that even if they faced some issues, they were 'more capable of overcoming those'[10] compared to other patient groups.

Previous research has also shown that immigrants frequently experienced discrimination in health care settings (cf. Wang and Kwak 2015; Derose, Escarce and Lurie 2007) or that tax-paying locals contested the deservingness of (poor) immigrants to access social benefits[11] (Calvo, Jablonska-Bayro and Waters 2017; Holmes et al. 2021). Since highly skilled migrants are less dependent on social benefits, they are not as exposed to these negative views as other groups. If my interlocutors mentioned that they felt they were treated differently in the United States, they usually assigned this to their insurance status (nine informants) or positive stereotyping (five informants) rather than discriminatory behaviour (three informants). There were, however, some differences in the reasons my informants gave across all three groups. For example, positive stereotyping ('I have experienced kind of discrimination. But it is positive discrimination')[12] was not mentioned at all by any of my German interlocutors, but only experienced by a few of my Japanese and several of my Indian informants ('People have this stereotype image, and when you come from India, usually people assume that you are this brainy, sharp kind of people').[13]

In many cases, however, their ability to handle communication barriers might also be directly related to the international experience many of my informants had at the time of the interview. Two thirds of the Germans I talked to had worked or studied abroad before, by far more than the other two groups. Half of the Japanese (53%) had experience of working abroad before their time in the United States, but only four Indians I spoke to had had previous international work experience (22%). One reason why Indians had fewer issues in the physician–patient encounter despite having had less international work experience might be their high level of English language confidence or the fact that many physicians are Indians themselves (as three informants pointed out).

Lacking insurance and health care costs

Lacking insurance, not being sufficiently insured ('underinsurance') or otherwise struggling with costs associated with health care such as co-pays or even transportation are another set of barriers that are frequently seen, particularly among low-skilled labourers or undocumented immigrants, as Ku (2009) documented by analysing data from the 2003 Medical Expenditure Panel Survey on insured immigrants in the United States. Also, a study by Grineski (2011) showed the significant effect underinsurance has on how low-income Mexican immigrants in the border area of the US seek health care for their children. Thus, even if immigrants are eligible for health care services, many find it frustrating and difficult to find out what they are and where to access them (cf. Calvo, Jablonska-Bayro and Waters 2017).

Most of the highly skilled migrants who were part of this study, on the other hand, had come to the United States for a particular job that included health insurance or, in the case of international students, were covered through their universities (see Chapter 3). While lacking insurance and struggling with costs may thus seem to be irrelevant for highly skilled migrants, many still experienced these issues and frequently mentioned them throughout the interviews.[14] And although none of my informants were uninsured, not having enough information on how insurance worked in the United States affected several of my informants and caused many of them to incur more health care costs than necessary.

Generally, costs did not prevent any of my informants from accessing and utilizing health care in urgent cases, as might be the case for other groups, although what was considered 'urgent' was also at times reinterpreted by my informants within the context of the US health care system: several of my interlocutors decided not to seek care in situations where they would have gone to see a physician in their home country, a strategy that I will also discuss in more detail in Chapter 6. In this sense, health care costs did shape the type of health care immigrants were seeking and how they chose to utilize the US health care system, as the story of 31-year-old Alia, a former research assistant who had followed her husband from India as trailing spouse and was not eligible to work in the US at the time of our interview, highlights:

> I mean, it's not like you get an orientation course what is preexisting conditions and deductibles and all of that, right? . . . I started getting a rash two weeks ago and my husband said maybe we should go and get it checked . . . I just use topical steroids am fine with it, I can't afford a dermatologist. Because that's the thing. Because you need to start looking into who fits into your insurance policy and . . . it is a lot of homework to do for something that should be more accessible.
>
> (Alia, Indian female, J2 visa, in the US since 2016)

My informants' choices often seemed correlated with the health system setups in all three origin countries. For example, as we have seen in Chapter 3, German and Japanese transmigrants have access to health care in their home countries free of charge and might thus be less aware of the costs than Indians, who are used to fee-for-service health care from their home system. Despite this, Indian highly skilled migrants also seem to experience health care in the United States as expensive, and more costly than in their home country. In some cases, dealing with often unexpectedly high costs – despite being insured – posed an additional 'culture shock', as was the case for 38-year-old Vihaan. At the time of our interview, the Indian IT specialist saw some of his initial fears from a better perspective, but having heard many disturbing stories of families and friends, he was still cautious of US health care, and finances continued to be an important issue for him:

> I'll give you another example. I had a relative visiting and she bumped her . . . toe . . . and I took her to the hospital, emergency room, and we waited for two hours, and then they just . . . they did

this [motions relocating a finger] and it was fine ... Just a dislocation. And they fixed it, it wasn't a big deal ... They did it, we came back home, they send a bill of $2,000. Two thousand dollars. And I am like, are you kidding me? So, so, they charged $2,000 and for a middle-class family it is a lot. Same thing in India, it would have been $3 ... When I just landed, and it's not just me, I talked to my friends, and everyone was scared ... to death. Because we were told horror stories, that one mistake or something bad happens to you, like you could be, you could be owing like $50,000, and you'll go bankrupt ... You know I was so scared of going to a doctor ... I didn't know how it [insurance] works ... I mean, I don't know a solution to this, besides saying: don't get sick. I'll say just try to get an okay health insurance and don't be afraid to use it, because I was afraid to use it.

(Vihaan, Indian male, waiting for Green Card approval, in the US since 2002)

Not being able to access health care in a familiar way was also often described as being very frustrating or confusing, especially because it was often associated with higher than anticipated costs. For example, getting simple medical advice was something that Priya, a 40-year-old academic from India, felt was not possible for her in the United States as it would have been back in India, mainly because 'the cost itself is so prohibitive, you are not sure whom you can trust'.[15]

Another typical example is the case of Ichiko,[16] who was quite uncomfortable in the US health care system, both because of communication difficulties and because she did not know how to navigate the system. Shortly after she arrived in the United States from Japan to marry her fiancé, a US citizen, she had an allergic skin reaction that made her very worried. Her first instinct was to immediately go and see a doctor like she would have in Japan, although her husband tried to persuade her to wait. Unsure how to act, Ichiko contacted her mother in Japan, who encouraged her to immediately see a doctor. Her mother's advice would make sense from a Japanese perspective, since there citizens have a free choice of physician and prices are regulated by the government, so everyone has easy and immediate access at all times with no additional costs:

One night, I got really swollen and I apply a lot of products to try to calm this down. But it didn't work well, so ... ahmm, I asked my husband, like I really need to go to the doctor. And then my husband says, 'Oh it's too late, there is no one up.' So he suggested me to wait. But I couldn't wait. And I talked to my mother on Skype. And she said me: 'You need to see a doctor right now, you need to go to the hospital right now.' And I believed her and we went to ER . . . But then the bill is so expensive, like $1000. In Japan, you go and see like emergency to the hospital, they don't charge you that crazy like that bill. They really just bill you just normal price. So, I just didn't know that.

(Ichiko, Japanese female, K1 visa, in the US since 2016)

This was an expensive lesson for Ichiko, and in retrospect she said, 'I should have listened to my husband.' Even though Ichiko had a trusted person to help her navigate, integrating into a new health system is not easily done. And having insurance coverage alone does not protect immigrants from facing obstacles that stop them from integrating smoothly into the US health care system. Her story also highlights that making assumptions about health care can affect satisfaction with US health care and thus presents a barrier in itself. For Ichiko, seeing a physician to get reassurance was an important part of health care. While she had initially assumed she could continue doing so in the US, the costs had proven to be too prohibitive.

Again, the financial difficulties that the informants of this research described do not prevent them from using health care in urgent cases, as may be the case for other, more disadvantaged groups. But they can cause hardships and lead many to rethink how they approach health care. This seemed particularly to be an issue for embassy staff or others that were not insured in the United States through a US-based insurance company but through private insurance from their home country. With this arrangement, they often have to advance large sums of money, then wait, often for months, until they are reimbursed. Also, since they appear as self-payers to the US health care system, they are charged higher costs than those with insurance, since no one negotiates on their behalf as the big US insurance companies do.[17] Anna, a 35-year-old former consultant who was working as a German-language instructor at the time of our interview, did not anticipate that life, including health care, would be as expensive in the United States. Having to advance money made her think twice before seeing the doctor, something she never had to do in Germany:

> I must say that, for example, here I do think before I go to the doctor. Because, because I have to pay for it first, and it takes so long till it is reimbursed and my life in general is very expensive here and

although my husband is a diplomat, and well paid, at the end of the month, we are really struggling. Because the apartment is, the rent is expensive, the daycare is expensive, and so, if I can avoid a visit to the doctor, I say maybe it will go away by itself. Of course, if I need to go . . . but I do think twice.

(Anna, German female, A1 visa, in the US since 2014)

For 37-year-old Julia, who was working as a political consultant in DC at the time of our interview, and her family, being a self-payer in the US had even more severe consequences. Her child, who had several medical issues, regularly incurred very high medical bills which she had to pay in advance and were a serious cause for concern for her family. And although Julia said that she never felt discriminated against because of her nationality, she thought being a self-payer made a difference to the way she was treated:

I just, I calculated and it was in the first half year we have had medical expenses of more than $100,000 . . . And for the first time that was kinda a shocking experience . . . Maybe I was treated differently because of our, because of our insurance? . . . So I think we get as we are listed there as self-pay patients and I think then you get higher, you get higher rates . . . this whole financial thing, I think, this is different to a US citizen but I don't think it's a question of nationality, it's a question of the, the insurance.

(Julia, German female, A1 visa, in the US since 2012)

But their biggest problem was after they were told their child would need surgery. Two or three days before the scheduled operation, Julia received a phone call from the hospital, informing her that due to their insurance status they would need to pay for the procedure in advance. Julia was told that as a generous gesture on behalf of the hospital they would only have to advance 50 per cent:

And I said, okay, but that's still $10,000 and we don't . . . we can't pay that in advance because we have our, we get all our salaries and anything in Germany. We would have had the money in Germany but only like the bank transfer takes about a week. So we wouldn't have, we wouldn't have received the money on time.

(Julia, German female, A1 visa, in the US since 2012)

In a panic, Julia then scrambled into action to come up with the sum to make sure the procedure would not be cancelled. After contacting the embassy, she says they were 'really lucky', as they were eligible for an advance payment 'directly from the embassy' for a scheduled procedure, and immediately contacted the hospital only to find out that they were no longer on the operation plan. Although they were finally able to have the scheduled procedure, it was now scheduled late in the day,[18] incurring even more costs because they then had to pay for their required overnight stay.

Julia was probably right to feel that her discovery that for certain procedures German citizens or embassy staff are eligible for financial support from the German government was 'lucky'. More often than not, a lack of information about the system, and unfamiliarity with it, gets newcomers stuck in the so-called 'expat bubble'. Their lack of experience makes them dependent on others to give them advice or point them to useful information and has also led many to seek alternative insurance coverage and other transnational health-seeking practices, discussed in Chapter 6. While being part of a closed network like an embassy can certainly be helpful, individual strategies often cannot be generalized and newcomers need to continue to be 'lucky' to hear about them on time – as Jonas's case illustrates.

At the time of our interview, 31-year-old Jonas was taking parental leave from his post at the German embassy. He and his wife, who is also a civil servant, arrived in the United States on an A1 visa in 2014 when they were transferred from a different posting due to the pending birth of their first child in order to profit from the better medical care in the US. Like other embassy staff, they appeared as self-payers in the medical system and were looking for a better way of dealing with the costs involved with the birth of their second child than 'using three different credit cards to block $20,000',[19] and asked their German private insurance if there was a better solution.

Jonas: And they said: 'Yes, there is.' They are working together with [name], an accounting firm, and what they do is, they appear to pay in advance and say this patient is insured with us. This is legally not so, but the Americans accept this and send them all documents, like all bills . . . they beat down the price by 40 per cent and negotiate, also because they are well versed and have the experience and they say: 'Well, no, this costs this-and-this much.' We would just accept that without comment. Also because . . . because I would not privately start negotiating with

	the hospital, also because it doesn't affect me, or it affects me financially only for a certain time and then they in turn sent the bills to [German insurance company], our private insurance and they pay [the US accounting firm].
Nina:	How did you find out about this?
Jonas:	Oh, a colleague in Berlin who also had a baby in the US told us. But the . . . the insurance company doesn't approach you and says: 'Listen!' Like all too often, you really need to have a word-of-mouth recommendation![20]
	(Jonas, German male, A1 visa, in the US since 2014)

Like Julia, Jonas was lucky enough to find a way to receive assistance with medical costs due to his insurance status on time, before large costs were incurred. However, when he tried to inform others at the embassy about his discovery, he realized that it would not even apply to all of his co-workers due to differences in insurance providers.

Learning how to be a patient in the United States seems to come quite literally at a cost, and the learning process can differ substantially from one individual to the next. While some of my informants, such as Jonas and Julia, have benefitted from lucky tips, others like Ichiko have had to 'learn the hard way'. Although the consequences of communication and financial barriers, for example misdiagnosis, avoiding physicians or differences in health status reports (cf. Flores et al. 1998; Sime 2014; Shetterly et al. 1996), tend to not be as dire for highly skilled migrants as for more vulnerable groups, these issues shaped how highly skilled immigrants utilized health care and their satisfaction levels. As newcomers to the US health system, many simply had too little knowledge about the system to use it to its full potential and made assumptions about health care and health insurance which inadvertently led to more confusion or incurred more costs. I would thus argue that lacking a common-sense understanding of US health care presents an additional barrier for immigrants, irrespective of their socioeconomic and educational background.

Do immigrants lack 'common sense' in health care?

As we have seen in Chapters 3 and 4, health care and health insurance systems can only fully be understood within a framework of local knowledge (cf. Ahlin, Nichter and Pillai 2016; Dao and Nichter 2016; Wolf 2012). They represent very local constructs, influenced by social, political, historical and economic factors, that shape the system's setup and can influence health behaviours: how and when individuals seek health care, the prevalence of self-care and so on. Each country's specific health care setup thus arguably gives rise to a set of 'common-sense' assumptions on health culture and health insurance that make sense locally, but this knowledge is not easily recognized or learned – and therefore impacts immigrants' abilities to successfully integrate and utilize health care. Being unable to grasp the rules of the new health system can make patients reluctant to seek health services and negatively affect them emotionally. Choi (2013), who looked at the health care service use of recent Korean migrants to the United States, found, for instance, that the differences in the health care systems presented the biggest barrier in seeking health care, in particular the long waiting periods for insurance approvals and the costs of insurance premiums, which was further exacerbated by the fact that most of her informants had lost access to health insurance in the United States after having experienced public insurance in South Korea.

Of common sense Clifford Geertz says:

> It is, in short, a cultural system, though not usually a very tightly integrated one, and it rests in the same basis that any other such system rests: the conviction by those whose possession it is of its value and validity. Here, as elsewhere, things are what you make of them.
> (1975: 8)

Looking at health cultures and health insurance systems with the common-sense assumption in mind is a worthwhile exercise, since the conclusions people draw by 'living their lives' can be vastly different (Geertz 1975: 9). Thus, arguably the 'common-sense' assumption of how to access health care will be very different for someone who has come to the United States from a system where no prior approval of insurances is necessary, or no additional charges can be incurred, compared to someone for whom these aspects are familiar. Immigrants will therefore need to learn not only how to successfully utilize the US system, but also that they might be making health care decisions based on certain assumptions – that may or may not hold up in the United States. Lacking an understanding of the local system and not being able to make common-sense assumptions on how to access health care can thus increase immigrants' dissatisfaction and leave them frustrated. Furthermore, while locals tend to be more 'well familiarised with pathways of access to healthcare and cultural practices in terms of service providers' expectations and rules of engagement' (Sime 2014: 87), migrants need to acquire such knowledge and often lack the resources to do so (Gideon 2011).

For some migrants, seeking advice in 'negatively functioning networks' (Sime 2014) among their immigrant peers can even disseminate incorrect beliefs about how local systems work. The negative experiences of their fellow immigrants can have an impact on whether or not they attempt to access care themselves. Several of my interview partners had very negative views of US health care – often based on stories from friends and families (as Vihaan mentioned above) – yet, misinformation through networking was not a big concern. However, many of my interlocutors were so baffled by how the US health system worked, that they felt they were set up to fail. This feeling that the system was specifically designed to see patients fail, however, was only mentioned by my Indian informants, who repeatedly referred to the US health care system as 'a big scam'[21] characterized by the fact that there are 'always . . . rules and hidden things'[22] and 'all into fuzzy ways to make money'.[23] The fact that many of my Indian informants did not understand the way the health care system in the United States worked was, however, not necessarily because they were not interested or informed. Ayaan, a 34-year-old economist, for example, who was very knowledgeable about health care financing, still experienced the US system as deliberately 'opaque':

> As I said, it is kind of extremely opaque. No one has any incentive to keep costs really down . . . Like in India, for example, most individuals don't have insurance, so they try to keep costs down. So if a drug is extremely expensive, there won't be enough sales. In the US, because it is paid indirectly through a payer insurance mechanism they are overpriced and people don't really know what they are paying.
>
> (Ayaan, Indian male, G4 visa, in the US since 2013)

Krish even mentioned specifically that he felt the system was set up to cheat people and was not meant to be intelligible even for highly educated individuals like him:

> It is pretty rigged, I would say. In terms of this, it is like, I would say, again, vendor system, multiple vendors, bargaining, nobody knows what is happening, so the system is pretty much not clear to

the public. I tell you, the most highly educated person cannot understand American insurance here. Is it not a shameful thing? Why are they doing that? What is the motive behind it? Because they cheat people, that is the bottom line.

(Krish, Indian male, US citizen, in the US since 2000)

In addition to these more fundamental concerns with health insurance costs, several informants also had trouble with health care bills and their reimbursements. While billing errors that take months to reimburse or being overcharged may not be financially devastating to this group, it can certainly lead to distrust in the system and feeling dissatisfied with it, as was the case with Nobu, an economist from Japan. The 37-year-old came to the United States in 2012 to work at a major international organization. As a father of two, he has had several issues with his health insurance in the US, including not being aware of charges about 'out-of-network' physicians. This left him feeling overcharged and made settling billing 'mistakes' difficult.

Another good example of the impact of wrong assumptions on health care is Simone's story. At the time of our interview, the 37-year-old trailing spouse from Germany had just started working as a language instructor, and prior to that position had been a stay-at-home mother of two. She had assumed she would be able to see a physician once the need arose – as she would have done in Germany ('I didn't think it would be so difficult to get a physician'[24]). However, when Simone had an infection, she was not able to visit a physician because she had failed to register as a patient ahead of time, and was forced to go to the ER instead. Although the costs she incurred were not as catastrophic as they might have been for other groups of immigrants, her experiences left her feeling confused and frustrated.

A sense of frustration with their lack of knowledge of the system had also made a group of poor working immigrants that Calvo and colleagues spoke to distrustful of the system and less willing to ask for support. Their experiences with US health care were also an important factor for their sense of belonging and influenced how many 'derived meaning of their place in American society' (2017: 2031). While none of my informants were in as vulnerable a position as immigrants applying for Medicaid, several mentioned a sense of distrust and certainly frustration caused by their lack of a common-sense understanding of US health care. The difficulties were sometimes also experienced as excluding, and left them struggling to find support in navigating the system. 31-year-old Christine, who had come to DC to live with her partner, an American, became quite frustrated when she realized that she 'had no idea about any of this, how any of this works'[25] and that she had to put a lot more work into learning how to navigate the health care system. However, despite her willingness to reach out for help, she felt that 'no one seemed to be responsible for this', and ultimately, she was unable to find somebody to guide her.

One of the main themes my informants brought up when I asked them about their opinions on health care was that they had previously understood it as a 'given'; many mentioned that they had 'never thought about it before',[26] that they had taken their home country's health insurance system 'for granted'[27] or that they now 'appreciate it more'[28] since having experienced the health system in the United States. Several informants also pointed out that their stay in the US had made them aware of differences and enabled them to compare the two systems, often leading them to point out advantages and disadvantages in both systems. When the informants were asked whether they had changed their opinions about their home insurance system since they had come to the United States, the vast majority reported that they had a better opinion of their home health insurance system after experiencing the US system, or that they had always had a very good opinion of their home insurance system (11 Germans, 8 Indians and 8 Japanese). Far fewer felt that US health care was better or that they now can see negative aspects of their home health care system better (5 Japanese, 3 Indian and 2 German informants). This may not necessarily be ascribed to the objective advantages or disadvantages of the differences in the systems, but, I would argue, is due to them becoming aware of their common-sense assumptions not holding up in the US system. Their fairly consistent positive evaluation of the home health system is thus likely to also be informed by their being more familiar with it. They have learned to navigate it and thus know what they can expect – not knowing enough thus negatively influences how favourably they experience the US system.

Physicians' views of highly skilled migrants' barriers to health care

As we have seen in the discussion on US health care and particularly its health insurance system (Chapters 3 and 4), the US health system has been rated as particularly complex (cf. Schoen et al. 2013), and even many US citizens lack the necessary knowledge to choose the most suitable plan from the many options available. A recent survey also found that many Americans do not understand the meaning of important health system words such as 'co-pay' or 'deductibles' or could not answer how US insurance worked. Unsurprisingly, those without insurance – and thus with less health insurance experience – fared far worse in answering the survey questions than insured individuals. As Levitt argues, the 'lack of health insurance literacy . . . has important implications for how effectively people use health care services and their insurance' (2015: 556) and ultimately how much they end up paying. According to the chief executive of the International Federation of Health Plans, the high level of fragmentation of the US health care system leads to a situation where 'American health care providers and pharmaceuticals are essentially taking advantage of the American public'.[29] However, the risk of being taken advantage of – not knowing how to successfully navigate the system or paying too much – is particularly true for those who have no previous experience with the system. Dr Brown, a 50-year-old internal medicine specialist working in a hospital setting, confirmed that 'paying for mistakes' was in fact a common occurrence among his immigrant patients, as they 'have no concept'[30] of the costs involved or an understanding of what deductibles are. Many of his patients also didn't realize that seeking care in the ER should be avoided, although he thought patients tended to 'only make that mistake once'.

In fact, when I asked the physicians interviewed for this study about the possible barriers regarding the successful integration of highly skilled migrants into the US health care system, only a few (5 out of 17) felt that highly skilled patients did not face barriers to health care. Some of them felt highly skilled migrants possessed the necessary skills and education to use the system to their advantage, and others thought that highly skilled migrants should not have any issues, since they had employer-provided insurance. Dr Gross, a 44-year-old dentist with 18 years' work experience, assumed that it was a common-sense approach to look at the fine print of insurance coverage to ensure satisfactory access; however, this was not how the majority of my informants approached their insurance:

> If you have an employer and use your health insurance, you have the same health insurance as any other American employee . . . It's all straightforward. I mean, you get a job, you have the insurance and it's like, you know, like in life. Always it is, you have to look at small print. And see what you get.
>
> (Dr Gross, Dentist)

Table 5.2 Key barriers for highly skilled migrants as perceived by their US physicians

Lacking system literacy: Not knowing how to effectively use the system, too much choice, pharmaceuticals	6
Language and cultural barriers	2
Difficulties finding trustworthy physician	2
Short duration of stay in the US	1
Racism	1
No significant barriers	5

The majority of my interlocutors (10 out of 17), however, reported that their highly skilled migrant patients faced at least some barriers, particularly regarding their minimal knowledge of the US health system or cultural or language barriers. Table 5.2 above summarizes some recurring themes in their narratives.

Although the short stay of many highly skilled immigrants was only mentioned as a distinct barrier by one, several physicians agreed that the time and effort going into learning and integrating into the US health care system may actually put short-term migrants at an additional disadvantage, since they might not get too involved with their health care in the United States, as they lack time to gain the necessary knowledge or to learn from their mistakes. Dr Costas, a paediatric resident in his late twenties and a recent immigrant himself, for instance, had a very detailed view of how the short duration of some of his patients' stays in the US presented a barrier:

> Because they come here for just two, three years they don't even think of really being involved in these issues, because they know that it's something that could be very money consuming and they just hope they gonna be healthy . . . And most of them travel also frequently so they might access some type of care back in their home country. So they are here just in case something goes wrong. But then they might seek the rest of their health care back in their country . . . So that is maybe one barrier, the fact that they are temporarily here and not for a long period of time.
> (Dr Costas, Paediatrics)

While the short duration of some immigrants' stays in the United States was often identified as a reason why getting to know the system sufficiently is difficult, finding a doctor that is invested in your care was also mentioned several times. Dr Stein, a 50-year-old university hospital professor of family medicine, for example, told me that because many of her highly skilled migrants leave after a few years, she experienced them as 'more transient',[31] and admitted that this could lead to 'maybe less of an emotional investment in the care'. Similarly, 59-year-old Dr Bauer, who had emigrated from Germany 15 years ago and who had established himself in the United States as a paediatrician at a large hospital, shared with me that he was particularly wary of the highly skilled patient populations. He felt they were reluctant to assimilate and accept US health care, for example by trying to avoid vaccinations and orienting their health decisions towards their home country:

> It's a peculiar population group in particular if you talk about those who come here for two or three years . . . they are not interested in assimilating in the local community . . . so I am also critical of that kind of population . . . They will come to me and say we don't want to immunize our kids, because in Germany we don't need it and, and you know, they, they refer to their or explain their decisions, their health care decisions, with how life is back home in their country of origin. Rather than with how their life is here. And that's different for those ahmm foreigners who come here to stay. You know, people like myself.
>
> (Dr Bauer, Paediatrics)

While, as Dr Bauer noted, transnational patients often take their access to their home medical system into account when they make health decisions, none of my international interview partners mentioned to me that they made these decisions because they are 'not interested in assimilating in the local community', but for a variety of reasons that I will discuss in more detail in Chapter 6. However, it seems highly probable that an interpretation of patients' actions such as Dr Bauer's reinforces miscommunication issues. This then goes to show that we need a greater understanding of the patients' experiences and expectations to better identify the reasoning behind their health decisions.

Unsurprisingly, however, the most common barrier mentioned for this group of patients was choosing the right options from an excessive amount of choices or knowing what requirements needed to be met for insurance cover to kick in. Several others mentioned that cultural customs prohibited some groups of patients from taking full advantage of their choices, such as seeking a second opinion, out of fear of being perceived as rude, which prevented some patients from receiving the best care. For example, being pushier and taking responsibility for their health and their treatments might be quite unusual for some immigrants, while others might find such 'necessary' behaviour inappropriate or rude. Dr Wang, who had a very sobering view of the US health system in general, felt that immigrant patients were often not aware of these requirements and that there was 'not a lot of handholding in the US health system',[32] leaving patients alone in navigating a very complex and difficult system.

This feeling of being left alone to navigate a complicated system was also reflected in some of my informants' experiences, most notably Christine (see above), who was the only one of my informants insured through the ACA (Obamacare, see also discussion in Chapter 3). During our interview she told me how taken aback she was about how little support she received:

> Here I found the access really complicated . . . There was no real help or support for me to figure that out . . . So yeah, I found that very surprising and disheartening. Because I remember thinking, I mean I know, I know I am in a very privileged position here, as a white immigrant from Europe who speaks and understands English pretty well, so I remember thinking how hard it must be for immigrants who don't have that, who don't have these, resources.
> (Christine, German female, Green Card holder, in the US since 2015)

This begs the question how newcomers to US health care can learn how to become successful patients. Sarah Kliff, a health care journalist and editor, experienced herself how important it was to have a firm grasp on US health care in order to be a successful patient. In fact, in her article 'Unpaid, stressed, and confused: patients are the health care system's free labor',[33] she writes that patients in the United States are 'the secret glue that holds the system together'. She concludes that the job of patients in the US system is like a part-time job with high stakes, with responsibilities including transporting medical records, finding pharmacies for filling prescriptions and checking with one's insurance to see if a procedure or medication will be covered. Several of the physicians I spoke with seemed to have similar misgivings about what was expected of their patients. For example, 42-year-old Dr Griffith, who at the time of our interview was working as a general physician at an office associated with a DC area hospital and had over 14 years of working experience, felt that patients in the US system 'are expected to understand too much', given that this was not their only job in life:

They [patients] are given very little information about what that entails and they are expected to understand too much. You know, health care is not their business. Right, how do they know which tests they should or should not get coverage for? So people are expected to understand too much, even people who are competent. You know, it's not the only thing they do in their life.

(Dr Griffith, Family Medicine)

Interestingly, my transnational informants generally did not refer to the many different jobs they had to perform as US patients, but were much more likely to mention their difficulties in accessing or navigating a system they did not understand. This was possibly because they did not fully understand what the patient's 'job' in the United States entailed. Thus, while being a good US patient is tedious, frustrating, time consuming and difficult for some, it can be almost impossible to navigate for those who already face barriers to health care like language skills or aren't knowledgeable about the system. And having to take on an active role as a patient and 'to take responsibility'[34] is not necessarily the common-sense assumption many immigrants make, as Dr Das, a paediatrician and geneticist in her forties at a health care centre who had immigrated to the US from Southeast Asia in 2007, explained to me.

Being aware of how to be a good patient or an 'ideal user' – that is, someone who matches 'the precise set of competencies and resources' (Dixon-Woods et al. 2005: 7) – is extremely important in order to succeed in the US health system. Immigrants, however, are rarely informed on what their 'job description' is, and Dixon-Woods and colleagues argue that often there is additionally a 'discord between the cultural norms of health care organizations and their imagined ideal user' (2005: 151) when it comes to minorities or immigrants and that many health care providers simply 'rely on implicit assumptions about the "ideal user"' (2005: 53). This is not only true for low-skilled immigrants, but also for the group under investigation here, since physicians often (rightfully) assume that they possess enough health literacy to '[n]avigate the healthcare system, including filling out complex forms and locating providers and services'.[35]

As we have seen, however, being health literate does not necessarily translate from one system to the next. In fact, some of the barriers highly skilled migrants experience could also be described as them lacking what Shim called Cultural Health Capital, meaning 'the repertoire of cultural skills, verbal and nonverbal competencies, attitudes and behaviours, and interactional styles, cultivated by patients and clinicians alike, that, when deployed, may result in more optimal health care relationships' (2010: 1). While the well educated and the middle class are the most likely to capitalize on Cultural Health Capital, these skills are always specific to time and place, and as such, they are not necessarily accessible to highly skilled migrants, even though they might have this skill set in their home country and are probably expected to also be able to use these skills in the host country setting. Adapting to a new system, a process that Dr Gonzales, a paediatric resident in her late twenties, described as 'mental translation', is heavily dependent on what basic assumptions immigrants bring with them from their home health care system setup:

> They need to know how to navigate the system, because insurance sometimes covers this and doesn't cover that. And for example, when you come from a public health system like Germany it's really hard to translate mentally, where are you able to go, which hospital do you have access, which hospitals you don't have access to.
>
> (Dr Gonzales, Paediatrics)

These different aspects of taking on the role of a US patient were also reflected when I asked the participating physicians to talk freely about what they thought their highly skilled patients need to know. Overwhelmingly, they considered knowledge of functional and structural aspects of US health care more important than cultural aspects (see Table 5.3 below).

I would argue that cultural factors were less frequently mentioned as a 'need to know' fact, because the patient group in question was 'highly skilled'. In fact, there is some evidence that cultural barriers are generally assumed to be more likely to affect minority or poorer

Table 5.3 Recurring themes of what physicians think their patients need to know

How the system works in general: establishing a doctor relationship, getting second opinions, how to access health care	7
How US insurance works: coverage, co-pay, in- and out-network physicians, referrals	6
How to be a patient: be proactive, educate yourself, get advice, how to communicate with doctors	4

immigrants. For example, Johnston and Herzig (2006) found that Mexican agricultural labourers were much more likely to cite structural barriers to accessing health care, while their health care providers were more likely to ascribe cultural differences as the main reason for any difficulties in their health care encounters. For this group of highly skilled migrants, on the other hand, we have seen above (Table 5.2) that several physicians (wrongly) assumed that they do not face any cultural or linguistic barriers.

Conclusion

Previous research on barriers to health care has rightly focused on many of the debilitating effects these have on the most vulnerable groups. However, as this research has demonstrated, highly skilled migrants, as newcomers to the health care system, are affected at least to some degree by these barriers as well, regardless of their socioeconomic and educational background. This also included linguistic and financial hurdles usually not associated with this more privileged group. And while some physicians generally were aware of the difficulties newcomers to the system may face, highly skilled migrants are usually not assumed to be in need of any additional support, leaving many struggling to integrate successfully into the system. I have also argued that lacking a 'common-sense' understanding of US health care presents a significant barrier, which has frequently been overlooked in discussions of transnational health care, when more pressing barriers such as a lack of insurance, costs or inadequate language skills dominate the discussion. Yet, this can impact immigrants in two ways: first of all, health care and health insurance providers normally see the system as a given and thus fail to realize the immigrant's need to negotiate their understanding of the system; the assumptions providers make about immigrants lead to a cultural dissonance which creates new or enhancing existing barriers, as argued by Dixon-Woods et al. (2005). Secondly, immigrants bring their assumptions on how health care and health insurance work with them, and find it difficult to learn the rules of the new system and often end up 'learning by doing' (which leads to many paying for 'mistakes', as happened to, e.g., Ichiko). Some of Horton's interview partners had similar experiences, including a trip to the hospital that did not shed light on the patient's condition but instead taught her to 'stay away from hospitals' (2013: 423).

The impact barriers have on health-seeking behaviour also depends on immigrants' home health care setup and their previous experience with regulations, requirements and coverage. Since barriers not only affect satisfaction and health outcomes but can also have an impact on immigrants' sense of belonging (cf. Horton 2004; Calvo, Jablonska-Bayro and Waters 2017), the study of them becomes an important aspect of integrating immigrants into the host society. Excluding a subset of transmigrants from this research seems not only problematic, but also unwise. Future research should focus on a more detailed analysis of how diverse groups of immigrants can more effectively learn to use the new system without having to pay for their lack of experience. At the same time, the vast majority of immigrants already employ an array of alternative health care seeking strategies and practices to navigate barriers and to access their preferred style of health care, which I will discuss in the following chapter.

Notes

1. The quotation in the chapter title is from my informant Anna (German female, A1 visa, in the US since 2014).
2. As such, the scope of this chapter prevents me from discussing these barriers in detail; for more information, see, e.g., Scheppers et al. 2006; Derose et al. 2007; Sime 2014; and Gideon 2011.
3. We should keep in mind, though, that admitting to linguistic barriers might have been more comfortable for my informants than to cultural barriers. Krish, one of my Indian informants, pointed out that he did not have cultural misunderstandings 'Because I am not, I am not . . . like a villager from India, where . . . I have seen many cities and stuff' (Krish, Indian male, US citizen, in the US since 2000).
4. (Takeshi, Japanese male, G4 visa, in the US since 2013).
5. (Jana, German female, Green Card holder in the US since 2014).
6. Other approaches to specifically circumvent the difficulties they encountered in the physician–patient encounter included getting reassurances from doctors back home or even avoiding going to seek medical assistance at all, which will be discussed in more detail below in Chapter 6.
7. (Shun, Japanese male, G4 visa, in the US since 2004).
8. (Dr Thomas, Paediatrics).
9. (Dr Gonzales, Paediatrics).
10. (Dr Wang, Family Medicine).
11. Despite the fact that most 'deserving' immigrants often pay more taxes into the system than they receive in services (cf. Dickman, Himmelstein and Woolhandler 2017).
12. (Haruka, Japanese female, F1 visa, in the US since 2012).
13. (Salman, Indian male, H-1B visa, in the US since 2007).
14. Since these costs, language and cultural barriers are usually not associated with this group of immigrants, struggling with these might even be a source of social stigma (cf. Dean and Wilson 2009; see also Stodulka 2015).
15. (Priya, Indian female, G2 visa, in the US since 1995).
16. Ichiko was one of the informants who chose not to disclose her age to me.
17. http://www.nytimes.com/2001/04/02/us/medical-fees-are-often-higher-for-patients-without-insurance.html (accessed 11 February 2022).

18 The original procedure was planned for the early morning, because no food or drink can be given prior to the operation. While this can be tolerated better by older children, Julia and her family had to wait till the early afternoon and were not allowed to feed their six-month-old baby.
19 Translation of the original German by the author: 'um nicht mit 3 verschiedenen Kreditkarten 20.000 Dollar auf einer Kreditkarte zu blocken'.
20 Translation of the original German by the author: 'Die haben gesagt: ja die gibt es. Die arbeiten hier mit einer Rechnungsprüfungsfirma zusammen, [name], und was die machen, die treten quasi in Vorkasse und sie sagen, der Patient ist bei uns versichert. Stimmt rechtlich nicht, aber die Amis akzeptieren das erstmal so, schicken dann denen alle Unterlagen, also alle Rechnungen . . . die drückt den Preis um 40% und verhandelt, auch weil die Ahnung haben und Erfahrung und sagen: "Ja nö, soundso das kostet so viel". Wir würden das einfach kommentarlos akzeptieren, ja. Weil wir . . . also, weil ich nicht privat anfange mit dem Krankenhaus zu verhandeln, auch wenn's mich gar nicht, mich trifft's finanziell nur 'ne Zeit lang und die schicken dann wiederum der [Krankenkasse], unserer privaten Versicherung ne Rechnung, und die bezahlt dann die [Rechnungsprüfungsfirma] [Ja aber woher habt ihr das rausgefunden?] Oh, das hat uns ne Kollegin in Berlin erzählt, die auch in Amerika ein Kind gekriegt hat. Aber das . . . da kommt die Krankenversicherung nicht auf einen zu: Hier, passt mal auf! Wie so oft, muss man über Mundpropaganda das dann rausfinden!'
21 (Salman, Indian male, H-1B visa, in the US since 2007).
22 (Priya, Indian female, G2 visa, in the US since 1995).
23 (Irrfan, Indian male, Green Card holder, in the US since 2002).
24 (Simone, German female, E1 visa, in the US since 2015).
25 (Christine, German female, Green Card holder, in the US since 2015).
26 (Anaya, Indian female, Green Card holder, in the US since 2006)/(Ayami, Japanese female, Green Card holder, in the US since 2010).
27 (Hitoshi, Japanese male, J1 visa, in the US since 2014)/(Nobu, Japanese male, G4 visa, in the US since 2012).
28 (Stefanie, German female, G4 visa, in the US since 2012).
29 http://www.vox.com/cards/health-prices/america-is-getting-gouged-on-health-care-prices (accessed 12 February 2022).
30 (Dr Brown, Internal Medicine).
31 (Dr Stein, Family Medicine).
32 (Dr Wang, Family Medicine).
33 http://www.vox.com/2016/6/1/11712776/healthcare-footprint (accessed 31 December 2021).
34 (Dr Das, Paediatrics and Medical Genetics).
35 This quote, last accessed in October 2018, was originally posted at the following URL, though it is no longer available: https://health.gov/communication/literacy/quickguide/factsbasic.htm#one. See also Kickbusch 2001.

6
'Take a vacation, go back to India and get a treatment there': transnational health care practices and strategies navigating US health care and health insurance culture

> I think for me it has been really useful to have a physician in India I could always check back with . . . to have a personal physician I could call and say, you know, 'I am having this really bad throat'. I wouldn't go to the physician here, if I had to, if I just had a cold or cough or anything like that. If it is something, I guess if it is something that is more serious, more chronic I wouldn't go to a doctor here . . . in India, I would definitely go and check, because like I said, it is just like getting a cup of coffee.
> (Alia, Indian female, J2 visa, in the US since 2016)

Introduction

Highly skilled migrants are not only affected by the same kinds of structural and economic barriers to health care as other groups of immigrants (see Chapter 5); they also share many unmet treatment expectations and 'nostalgia' for a certain style of medical practice (Horton 2013).[1] Thus, immigrants often choose not to use the (biomedical) health care services available in the host country, even if they would be entitled to use them or could afford them, but rather engage in transnational health care strategies and practices in order to access their preferred style of care. These include delaying health care seeking, continuing treatments with medications obtained from one's home country or going for regular check-ups on visits back home (cf. Wang and Kwak 2015; Gideon 2011). Which strategies and practices are used, and how often, is determined by a range of factors, such as immigration status, income, gender, age and health status, but also the immigrant's 'knowledge of transnational opportunities' and the ability to use two health care systems to their advantage (Lee, Kearns and Friesen 2010: 110; cf. Yang 2010; Messias 2002; Grineski 2011). Most of the time, immigrants engage in one or more of these transnational health care seeking strategies and practices simultaneously, in addition to (biomedical) services in the host country.

Of everyday practices, De Certeau writes, there are two oppositional types: strategies, which represent a tool of power, dependent on 'a specific type of knowing' (1980: 5), and tactics, which are 'an art of the weak' (1980: 6) used in the absence of power and by those dependent on seizing opportunities. Loosely following this definition, I will use the term 'strategy' for the more active choices immigrants make in their health care seeking, such as planning medical treatment in their home country or engaging in pre-emigration health. I will refer to their more passive choices, such as continuing treatments with medications obtained from one's home country or continuing regular check-ups on visits back home, as 'practices'.[2]

To date, research on these transnational care strategies and practices has focused neither on highly skilled migrants in general, nor on transnationals moving from one industrialized country to another in particular, such as the informants from Germany or Japan in this study (cf. Villa-Torres et al. 2017). While several transnational care strategies and practices are more common in some groups of immigrants than others, the vast majority of highly skilled migrants in the research at hand made similar choices that to date have only been described for less privileged immigrant groups, although their motivations for employing these options differed substantially across groups. I argue that an analysis of these strategies and practices is necessary to gain an in-depth understanding of when and for what reasons immigrants employ transnational health care seeking, particularly because they not only influence health care decisions taken by the patients, but also impact the physician–patient relationship (cf. Gonzalez-Vazquez, Pelcastre-Villafuerte and Taboada 2016). In this chapter I will thus discuss the different strategies and practices used by transnationals to overcome some of the barriers outlined in the previous chapter and their different motivations for engaging in them as well as the risks and benefits associated with transnational health care seeking.

What are transnational health care strategies and practices?

With the ever-increasing globalization and mobility of individuals, it is not surprising that transnational health care and health care seeking are on the rise as well. This 'medical globalization' (Dilger and Mattes 2018) is not only restricted to the movement of patients and physicians, but can also 'describe the movement of health-related resources, ideas, finances, and objects – both afflicting and healing – that are important elements of migrants' identities and health practices between home and host countries' (Langwick, Dilger and Kane 2012: 8; Tiilikainen 2012; Giordano 2013). The most common reason why immigrants seek transnational health care is to overcome the barriers they experience when attempting to access health care in the host country, as outlined in Chapter 5, including communication barriers, health care costs, insurance coverage and unfamiliarity with the local health care system. Although this tends to be more common among uninsured or low-income individuals (cf. Choi 2013), the vast majority of immigrants experience some degree of uncertainty or fear of biomedical treatments, perceptions of unreliability or untrustworthiness of diagnoses made by physicians, worries about the impact of Western lifestyle or unfamiliarity with the environment in the host society – regardless of their socioeconomic background (Tiilikainen 2012; Messias 2002). Therefore, many immigrants employ a variety of transnational strategies and practices in order to access their preferred type of health care. This flow of patients, healers and medicine is not only bidirectional (cf. Dilger, Kane and Langwick 2012); it can also directly shape immigrants' health care choices through their 'knowledge of transnational opportunities' (Lee, Kearns and Friesen 2010: 110) and their 'transient mindset' (Messias 2002: 191). The research at hand indicates that these transnational practices and strategies are not merely a reaction to socioeconomic or cultural aspects of patients' experiences, but an integral part of the transnational experience or their flexible migrant identity (cf. Gonzalez-Vazquez, Pelcastre-Villafuerte and Taboada 2016).

The vast majority of transmigrants seem to engage in both strategies and practices as well as utilizing health care services in their host society, including (1) bringing medications and using self-diagnosis and self-medication, (2) returning home for medical treatment, (3) pre-emigration health care, (4) delaying health care seeking and (5) seeking trustworthy health care (providers).[3] There are, however, also health care seeking activities, such as (6) alternative care options, that seem to be mainly employed by less privileged groups. These typically include communal sharing of information on where to get alternative medications and how to prepare home remedies, or using the community network to bring herbs or other alternative medications from the home country. The willingness to resort to using predominantly alternative health care might also be related to a lack of insurance or other barriers to accessing biomedical health care services, and is an important aspect of what Krause (2008) described as a 'Transnational Therapy Network' or TTN, in which medicines, treatments and ideas are exchanged. In this chapter I will argue that TTNs seem to be a less important source of health care for highly skilled migrants, possibly since such a network tends to be rooted in strong community ties, which are less common among this group,[4] and because TTNs might be particularly helpful in navigating barriers uncommon among the highly skilled, i.e. lacking resources or insurance coverage (cf. Messias 2002).

Unlike less privileged immigrant groups, the highly skilled migrants in this research tended to use transnational strategies and practices more out of convenience or comfort, or for added advantages, rather than necessity, although many also experienced substantial barriers to health care in the United States (as discussed in Chapter 5). However, to fully enjoy the benefits of being able to use more than one health care system to satisfy one's health care needs, immigrants need to have the knowledge to comfortably navigate the health care systems in both the host and home country, the necessary paperwork and documentation, and adequate language skills. Grineski (2011) refers to this skill set as 'Transnational Cultural Capital' (TCC). TCC allows patients to consider different health care opportunities and options across countries and gives them 'the power to acquire what one perceives to be best in a healthcare field that spans borders' (2011: 258). So, while most of the highly skilled migrants did not have access to TTNs, TCC was available to all of my informants at least to some degree. Their TCC also allowed them to engage in (7) alternative insurance coverage as a transnational strategy, which seemed to not be an option for immigrants with fewer resources at their disposal.

However, while most strategies and practices were shared among all groups of immigrants, the motivations for engaging in them differed across the different groups under investigation here. One explanation for this might be their differences in language skills and how differently US culture and US health care quality were rated, as well as the length of stay in the United States and previous living experiences abroad. For example, the need to bring medications or see a physician back home may be

Table 6.1 Closed question results of questionnaire: differences in language and culture, opinion of US health care quality, length of stay in the US and first time living abroad

	Germans	Indians	Japanese
Average English language confidence on a scale of 1 to 5	4.2 [1.5–5]	4.9 [4–5]	3.8 [2.5–5]
Average of cultural difference between US and home on a scale of 1 to 5	2.9 [2–4]	4.11 [3–5]	4.13 [3–5]
Average ranking of US health care quality on a scale of 1 to 5	4 [2–5]	3.4 [2–5]	3.6 [1–5]
Percentage of whom had worked/lived abroad before	66%	22%	53%
Average of how many years in the US	4.13	10	5.2

correlated with how US health care quality is perceived. As the questionnaire results in Table 6.1 above show, Germans were on average not as confident speaking English (4.2 out of 5) as Indians (4.9 out of 5); however, their rating of the US health care quality was the highest, and the cultural differences between Germany and the US were the lowest.

My German informants also had the highest rate of international experience before coming to the US (66 per cent had lived abroad before). This might account for the fact that Germans tended not to engage in transnational health care seeking practices as often as the other two groups. The Indian and the Japanese informants of this study rated the cultural differences between their countries and the US similarly (4.11 and 4.13 respectively), and also had similar opinions about US health care quality (3.4 and 3.6 respectively). However, while the Japanese had more international experience (53 per cent had lived abroad before), they ranked the lowest across all groups in their English confidence (3.8 out of 5). These differences may be responsible for some of the different motivations Indians and Japanese informants gave for engaging in these strategies and practices.

Although many of the strategies and practices were used in combination or are interlaced to such a degree that it can be difficult to view them as separate practices, in the following section I will discuss each one separately in order of how often they were used by my informants.

Bringing (biomedical) medications, self-diagnosis and self-medication

Many immigrants either bring biomedical medications with them from their home to the host country, have friends or family members bringing or sending them, or share medications in their network (the use of alternative medications such as herbs will be discussed below). They also use these medications to self-medicate after self-diagnosing. Previous research frequently cites having familiar medicine on hand as a way to feel prepared in cases of medical emergency and as a sensible way to delay going to a doctor. Brazilian women in the United States, for example, bought a 'stock of Brazilian prescription drugs' (Messias 2002: 187) because many felt US physicians did not prescribe the right medications. Having medications at home also allowed them to avoid having to seek expensive health care services in the United States. Similarly, immigrants often brought medications with them from home because they felt they had less access to the more regimented prescription drugs in their chosen country, like Latin Americans living in London (Gideon 2011), or to avoid costly medications, as was the case for many South Koreans in Canada (Wang and Kwak 2015). While this reasoning has most frequently been reported for uninsured immigrants, 39 out of 48 of my interview partners had brought medications with them and cited similar motivations for doing so. Among my informants, bringing medications was mainly employed to navigate the barriers regarding timely access to a physician and long waiting times (i.e. by being able to self-medicate instead of seeking medical care), the costs of medications in the United States as well as a lack of medications in the right dosages. For others, bringing their own medications was also a way to compensate for their lack of knowledge about the US health care system. For Silke, for example, a German lawyer in her mid-thirties, bringing her own medications for her child was much easier for her than trying to find the specific one she wanted in the United States, mainly because she 'couldn't find . . . the specific nose drops which I like here in the US'.[5]

The medications my informants brought with them were usually over-the-counter medications ranging from painkillers and cold medication to nose or eye drops and, in a few cases, also antibiotics, birth control or homeopathic medicines. While all informants in this research had the ability to utilize more than one health care system to their advantage – that is, to use their TCC – there was a difference in how often the different groups engaged in this practice, as Indian (89%) and Japanese (80%) informants were more likely to bring medications than

German informants (73%). Unsurprisingly, my Indian and Japanese informants were also more likely to refer to costs and access as more substantial barriers to health care than my German informants.

In fact, while both the Indian and Japanese informants often mentioned that US brand medications did not work for them, the Indians specifically felt that the US medications did not work on their body types or were not as effective as the medications they were used to from home. They were also much more likely to use home medications to address their issues with the restrictions (i.e. over-the-counter medications only being available as prescription drugs in the United States) and costs of medications. Having medications at home was also a good way to self-medicate in non-emergency situations and to address issues with access and waiting times, not being able to get a same-day appointment often being a source of frustration for many informants. A good example of this is the experience of Aishwarya, a software engineer who at the time of our interview held an H-1B visa. When she had a 104°F (40°C) fever, she wanted to go and see a doctor but couldn't get a same-day appointment. Since going to the ER was then her only option to get care, and because she knew her case was not an emergency, she opted for self-medication with 'back-up' medications:

> When I came to the US, I figured out that you . . . need to make an appointment with the doctor . . . So that was like, really surprising for me because if I get the same thing, I just go, you don't have any appointment you just walk in. Sit in that queue, the doctor will attend to you . . . What I did is, as a back-up plan, I get medication from India because I can take that and be done with it. I don't need to go to emergency room, for something that simple.
> (Aishwarya, Indian female, H-1B visa, in the US since 2002)

Several others also mentioned that bringing medications from India, or asking friends or family to bring some when they were visiting, was important, since US medications either had the wrong dosage or, as Irrfan, a software engineer in his forties, mentioned, the 'formulation is different in India'. About this he said 'it works better for my body than the ones here'.[6] Having medications from home handy also meant that he felt confident to self-medicate with the appropriate medications if the need arose.

While my Japanese informants usually did not cite regulations and few of them mentioned the costs associated with US medicine, many felt they had to bring Japanese drugs with them, because US medications frequently caused side effects. Ichiko,[7] for example, who had come to the United States to live with her American husband and was at the time of our interview waiting for her work permit, thought drugs in the US are 'too strong for me sometimes . . . and as soon as I took the medicine, I got fainted'.[8]

Several others also felt that US dosages were different and did not work well for the Japanese because they are 'smaller than average size American',[9] and it seemed to be common knowledge among my Japanese interlocutors that in the US 'the medicines tend to be stronger'[10] and that one should bring several medications for 'regular diseases . . . like cold, and headache and stomach ache' when travelling to the US. And although some Japanese informants felt that self-care or self-medication was a good option to deal with costs or long waiting times, they were more commonly used as a way to actively avoid physicians in the US ('I think I will try to, you know, ahmm, lying on the bed and try to believe in my kind of inner power and try to overcome'[11]).

Germans, on the other hand, usually did not mention waiting times or that US medications did not work, but rather brought medications out of convenience, because they felt familiar with the products. The 32-year-old researcher Tobias, for example, had brought some cold medications, anti-histamines and painkillers and explained to me why his parents had 're-supplied' him when they visited instead of buying US medications: 'because it works really well and I just like to stick with what I have'.[12] Furthermore, since several medications that were available over the counter in Germany needed prescriptions in the US or were much cheaper in Germany, many saw no incentive to change a medication that they knew worked for them, as 31-year-old Jonas, who was at the time of our interview on parental leave from his job at the German embassy, told me:

> . . . it's cheaper. Well, all sort of stuff. General cold medications and also suppositories for the kids or simply just lozenges or . . . and I also think it is easier to recognize, regarding the active ingredients. You just know the things . . . it is just more convenient. You just know the things, you know what effect they have on you.[13]
>
> (Jonas, German male, A1 visa, in the US since 2014)

Returning home for medical treatment

Transnationals sometimes engage in what has been called 'medical return' or 'medical travel' during their stay in the host country to receive medical treatment in their country of origin either on scheduled home visits that they were already organising, where they get regular or preventative check-ups, or via planned treatments on additional visits solely or primarily for the purpose of getting medical services. Others temporarily return home specifically in order to get a more urgent procedure done. This is often done to avoid high medical costs in the host system, because transnationals trust the medical professionals and their advice more in their home societies, or because they feel 'facilities are way better than here'.[14]

However, Horton and Cole rightfully point out that few studies have explored the various factors influencing the decision to travel back home for medical care or the 'distinct circumstances under which each group returns as well as their differing relationships to their "home" health care systems' (2011: 1852; cf. Gideon 2011). Since the reasons and circumstances for (temporarily) returning home for medical treatment are particularly dependent on the type of group under investigation, any study on this strategy needs to be heavily contextualized to get a fuller picture of these medical returns (cf. Horton 2013). The following discussion therefore has to be seen in the context of the transmigrants' experiences and expectations of health insurance and health care, as discussed in Chapters 3 and 4 above.

The majority of research on medical travel from the United States focuses either on South American immigrants, who are often described as being 'forced' into using health care across the border mainly due to a lack of insurance, or on patients from the Global North engaging in 'medical tourism' abroad to get access to procedures that would otherwise be too costly. To my knowledge, the category of highly skilled migrants, who fall into neither group, has so far been missing from research. While there are many different reasons why immigrants opt for medical returns, the ones mentioned the most are to address immigrants' financial barrier to health care by allowing them to gain access to low-cost care or to supplement limited or non-existent health insurance in the US[15] (Ormond 2014). Medical travel also seems to be a means of dealing with dissatisfaction with US health care, as well as reducing cultural and linguistic barriers. Lee and colleagues (2010), for example, suggest that South Koreans travel back home to receive not only effective but also 'affective care'. In Korea they could receive 'culturally comfortable' health care where 'notions of being "in-place", trust and familiarity are significant factors in promoting feelings of well-being'. This was of such importance that even the better-off, skilled Koreans temporarily returned home for medical care rather than seeking health care in their host country,

New Zealand (Lee et al. 2010: 108, 114). Similarly, when I asked Ichiko, one of my Japanese informants, if she had been to see a physician on one of her return visits to Japan, she told me that she had done so both because of her language barrier in the United States and because of her greater familiarity with Japanese health care:

> Yes, to a doctor I can speak to . . . I just suffer to express in other language, the really the detail . . . Well it is just, I think that the reason why I feel uncomfortable with the health care here is that I just don't know much about health care. So, if I don't know the system, or how the hospital or the doctor will take care of me and then I can make a decision with the right information but I just don't have it.
> (Ichiko, Japanese female, K1 visa, in the US since 2016)

This 'culture of medicine' (Horton and Cole 2011), or even 'nostalgia for a style of medical practice and organization of the health care system with which they are familiar' (Horton 2013: 430), arguably affects all returnee patients, regardless of their socioeconomic position, visa status or level of insurance, and has been frequently mentioned by the informants in this research (this 'nostalgia' can also affect immigrant physicians, as Schühle (2018) demonstrated). However, other factors may play a role, such as the planned length of stay in the United States, which can influence immigrants' willingness to adopt a new 'medical home' or their preference for regular check-ups in their home country. Additionally, practical factors may be at play here, such as how easy it is to travel back home, which may put those who live near the border at an advantage, or those that have frequent home visits paid through their work, for example intra-company transferees or embassy staff. Returnees might also choose this strategy to avoid discrimination or to be close to family and friends in cases of serious injury or illness[16] (Ormond 2014: 2; Rajeev and Latif 2009).

Using home visits for check-ups or planned treatments was frequently mentioned by my informants, and approximately half of the group (25 out of 48 informants) had been to see a physician in their home country since arriving in the United States or were planning to do so on their next visit home. However, two of the common reasons for medical travel discussed above were not relevant for the group under study here, since none of my informants lacked insurance coverage in the US and their home regions were not in close proximity, making travelling home time-intensive and expensive. The Indian (11 out of 18) and Japanese (9 out of 15) participants were almost twice as likely to use a visit back home for medical treatment as the Germans (5 out of 15). And not only the frequency but also the reasons given differed across the three groups. Although a lack of insurance coverage was not in itself an issue, many informants felt that despite their coverage, the cost of medical services was much higher in the United States than in their home country. Thus, a financial barrier – which is usually assumed to be a typical motivator for uninsured or underinsured migrants – was among the most frequently mentioned motivations for medical travel across all groups. As discussed above, better access and cheaper medical care ('so, yeah, I have check-ups, I have done lab tests . . . just for the sake of it, because it's so cheap'[17]) were most commonly mentioned by the Indian informants.

Some Indian informants even mentioned that they were not planning to use medical services in the US and would rather get all their check-ups done back home. Many also felt that their restricted access to care in the United States, the lack of a personal connection to a family physician and the costs associated with health care despite insurance were the main reasons why they treated the US health care system as an emergency back-up (discussed further below). The Japanese informants, by contrast, were much more likely to give linguistic and cultural factors as the main reason for going to see a physician at home (see Ichiko's story above). Although cost was also one of the reasons why Himari, who was working in a leading position at a US company at the time of our interview, chose not to visit a US dentist, linguistic and cultural barriers were just as important in her decision. For her, paying out of pocket for those services in Japan was cheaper than in the United States, even with insurance coverage. She felt that going to the dentist in Japan once a year also 'makes sense'[18], because her dentist in Japan had her medical history and she would feel more in charge of her treatment options.

For most of my German interlocutors, their greater familiarity with and sense of trust in the German system were the main reasons for seeking medical care there. For Julia, the 37-year-old political consultant, for example, being able to travel for medical care for her child meant that she could continue the treatment plan she knew from Germany and did not have to adjust to the US way. Her child periodically suffered from croup[19] episodes, for which she had visited the ER in both Germany and the United States. While she felt her doctor in Germany trusted her to use the prescribed medication at home, in the US she was supposed to return to the ER for each episode, despite the fact that a trip to the hospital – usually in the middle of the night, with a room full of doctors who would take the medical history, weigh her child or take his temperature several times during the night – worsened her child's symptoms. Although she was comfortable treating her child at home during these episodes, she felt her attending paediatrician in the United States thought she was acting irresponsibly:

> We deal with them [medical conditions of child] on our own now with the help of the medication that we get from Germany. And they ... it's hard to ... I, I think they [US physicians] kind of find it irresponsible that we don't take him to see a doctor here ... And that is also the reason why I went a couple of times to, to see doctors in Germany just to get reassured that it's not irresponsible, what we are doing. Ahmm, but I think what they are doing here in this situation is too much and is overreacting.
> (Julia, German female, A1 visa, in the US since 2013)

While costs, ease of access and some reservations towards US medical practices, such as over-prescription of antibiotics or excessive lab tests, were commonly cited across all groups, many also mentioned their lack of an established connection to a general practitioner or family physician or their medical records as one of the key reasons for planned visits on their regular trips back home. Some even mentioned that while they are in the US they try to 'only go to the doctor if it is really necessary'.[20]

However, medical returns also need to be seen in the context of the health care experiences returnees have had in their home countries and their returnee status.[21] The degree to which returnees can access health services in their home countries depends on the costs associated with health care, the insurance and coverage regulations and the returnees' legal status in their home countries, which also affects returning immigrant groups differently (Ormond 2014). It would also be false for migrants to think that they are returning to a familiar health care system. The act of migration can, for instance, accomplish a class transformation. For example, Lee, Kearns and Friesen (2010) found that even well-off Koreans who returned home were now able to receive treatments or levels of care that had previously been beyond their reach. Similarly, on their return visits, Mexicans might suddenly be able to afford private health care, turning formerly poor migrants into a new class category of cash-paying 'returning royalty'[22] (Horton 2013: 417).

On the one hand, many of my informants had the TCC skill set to be able to access their preferred care back home, which was in many cases cheaper, experienced as more trustworthy and not associated with linguistic barriers. Return visits also allowed access to treatments that would be unaffordable in the United States (as was the case for dental care for some informants). This strategy, on the other hand, might also force some medical returnees to pay for private services out of pocket, since US travel insurance does not cover non-emergency medical services, and as non-residents, they would not be covered by their home country's insurance, as some German or Japanese transnationals reported in this research. Furthermore, waiting until an upcoming visit home to seek medical care (discussed in more detail below) might also in some cases not be in the best interest of immigrants, regardless of their socioeconomic background. And although delaying health care seeking had caused none of my informants' health complications, several have suffered discomfort or uncertainty from untreated dental issues until their planned visit home (see Saki's and Alia's experiences below).

Pre-emigration health care

In order to prepare for their upcoming immigration process, many transnationals pre-emptively seek medical check-ups or treatments, and making use of such 'pre-emigration health care' was very common both in previous research and among my informants. This was mostly discussed as a way to address the barriers immigrants anticipated running into, such as costs, issues accessing health care and their general lack of knowledge of how the US system works. Unlike bringing medicines from home and visiting physicians during annual visits home, to utilize pre-emigration health care was one of the most common pieces of advice my informants would give their fellow countrymen regarding how to deal with US health care and health insurance and as such appears to be more of an actively chosen strategy to navigate US health care culture (see discussion below). At the same time, engaging in pre-emigration health care also often naturally led to return visits to the same physician, either for a follow-up visit or to continue treatment. In the interviews, this has most commonly been pointed out in regard to dental work and vaccinations as well as well-child care visits (*'U-Untersuchung/Früherkennungsuntersuchung'* in Germany), as Tobias experienced after he had gotten the first of two Hepatitis A vaccinations just before leaving for the United States:

> The doctor, who had been to the United States himself, told me that it has to be renewed after roughly six months or so, and he said, 'You know if you come home for Christmas, give me a call and drop by and I give you the second shot.'
> (Tobias, German male, J1 visa, in the US since 2017)

Messias suggests that most of the Brazilian immigrants she talked to had little knowledge of the US health care system and that '[p]re-migration health care practices were in part an acknowledgment of this lack of information' (2002: 186). I would argue that in many instances the opposite seems to be the case for highly skilled immigrants. Due to their imagined knowledge of US health care, for example through stories they had heard from family members or friends, many informants had actively tried to get complete physicals as well as dental check-ups before they moved, in an attempt to circumvent some of the disadvantages they thought they would have once they left their home health care system. In fact, getting medical check-ups before coming to the United States was often framed by negative stories of US health care, as discussed above. Unsurprisingly, a frequently mentioned 'standard piece of advice' Indian immigrants such as Rahul offered to those who were preparing to immigrate the US was to prepare by getting 'all your dental work done in India (laughs)' and 'get your eyes checked'.[23]

For others, pre-emigration health care was also an important aspect of feeling prepared, as was the case for Christine. The 31-year-old German-language instructor could no longer utilize the German health care system for return visits, as she had to give up her German insurance when she moved to the United States, which was one of the reasons why she felt it was extremely important to adequately prepare oneself for the US health care and health insurance system in advance. To do so, she recommended 'do[ing] as much research as you can' and 'get[ting] as many check-ups and medications and anything as you can (laughs)'[24] before coming to the US.

Delaying health care seeking

Another practice that is closely related to both medical returns and self-medicating is delaying health care seeking, for example until an upcoming visit home. Previous research has shown that delaying health care does not mean patients are not involved in their health and lifestyle. In fact, key drivers for this practice were barriers such as lacking insurance coverage and other issues surrounding time and available resources;[25] it was also found to be practised by those immigrants that are uncomfortable or scared of entering US health care. Delaying health care was very common among all participants in this research. However, while Germans and particularly Indians cited almost exclusively costs and their dissatisfaction with access to health care (i.e. long waiting times) in the United States, it was most commonly referred to by Japanese immigrants, who often cited cultural or linguistic barriers as their reason for trying to avoid contact with physicians in the US and instead rather saying that they would 'try to endure and try to overcome [a disease]'[26] by themselves.

Although highly skilled immigrants on a work assignment (e.g. through a company or embassy) did not lack insurance coverage as such, the fact that they were insured through their home country often made delaying health care a natural consequence of this particular setup. Also, for those who stayed in the United States for a short amount of time and thus often opted for only basic insurance coverage with higher co-pays and deductibles, the costs associated with health care seeking in the US were one of the reasons they would wait for an upcoming visit home, as was the case for Saki. As a visiting researcher who was in the US for only seven months, she decided to delay dental treatment until she was returning home because she lacked dental insurance in the US and knew, therefore, that dental care would cost her a lot:

Saki: My insurance didn't cover, cover the dental care. So I, I had a tooth ache, but I couldn't go . . . I couldn't see a dentist. So I went to CVS [name of pharmacy] and bought, and I bought a painkiller for my teeth.

Nina: Did you get your toothache fixed here or did you go back to Japan?

Saki: Oh, it was just a like a temporary cure. I just alleviate the pain and make it, and then . . . try not to chew on this side for the rest of the seven months (laughs). Because it happened in the first month . . . And after I went back, I went to see a doctor and they cured it.
(Saki, Japanese female, J1 visa, in the US since 2016)

Seeking trustworthy health care (providers)

Another set of strategies described in previous research consisted of the different ways in which immigrants sought 'trustworthy' care, either because they did not trust physicians' diagnoses or treatment plans or because they felt that they could not easily communicate with health care professionals in the United States. Instead, they would, for example, consult with doctors back home either through phone, email or texting programmes such as WhatsApp or shop around for 'culturally aligned'[27] physicians in the host country (cf. Gideon 2011; Wang and Kwak 2015; Dyck 2006; Kane 2012; Tiilikainen 2012).

Among my informants, connecting with physicians from home was mostly mentioned by my Indian interlocutors, who said that they continued to have close ties with their family physicians but also felt that they were lacking a connection with a US physician or felt that they were not as personable as back in India. Getting advice from physicians back home was often seen as less time consuming and much easier than getting medical advice in the United States. In fact, the perceived 24-hour availability of their family physicians – who 'respond like, right away'[28] and often without charging – led many to consult them as they would if they were at home. While some of my informants regularly consulted their family physicians back in India, either directly or through family members, others, such as Priya, an academic in her forties, specifically looked for Indian physicians in the US who would be able to provide a second opinion that was more in line with their expectations, and who 'would give you advice you would trust more'.[29]

German immigrants usually did not mention barriers such as costs or access but rather a distrust in US health care as the main reason for seeking second opinions or reassurances for medical treatments that they were uncertain about (see also Julia's experience above). While Jonas, for example, continued shopping around for a physician in the United States that he felt he could trust ('I have not yet found a family doctor of whom I could say that is THE family doctor'[30]), he relied on second opinions from Germany in the meantime. Interestingly, seeking 'trustworthy' care was usually not mentioned by my Japanese informants, although some did mention the lack of Japanese-speaking physicians in the DC area.

Alternative care options

Many immigrants use 'alternative care options' to ensure their access to treatments either due to lack of insurance, concerns over costs and legal status, language skills or unfamiliarity with US health care or because they prefer different health care services from those available to them in the United States (cf. Messias 2002; Krause 2008; Kane 2012; Tiilikainen 2012).[31] These strategies include, on the one hand, using alternative forms of health care seeking or 'human resources' (Gonzalez-Vazquez, Pelcastre-Villafuerte and Taboada 2016: 1192), for example visiting a traditional healer in the host society or back at home, or using unregistered or illegal private providers, such as foreign physicians or nurses who offer medical services or consultation in the United States. On the other hand, alternative care options refer to alternative medications and treatments or 'material resources' (Gonzalez-Vazquez, Pelcastre-Villafuerte and Taboada 2016: 1192), such as using medicines prepared by traditional healers, preparing home remedies oneself or bringing medical plants or other supplies from one's home country (cf. Dyck 2006; Gideon 2011; Thomas 2010). Sometimes specific herbal treatments can also be purchased in speciality shops, which in turn can become an important networking space and as such a health resource (Krause 2008).

These alternative human and material resources make up what Krause called a 'Transnational Therapy Network', in which not only medical supplies, treatments and advice are shared but also 'formal and informal contacts between people which become meaningful in the event of sickness, providing financial and practical support and help in finding the right treatment' (2008: 235; cf. Choi 2013). However, as discussed in Chapter 4, alternative treatments generally had a more supplementary character for my informants and were almost exclusively material in nature, such as using homeopathy, Ayurveda and herbal medicine and not 'human resources', such as visiting a chiropractor or acupuncture.[32] Furthermore, although the majority of my interview partners had mentioned that they used alternative medicines in their home countries at least once, many had discontinued using them in the United States.[33]

It thus appears that highly skilled migrants as reflected in this study do not typically engage in alternative care options in general or seek advice from traditional healers in particular. TTNs may therefore be more prevalent among low-resource immigrants in general or in particular immigrants who are not planning to return to their home countries and are thus trying to find local solutions to some of their health care needs (Krause 2008; cf. Messias 2002). While some immigrants have to rely on the support of friends and the local immigrant community, the insurance status, language skills and financial option to return home in emergencies give highly skilled migrants more options than others might have. At the same time, the often short duration of their stay in the United States as well as difficulties integrating into local communities might also be reasons why none of my informants mentioned relying on support from local networks. This might be particularly the case for Japanese and German highly skilled migrants in Washington, DC, as their diaspora networks are not as large or strongly developed as the networks of some other communities, such as Latin Americans (Singer, Wilson and DeRenzis 2009). This also means that highly skilled migrants miss out on some of the meaningful support that TTNs can offer immigrants during adverse events.

Alternative insurance coverage

Many of the more vulnerable immigrant groups need to supplement their often insufficient health insurance coverage in order to receive care at all (Horton 2013). However, US health insurance was a big issue for the majority of my informants as well (as discussed in Chapter 3), despite their more privileged status and the fact that they all had insurance coverage in the United States. Thus, in an attempt to address possible financial barriers due to the high costs of US health care and to maximize health care access, several informants resorted to 'alternative insurance coverage'. For example, 46-year-old Takeshi, who was working at the time of our interview at one of the international organizations in DC, actively relied on his Japanese health insurance for his health care needs and utilized its benefits when he was back in Japan for a visit.

Like many other informants, his TCC and transnational status allowed him to be rather flexible with his US health insurance coverage. This flexibility also supported many of my informants' approaches to US health care as an emergency back-up, as discussed above. One example of this is Rei's insurance setup. The 32-year-old economist from Japan, who had come to work at a large international organization, had both a public and an additional private health insurance for hospitalization coverage back home in Japan. While she did not pay for Japanese public insurance during her stay in the United States, she kept the private insurance as a back-up for her return visits to Japan and in case something serious were to happen. This and the fact that she generally felt healthy gave her the freedom to purchase a high-deductible plan in the US that she did not plan on using:

> So for the private insurance, I adjusted a bit the options because, you know, I already buy in the United States, so I tried to minimize, you know, the coverage also, the options I have. But I am still keeping it . . . Here, the insurance I buy of course you can choose the level since I am healthy, I buy the one with out of pocket.
>
> (Rei, Japanese female, G4 visa, in the US since 2014)

Others felt that alternative insurance coverage practices allowed them to discontinue some additional insurance (such as dental insurance) that they felt was expensive and not worth its price, and instead supplemented their care with home visits. Bernhard, a professor from Germany in his late forties, who was at the time of our interview working at a university in DC, told me that for his family 'it doesn't make much sense to have [dental insurance]' in the United States, and instead they decided to continue seeing their dentist in Germany, because 'you pay less, they also bother you less'.[34]

Several also used international insurances that would cover them both in the US and in their home country. While most mentioned alternative insurance coverage as a way to have access to health care in two countries, Varun, a 32-year-old researcher from India, also felt that it protected him from the 'exploitative' US health insurance system and would allow him to travel back to India if the need were to arise:

> **Varun:** . . . try to get a like an international insurance . . . the one which supports here and there . . . when I look at the bill also, they put charges for moving this pen from this side to that side, I would call it as exploitation, because this never happened in India.
> **Nina:** And an international insurance from India would not do that?
> **Varun:** Ok, at least you have some security, right? That in any case you can ask to go back and ask for that, right? Because it's compatible here and there, too. So, if you miss your chance here, at least you can go back and say hey this happened to me, I have been paying and this is the bills and take care of it.
> (Varun, Indian male, J1 visa, in the US since 2017)

This 'insurance juggling' allowed many participants of this study to optimize and customize their insurance coverage in the US and their home country, enabling them access to their preferred care and in many cases save money in doing so. Yet, at the same time, not having good insurance coverage in the country of residence will most likely reinforce many of the aforementioned practices such as delaying health care seeking, self-medication and medical returns. A good example of this is Saki's story discussed above. She had kept her Japanese insurance that she was free to use while in Japan, and had only gotten a basic international insurance in the US, mainly because, as she explained to me, this was the requirement for coming to the United States. This insurance, however, was very limited and did not cover dental treatments. For this reason, she let her dental issues go untreated for the entire duration of her stay in the US. While she had considered travelling back to Japan to deal with her toothache, she decided this was not feasible given the short period of time she had in the United States. Instead, she decided to delay her treatment and self-medicate with over-the-counter drugs. Because of her unfamiliarity with the medications, she ended up suffering serious side effects, as she 'was suffocating (laughs) and almost died [from using over-the-counter painkillers]'.[35] Using alternative insurance arrangements can thus negatively impact health. I further submit that this particular practice can also prohibit immigrants' successful integration into the US health care system, and it bears further research to establish how common insurance juggling is among transnationals and how this impacts health outcomes and access to services in the US.

What makes a health care practice a strategy?

While all the practices and strategies discussed above are widely used among highly skilled migrants, they might not necessarily be thought of as such by the immigrants themselves. As we have seen in many cases above, what is considered a 'strategy' in the literature – for example continuing the same type of medication or having annual check-ups during their annual visit home – can simply be a normal part of an immigrant's health care routine that results from their transnational setup without them thinking or planning around it consciously. When I asked my informants what advice they would give a fellow countryman who is coming to the United States, many of the above-mentioned practices were not among their key suggestions (see Table 6.2 below).[36] I will therefore describe them as more passive practices, whereas those that were also given as advice or took more active planning will be considered active strategies.

The majority of advice given also tended to be more structural or functional advice (get insurance, prepare an emergency fund) rather than cultural advice (contact a physician at home for advice). This could mean that overall, highly skilled migrants do not feel as pressed to resort to these strategies to access what they would consider adequate health care. And in fact, none of my interlocutors mentioned that their access to care was ever seriously threatened. For them, strategies might thus rather present a 'nice-to-have' way to get their preferred type of care and to expand their options regarding their health care routines.

In this list of 13 pieces of advice given, the most commonly given tip was to make sure to get good insurance coverage and to research all relevant information, ideally prior to the immigration process, which also speaks to the sense of agency many of the highly skilled immigrants

Table 6.2 List of most commonly given types of advice for a fellow immigrant to the US health care system[1]

	What advice would you give?	Germans	Indians	Japanese	Total
1	Advice on health insurance	8	13	8	29
2	Research & educate yourself	7	5	5	17
3	Medical returns/ pre-emigration health care	2	3	1	15
	Dentistry in particular	3	1	5	
4	Bringing medications, medical equipment	2	3	3	8
5	Emergency fund/ prepare to pay more	2	2	1	5
6	Don't be afraid/don't worry	2	1	1	4
7	Lower/adjust expectations	2	2		4
8	Alternative care options. i.e. lifestyle chances		4		4
9	Delaying health care seeking, i.e. avoiding doctors in the US	1	1	1	3
10	Seeking culturally adequate care, i.e. looking for an Indian physician in the US		2		2
11	Find a US doctor	1			1
12	Have a physician at home for advice		1		1
13	No advice/don't know	1			1

[1] Although this is not strictly speaking advice on health care, one of my Indian informants also mentioned reconsidering coming to the US in the first place in response to this question.

possess. Only about a third of my informants mentioned medical returns or using pre-emigration health care as an important piece of advice for fellow countrymen coming to the United States. Within this category, advice on dentistry in particular was mentioned most commonly, including suggestions that transnationals either get treatments done before coming to the US or wait until a home visit (cf. Calvasina, Muntaner and Quiñonez 2015). In several cases, receiving care in the home country is also an important way for transnationals to keep their records complete for when they return home after their stay in the US, and may be preferred in order to stake a claim to their right to receive care in their home country, possibly also motivated by a 'need to belong' (Villa-Torres et al. 2017: 76; Sun 2014). Another common piece of advice or active strategy – which has not often been mentioned in previous research – was preparing an emergency fund or preparing for additional costs, like Anna, a 35-year-old consultant who was working as a language instructor at the time of our interview. She mentioned that in the United States everyone should set 'a little bit of money aside'[37] in case something comes up, a piece of advice that she felt was necessary because she had not realized that living and health care expenses in the US would be so high.

Several informants also mentioned 'cultural adjustments' as a good piece of advice, for example to lower one's expectations of health care and to not be afraid of using US health care, despite some of the stories that are in circulation in expat networks. However, we need to keep in mind that many of the strategies and practices mentioned do not fall neatly within one or the other category. For instance, four Indians mentioned that healthy lifestyle choices are a good alternative to having to utilize US health care. While I have listed this advice under 'alternative care options', it is also a strategy to delay health care seeking. A good example of such entanglement was mentioned by Krish, who thought a healthy lifestyle was important, due in part to a desire to avoid the complicated system:

> I would tell them: stay healthy. Don't try to go to hospitals at all. Impossible . . . I'll tell them, the health care is very complicated here, so make sure what you are getting into.
> (Krish, Indian male, US citizen, in the US since 2000)

Most of the aforementioned practices and strategies are also used in combination and need to be seen more as a network of strategies that cannot always be disentangled easily, as Priya's story demonstrates. Priya decided to get check-ups for her children in India and treat them when possible with herbal medications that she also buys in India and then prepares herself in the United States. For herself, however, she also used US health care services whenever she needed to, but she also sought advice from Indian physicians, in the US as well as back in India, for second opinions on treatments that she deemed to be too 'aggressive' and would often self-medicate with medications she had brought from India. At the same time, she used trips back home for medical treatments; for example, after a car crash in the US she opted to have surgery done in India instead of the US, because she 'was there anyway for holiday'.[38] She also delayed medical treatment in order to get a second opinion back home when a US dentist told her she needed an emergency root canal; she did not follow up on this until she had received a second opinion from a dentist in India, who told her he would not recommend the procedure. The set of health care services Priya uses in the United States and in India seems to be a good example of her 'knowledge of transnational opportunities' (Lee, Kearns and Friesen 2010: 110) that allows her to access her preferred style of health care, rather than being a rejection of certain medical services available to her in the host society.

Risks and benefits of transnational strategies

It seems clear that the TCC that highly skilled migrants generally have allowed them to integrate many practices and strategies to deal with potential barriers or what they might experience as undesirable aspects of US health care. However, many practices, for example having the option to use health care services in more than one country, are more passive rather than actively chosen tactics to deal with US health care and tended to arise naturally from their transnational mindset. Messias argues that migration contributed to the expansion and blurring of immigrants' identities and that for her interview partners, being from Brazil had become a 'health resource'[39] (2002: 185). For highly skilled migrants, transnational health care seeking can indeed be seen as a 'health resource' or an asset, especially when it is used as an opportunity to get supplementary health care and '[get] the best out of both worlds'[40] (see also 'Physicians' views of their patients' transnational health care seeking', below).

Yet managing barriers to health care in this way can also be damaging to the health of transnationals and reduce their access to quality health care – despite their privileged status – by delaying health care seeking, self-medicating or simply not establishing a medical home in the US. This was the case for Alia, who was unable to 'afford a dermatologist' in the United States and was generally more comfortable getting medical advice from physicians back in India. Thus, while having this option to employ strategies, such as seeking trustworthy physicians' advice at home, may be an advantage for her in many situations, it may also cause her to delay health care seeking and not get timely medical care for conditions she does not recognize as 'something that is more serious'[41] (see also the experience of Hitoshi, who had avoided seeking medical care in the US altogether, discussed in more detail above in Chapter 5).

In general, it seemed that particularly those who see the US only as a way-station in their international career, or those who are in the US only for a very short time, were the most likely to choose transnational health care strategies over health care in the host country. Some even mentioned that they considered the US health care system as only an emergency back-up, as Chetan, a 39-year-old procurement officer who had come from India in 2013, made very clear to me:

> But I always tell this, if I have anything serious, medically, I would take a flight and go home. I am not gonna get treated here, for sure. No chance.
> (Chetan, Indian male, G4 visa, in the US since 2013)

Yet many simply feel that they are lacking access to information on how to best use the system and which doctors to visit, i.e. lacking access to TTNs (Krause 2008). Emi, a Japanese researcher in her mid-thirties, told me, for example, that her Chinese co-workers had the advantage of having a large community including physicians and an information network available to them. As a Japanese citizen, however, she felt she was directly affected by the temporary status of many Japanese transnationals in the DC area, impacting the ease with which she could integrate into US health care for the duration of her stay, since she thought most of them didn't 'so much care about [the] long term'.[42]

In this context, I would argue that further research is needed to investigate whether an adaptation to US medical care, including the usage of local medicines, should be seen as an indication of a sense of settling and adapting to the United States and a willingness to transition from being an outsider to a local (cf. Messias 2002). In fact, especially for non-permanent residents, who might not benefit from TTN, deciding not to use their TCC or giving up a 'transient mindset' may actually reduce their access to quality health care. I argue that a broader understanding of this phenomenon among medical care providers could enhance the health care experience for both sides.

Physicians' views of their patients' transnational health care seeking

As I discussed in Chapter 5, most of the physicians I spoke with for this research (12 out of 17) felt that highly skilled migrants did face some barriers to health care. However, while my interlocutors often (wrongly) assumed that cultural and linguistic barriers were not an issue among the 'highly skilled', they frequently acknowledged structural and functional barriers, such as the difficulties newcomers might face when trying to navigate the very complex US health insurance and health care system (cf. Table 5.3). It is thus somewhat surprising that most physicians were not particularly aware of the many strategies and practices their transnational patients were engaging in. In fact, during the interviews, my interlocutors mainly mentioned that their transnational patients had returned home for medical treatments or check-ups and/or had brought medications with them. Dr Banik, a 43-year-old psychiatrist, for example, who had come to the United States from South East Asia in 2000 and was at the time of our interview working in a cancer clinic in the suburbs of DC, thought this was mainly due to the fact that 'in the US, you know, fewer medications are approved in psychiatry than the rest of the world',[43] which led to his patients frequently resorting to bringing drugs that were not approved there.

Dr Stein, a family physician in her fifties who was working in a hospital setting, had had similar experiences with her patients and was aware that many brought medications or returned home for medical treatments, which she usually didn't mind, as long as it is 'a similar group of medications or class of medications that we have here'.[44] She told me that some of her German patients brought medications to the US either because they could not get what 'they always use' or chose to bring medications because of the higher costs in the United States.

Although none of her Japanese patients had openly discussed taking medications from home instead of those she had prescribed, she felt that they seemed to take their medical care into their own hands when they would use a home visit to do 'ultrasounds for every little aches and pains, all kinds of MRIs',[45] which she did not administer because she felt they were 'unnecessary'. Her patients' willingness to obtain their preferred medical care ('regardless of what I say') can thus probably also be seen in light of the highly skilled migrants' sense of entitlement and agency, as discussed in Chapter 5.

While Dr Banik and Dr Stein did not find these strategies particularly problematic, others did. For example, 40-year-old Dr Wang, another family physician working in a hospital setting, sometimes felt uncomfortable accommodating the different medication plans of his patients, especially if his patients 'bring medications that are purchased in India, which I then have to decipher what they really are. And sometimes they are not, I mean, sometimes they might not be something I might be familiar with.'[46]

While it is understandable that he was reluctant to allow the patients in his care to continue their treatment with medications he was not familiar with, this might also cause his patients to feel misunderstood or indeed continue seeking transnational health care such as delaying health care or returning home. Similarly, the fact that Dr Stein had dismissed her Japanese patients' interest in additional tests might leave transnational patients feeling that they are not taken seriously (see Chapter 4). It is, however, important that physicians are aware of all of their patients' medications and treatments – including transnational ones – in order for them to provide adequate care, as Dr Griffith, a family physician in her forties, pointed out to me:

> They tend to come and tell me, they will be more likely to tell me what they are doing instead of what I have prescribed . . . And that's really helpful, so I can, you know . . . It's much more helpful to know what someone is actually doing.
>
> (Dr Griffith, Family Medicine)

Thus, while it might not be necessary for physicians to be aware of all transnational health care seeking, I argue that it is important for them to have some knowledge of these strategies and practices, their patients' motivations for engaging in these and the potential benefits and risks associated with such strategies, in order to improve immigrant health outcomes.

Conclusion

While previous research has investigated the motivations of many vulnerable immigrant groups when engaging in transnational practices and strategies, this research has shown that highly skilled transnationals seem to extensively utilize many of the same practices and strategies despite their more privileged socioeconomic background. The reasons for practising transnational health care seeking span economic, structural and cultural factors and include both active strategies and more passive practices to navigate difficulties in accessing health care. The former include seeking out a culturally aligned physician for second opinions or getting check-ups prior to the immigration process and the latter include continuing with the same medications or having a follow-up visit during a home vacation. As such, these strategies can be an important way to 'augment or expand their options for meeting their health needs and to reestablish a relationship with their countries of origin, particularly later in life' (Villa-Torres et al. 2017: 77). This seems particularly relevant for those immigrants who are in the United States only on a short-term basis, for whom integrating successfully into the US health care system might not be a high priority. For others, it might not even be the most sensible idea, particularly if they feel the need to keep their medical histories up to date in their home countries and have a continuing relationship with their family physicians for when they ultimately return (cf. Bilecen, Çatir and Orhon 2015; Sun 2014).

To address the extent to which some transnationals have to rely on transnational health seeking, Gonzalez-Vazquez and colleagues (2016) suggested putting a variety of procedures in place that will help the most vulnerable immigrants with navigating the US health care system, for example training community members, providing culturally suitable information and educating immigrants on some of the benefits of biomedical treatments. While these are certainly important points for many transnational patients, they might not work for all groups of immigrants. Messias (2002) argues that physicians should enquire not only about the migration experiences or medications their transnational patients are taking, but also about their pre-migration health practices – and I would argue that this should include enquiries about the other strategies discussed here as well, in particular transnational patients' tendency to delay health care seeking or to seek advice from physicians back home, who might not be able to diagnose their patients accurately from abroad. In fact, it seems clear that a better understanding of these strategies and practices and the motivations for engaging in them might have a positive impact not only for health outcomes and health care satisfaction, but also for the overall level of satisfaction in the physician–patient encounter. They are thus just as important for our overall understanding of immigrant health care needs as the structural and cultural differences of health care systems, as well as the persisting barriers immigrants experience – regardless of their socioeconomic background.

Notes

1 The quotation in the chapter title is from my informant Kareena (Indian female, H4 visa, in the US since 2015).
2 Although De Certeau (1980) discusses strategies and tactics as the two 'oppositional practices', the vast majority of literature on transnational health care seeking (1) uses the terms 'strategies' and 'practices' interchangeably and (2) does not use the term 'tactics'. In this book I will thus continue using the terms strategies and practices instead of tactics.
3 Although there are also strategies employed by transnationals who cannot travel or cross borders for various reasons (cf. Villa-Torres et al. 2017), the scope of this chapter allows me to focus only on the health seeking practices available to those that can travel and seek health care abroad, as was the case with all of my informants.
4 However, 'ethnic enclaves' in the host country have been found to be very important for immigrants, putting those who might not benefit from it at a disadvantage, as they can offer many different resources and 'mediate [immigrants'] interactions with the host society at large, thereby buffering them from the strains of dislocation' (Viruell-Fuentes 2007: 1532; cf. Ryan et al. 2009; Ormond 2014).
5 (Silke, German female, F1 visa, in the US since 2014).
6 (Irrfan, Indian male, Green Card holder, in the US since 2003).
7 Both Aishwarya and Ichiko chose not to mention their age during their interview.
8 (Ichiko, Japanese female, K1 visa, in the US since 2016).
9 (Ayumi, Japanese female, G4 visa, in the US since 2016).
10 (Saki, Japanese female, J1 visa, in the US since 2016).
11 (Hitoshi, Japanese male, J1 visa, in the US since 2014; see longer quote in Chapter 5).
12 (Tobias, German male, J1 visa, in the US since 2017).
13 Translation of the original German interview by the author: '. . . weils günstiger ist. Naja so alles Mögliche. Allgemeine Erkältungsmedikamente und oder auch für die Kinder Fieberzäpfchen oder einfach auch nur Lutschtabletten oder . . . und ich finds auch einfacher zu erkennen, von den Wirkstoffen. Man kennt die Sachen halt . . . es ist halt einfach bequemer. Man kennt die halt die Sachen, man weiß wie sie auf einen wirken.'
14 (Krish, Indian male, US citizen, in the US since 2000).
15 Brown (2008) even suggests that the high numbers of uninsured Mexican immigrants in the United States are caused by the ability of those individuals to return home for health care, particularly in a crisis situation, making their close proximity to home the more decisive factor than cultural preferences.
16 At the same time, we have to keep in mind that this strategy clearly is only available to a subset of transnationals that can afford a home visit fairly regularly. Many so-called highly skilled migrants can only afford to travel once every few years. And of course, many of the less privileged groups of immigrants may not have the ability to pay for such a trip home at all, are not able to take time off work or, in the case of some immigrants, would risk not being able to return to their host country if they did so. These consequently cannot enjoy the benefits of medical travel (cf. Gideon 2011).
17 (Vihaan, Indian male, waiting for Green Card approval, in the US since 2002).
18 (Himari, Japanese female, US citizen, in the US since 2005).
19 A relatively common respiratory infection in children. It is often recommended to keep the sufferer calm during episodes to prevent agitation of the affected airways; cf. https://www.mayoclinic.org/diseases-conditions/croup/symptoms-causes/syc-20350348, as well as https://www.webmd.com/children/understanding-croup-treatment. Both accessed 31 December 2021.
20 (Jonas, German male, A1 visa, in the US since 2014). Translation of the original German interview by the author: 'Hier gehen wir nur zum Arzt wenns wirklich notwendig ist.'

21 The status returning immigrants enjoy in their home country – including the additional services that they may have access to – is dependent on a multitude of factors, including the cultural and economic importance of returnees. Returnees from typical sending countries such as Mexico or India, or those returning from the Global North to the Global South, probably enjoy a higher status back home than those returning to Germany and Japan from the US (cf. Horton 2013).
22 As such, they might be able to afford better services than locals or are catered to by providers specializing in the needs of time-pressed and frustrated returnees. Returning Indians and Filipinos in particular have become an important source of income and a driver for the medical tourism industry. Yet, while catering to their needs of having high expectations but limited time, they are often charged more than locals would be (Ormond 2014: 4; Horton and Cole 2011; Rajeev and Latif 2009).
23 (Rahul, Indian male, J1 visa, in the US since 2016).
24 (Christine, German female, Green Card holder, in the US since 2015).
25 Others have even suggested that immigrants (particularly women) wait until their partner's needs as main bread winner or their children's needs are met before incurring costs for their own health care (cf. Messias 2002).
26 (Hitoshi, Japanese male, J1 visa, in the US since 2014).
27 (Maneka, Indian female, US citizen, in the US since 2001).
28 (Anaya, Indian female, Green Card holder, in the US since 2006).
29 (Priya, Indian female, G2 visa, in the US since 1995).
30 (Jonas, German male, A1 visa, in the US since 2014). Translation of the original German interview by the author: 'ich habe noch nicht einen Hausarzt gefunden, wo ich sagen kann, das ist der Hausarzt'.
31 In their research on Mexicans' usage of alternative medicine in the United States, Gonzalez-Vazquez, Pelcastre-Villafuerte and Taboada (2016) found that alternative medicine encompassed many of the strategies described in this chapter. It was, e.g., part of migrants' pre-emigration health care, and healers were consulted both on return visits and during consultations from abroad.
32 See Table 4.14 for the full list of services and treatments used by my informants.
33 Discontinuing alternative treatments seems to be not uncommon among immigrants. Dyck and Dossa (2007) described how South East Asian women, for instance, stopped using home remedies, such as *'desi'* medicines, since their use and preparation was closely linked to the networks they were part of back home and were not available to them in the host country, which could be described as a breakdown of Krause's TTN in the host society.
34 (Bernhard, German male, Green Card holder, in the US since 2016).
35 (Saki, Japanese female, J1 visa, in the US since 2016).
36 I listed all the advice given by how often it was mentioned. If items were mentioned the same number of times, those that were mentioned across the three groups were ranked higher.
37 (Anna, German female, A1 visa, in the since 2014).
38 (Priya, Indian female, G2 visa, in the US since 1995).
39 Gonzalez-Vazquez et al. also argue that transnational strategies strengthen the networks between immigrants with similar needs and help them preserve their cultural identity in a potentially 'adverse, anti-immigrant context' (2016: 1195), although this did not appear to be an important aspect among the group under study here.
40 (Dr Das, Paediatrics and Medical Genetics).
41 (Alia, Indian female, J2 visa, in the US since 2016).
42 (Emi, Japanese female, J1 visa, in the US since 2013).
43 (Dr Banik, Psychiatrist).
44 (Dr Stein, Family Medicine). Dr Stein also referred to their highly skilled status as a possible facilitator for engaging in these strategies, although I did not discuss with her or any of the other informants whether or not they thought highly skilled migrants were more likely to engage in transnational health care seeking than other groups of patients.
45 (Dr Stein, Family Medicine).
46 (Dr Wang, Family Medicine).

7
Conclusion and outlook

Summary of key findings

The aim of this research project has been to question the wide range of largely unexamined assumptions about the smooth and straightforward assimilation of highly skilled migrants into a host health care system, in this case the US American one. To this end, I have examined the specific conditions this group faces when navigating the US health care system, highlighting the persisting range of special constraints and barriers to access within it. Although members of this group unquestionably enjoy a more privileged status, experience fewer barriers and have more access to health care services both in the United States and in their home society than other groups of immigrants, we have seen that their socioeconomic and educational background did not shield them from experiencing difficulties when navigating US health insurance and accessing US health care services. By focusing on comparisons between the experiences of immigrants to the US, itself a Western, highly industrialized country, from, first, another Western, highly industrialized country (i.e. Germany), second, a non-Western industrialized country (i.e. Japan), and, finally, a non-Western non-industrialized country (i.e. India), it was further possible to scrutinize not only the cultural differences[1] but also variations in structural and functional barriers.

    The analysis and comparison of the different health care and health insurance systems should, however, not be seen in light of previous health policy research comparing the US health care system with, for example, its Canadian and European counterparts to learn from their respective strengths and weaknesses (cf. Schoen et al. 2005; 2007; 2010; 2013). This book has also not set out to investigate how satisfied people were with the quality and delivery of their home country's health care, or tried to answer the question 'Who has the best health care system?' (Blendon et al. 1995; see also Consumer Science & Analytics 2013; Blendon et al. 2012; Loh, Nihalani and Schnusenberg 2012). Instead, I have attempted to show that cultural, structural and functional differences in how health care is set up can have a significant impact on patients' expectations and experiences. The comparison of highly skilled migrants from Germany, India and Japan – all with roughly comparable socioeconomic and educational backgrounds in their respective home countries – has further allowed me to gain a nuanced insight into how changing from one biomedical setting to another impacts transnationals and their health-seeking behaviours.

In fact, a comparison between different groups has proven to be particularly fruitful, as previous research has repeatedly shown that the country of origin, as well as gender, race, ethnicity, religion and socioeconomic background, impacts the immigration process as well as whether or not individuals are categorized in the more or less prestigious categories such as 'highly skilled migrant' versus others such as 'refugee' or 'asylum seeker' (cf. Crosby 2006; Yuval-Davis, Anthias and Kofman 2005; Crawley and Skleparis 2018). While such categorization can have far-reaching consequences regarding foreigners' visa status and eligibility for health care services, this was less of an issue for the highly skilled migrants under investigation in this research. Yet many of my informants were keenly aware of the discriminatory nature of such categories ('You have to be 20 times better than people here to succeed')[2] and also often felt (positively or negatively) stereotyped by such labels ('They think I am rich, I am very intelligent').[3] This also had implications in the health care setting, since their classification as 'highly skilled' tended to presuppose a privileged status that often failed to take their specific 'costs and constraints' (Favell, Feldblum and Smith 2007: 20) into consideration. For example, several of the physicians I spoke with did not recognize or acknowledge their transnational patients' issues with language barriers, their struggle with the costs of health care services or the implications their lack of understanding of US health care and health insurance had. Some also admitted that due to the short duration of their patients' stay in the United States, they had less of an 'emotional investment in the care'.[4] Many physicians were also under the impression that highly skilled migrants 'have help from their employer institutions and receive plenty of advice'[5] and 'have wonderful benefits'.[6] This, however, was generally not the experience of the informants I spoke with. Based on their experiences, I have thus argued that although highly skilled migrants are generally a more privileged group, their classification as global elite by previous research does not adequately capture their experiences. Instead, the classification of this group as 'middle-class migrants' (Voigt-Graf 2005: 367) or 'middling transnationals' (Conradson and Latham 2005b: 229) often seems more appropriate, as it better reflects that this group's mobility has its own costs and constraints. And since many of the barriers middling transnationals are confronted with are similar to those of other, less privileged groups of immigrants, I argue that their integration into US health care should be scrutinized with this in mind.

In regard to health insurance, the costs and constraints of these middling transnationals were not so much due to a lack of coverage or underinsurance, as none of my informants lacked health insurance in the United States, but stemmed from unmet expectations caused by differences in the health insurance cultures present in the different countries under investigation here. Although some of the physicians I spoke with again felt that their insured transnational patients should not have any difficulties and in fact 'have all the same options that a US citizen has',[7] the majority of my informants reported that by and large they *had* had negative experiences with US health insurance, often depending on the expectations they had formed on the concept in their home society. For example, several of my Indian informants did not 'know how the concept works'[8] or did not even accept the premise of health insurance ('Why do I need this?').[9] My German and Japanese informants, who were more familiar with the concept, were 'really shocked'[10] or even 'scared'[11] when they realized that certain treatments, services or medications they had expected to be available to them were either not covered by their US insurance or were associated with much higher costs. The impact of my informants' lack of understanding regarding US health insurance culture was most consequential when they unwittingly accrued unnecessary medical costs, for example for requesting health care treatments that were not covered by their insurance ('I never knew when I had to pay and for what')[12] or visited the ER for minor issues, as they had done in their country of origin. Unsurprisingly, this dissonance between my informants' expectations and their experiences in the United States led many to be dissatisfied not only with their access to US health care but also with health care delivery. Based on my informants' experiences, I have thus argued that a better understanding of health insurance culture is a crucial aspect in understanding immigrant health care seeking behaviour, following previous research that has shown that insurance can determine when and how often immigrants choose to access medical services (cf. Ahlin, Nichter and Pillai 2016).

Yet, unlike other, less privileged immigrant groups, all of my informants at least met the formal requirements for accessing the US health care system by being covered either by US health insurance or international insurance from their home country. However, this also meant that, in addition to the issues arising from the differences in health insurance culture, they were confronted with the 'Americanness' (Fox 2005) of the US health care system. This, I have argued, affects highly skilled migrants in a similar manner to other immigrant groups regardless of their privileged socioeconomic and educational background, as many of the arising dissonances can be traced to structural and functional differences in how health care systems are set up, ranging from differences in the accessibility of physicians or medical devices to the availability of biomedical and alternative medicines and the role hospitals take on in health care delivery (cf. Mossialos et al. 2016).

And in fact, 'perceived and actual differences' in the host country's health care system (Lee, Kearns and Friesen 2010: 109) have been shown to shape the health care decisions of middle-class immigrants. My informants from India, for example, who were used to a health care system with a much lower ratio of medical devices (such as MRI units or CT scanners) per capita compared to the United States, often remarked that they felt that in the US 'physicians are mostly relying on diagnostics'[13] and are therefore often 'much more interventionist than it would have been in India',[14] making them at times reluctant to see physicians in the US. Their experiences were dramatically different from those of my Japanese informants, who were used to a health care system that provides the highest ratio of medical devices per capita worldwide. And indeed, for them US health care did not offer nearly enough 'tests, cancer test, cancer check or a blood check'.[15] My Japanese interlocutors thus often used visits back home to get additional check-ups done there. Although my German informants generally experienced fewer differences in regard to the health care services and medications provided, they also felt that 'what you get on a standard basis, get prescribed here and in Germany is different'.[16] These differences not only shape immigrants' expectations and experiences but can also impact their medical encounters with physicians, as any out-of-the-ordinary requests are prone to be interpreted as 'cultural peculiarities' (cf. Johnston and Herzig 2006) and can become the causes of miscommunications and unmet treatment expectations ('You have to use more, more talk-time to explain them why you want to do this or that').[17]

These structural and functional differences in health insurance and health care setups are, however, not the only barriers immigrants experience in the health care setting. And although issues such as costs, cultural and linguistic differences or lacking sufficient insurance coverage have been mainly associated with low-skilled or ethnic minority immigrants (cf. Gideon 2011; Horton and Cole 2011; Ku and Matani 2001), most of my informants reported experiencing similar difficulties. In addition, the successful integration of highly skilled migrants might even be negatively affected by their usually short stay in the United States ('Because they come here for just two, three years, they don't even think of really being involved in these issues')[18] compared to other groups of immigrants that do not intend to move back to their country of origin.

The barriers my informants mentioned also differed across the groups under investigation in this research project. For example, while cultural or linguistic 'communication issues'[19] were frequently mentioned by all of my informants, it was mainly the Japanese who struggled with language barriers to such a degree that they would 'try to overcome the disease without seeing the doctor'.[20] Also medical costs were a common theme across all groups, yet the fear that 'you'll go bankrupt'[21] was mainly mentioned by my Indian informants – presumably because of their more limited exposure to the concept of health insurance.[22] However, some of my German informants struggled with health care costs, which kept them from utilizing health care in the same way they would have in Germany, making them 'think before [they] go to the doctor'.[23] These barriers thus not only affected my interlocutors' ability to access health care but impacted their satisfaction levels and even health outcomes. I have therefore argued that one of the most common, yet frequently overlooked barriers in transnational health care is immigrants' lack of a 'common-sense' understanding of the local health care culture ('I mean, it's not like you get an orientation course what is preexisting conditions and deductibles and all of that, right?').[24] In fact, the (wrong) assumptions immigrants make about the US health care system can even reinforce other barriers, such as leading them to accrue unnecessary health care costs, risking worse health outcomes by delaying necessary treatments and generally restricting their ability to use the health care system to their advantage, as they might have been able to in their country of origin. And the fact that physicians were less likely to acknowledge these persisting barriers for highly skilled migrants ('they are more adept to getting over those barriers')[25] can even present an additional source of dissatisfaction or unmet treatment options.

It is thus not surprising that highly skilled migrants engage in transnational health care seeking practices which are similar to those that – to my knowledge – have to date been described only for less privileged groups of immigrants, although the extent and the reasons for doing so differed substantially across the three different groups under investigation here. Many of my informants, for example, delayed seeking care and returned to their home country to see physicians or get certain treatments (particularly dental treatments) or brought their own medications from their home country and self-medicated. While Indians usually did so because the 'US has a lot of restrictions'[26] on drugs and the Japanese because 'the medicine is too strong'[27] in the United States, my German informants mainly brought medications from home because 'it is just more convenient'.[28] These choices might be an indication that highly skilled migrants are more likely to use such transnational health care practices in order to get 'the best out of both worlds'[29] rather than out of strict necessity, as might be the case for other groups of immigrants. The better socioeconomic position of the groups under investigation here was probably also the reason why they seemed to be able to supplement their health care by juggling health insurances in the US and their home country, a practice that is likely to be less common among other groups of immigrants. While in many cases transnational health care seeking allowed my informants access to their preferred style of care, for example by consulting physicians back home that 'would give you advice you would trust more'[30] or 'have check-ups . . . because it's so cheap',[31] transnational health care seeking can also carry some risks for highly skilled migrants. This could happen, for example, when health care decisions are made by contacting family physicians abroad without seeing health care providers in the United States or health care seeking is delayed until an upcoming home visit. At the same time, this research also indicated that immigrants do not always actively think about supplementing their health care by engaging in these practices, but do so because transnational care options organically arise from their transnational setup, such as seeing their family physician each time they travel home ('You know if you come home for Christmas, give me a call and drop by and I give you the second shot').[32] This was particularly the case for those who were in the US for only a shorter amount of time, as integrating into the US system is not only more difficult, but might also not be as high a priority for them ('because looking for a new doctor is also really time consuming'),[33] since they know they will return home soon.

Implications of this research

As I have argued throughout this book, transnational patients, who move between the medical setting in the United States and the one in their home country, frequently compare and contrast how medicine is practised and how care is accessed. Neither biomedical health care in general nor US health care in particular are 'neutral' concepts, but rather ones that can only be understood in a comparative framework. The experiences of transnational individuals such as the ones discussed in this research help us to understand some of the barriers that persist despite – or rather regardless of – the socioeconomic or educational background of health care seekers, which need to be addressed to promote patient satisfaction and equitable health outcomes. However, beyond this, their experiences also allow us to critically assess and examine these differences for their possible implications for broader health policy issues, such as access to health services and health care delivery.

Compared to its economic peer countries, the United States spends a lot more money on health care,[34] making the US health care system very expensive. As we have seen, these health care costs were experienced as major financial and psychological barriers to accessing care – even among my informants who are insured, highly skilled individuals who can afford to use US health care. What is more, while my informants acknowledged that they may have access to a high quality of care and benefit from the newest treatments or medical technology on the market, these were not experienced as indicators of good health care. In other words, the health care services they received were not worth their price, and did not translate into experiencing health care as good as or better than care in their home country. Instead, many of the transnational patients I spoke with mentioned that health care was experienced as 'good' when it provided patients at least some level of comfort or reassurance and was easily (and at least at times informally) accessible and convenient to use. At a minimum, they felt that it should not require a lot of research and 'homework' to understand. For most of my informants, either these standards were not met in the United States or, in some cases, achieving that desired level of care turned out to be cost-prohibitive.

Thus, many of the current attempts to help underserved patients with some of the biggest barriers to health care, for example by providing additional health insurance coverage (as the ACA has done for many Americans, cf. Fletcher 2016) or broadening access to health care services (e.g. free health clinics and multilingual clinics: Calvo, Jablonska-Bayro and Waters 2017), are crucial to ensure at least some access to health care for those most in need, but they do not guarantee successful utilization of the system. In other words, solving access, and specifically access to insurance, is not enough to address structural, functional and cultural barriers to care.

This book also joins the body of evidence demonstrating that being insured in the United States does not adequately protect patients from incurring dangerously high health care costs or missing access to health care services by delaying or avoiding seeking care. This is particularly problematic against the backdrop of the confusing and labyrinthine nature of the system, which, as my informants echoed, is not only difficult to navigate for newcomers (cf. Reid 2009; Wetzel 2011; Horton et al. 2014), but also for the general US public[35] (cf. Levitt 2015). The experiences of the patients in this study show us, therefore, that even under otherwise favourable conditions, the combination of high health care costs (even for the insured) and a health care system that is difficult to navigate leaves little room for patients to make mistakes in their health care seeking, and learning how to be a patient in the United States came at a steep price for many of them or their family members. It should thus come as no surprise that this also led to reliance on strategies such as importing medications and seeking care abroad, even at the price and potential risk of delayed care. The fact that access to care in the US was not experienced as a 'right' by my informants also highlights that any attempt to access care – or even being afraid to try to access care – can also have broader societal implications for those who are struggling, who feel that they do not belong or who do not feel successfully integrated into society (cf. Horton 2004). These patterns and risks can affect patients' lives very adversely and should be addressed by health care policies.

Future research

My goal in this research endeavour has not been to claim that highly skilled migrants are not in many ways privileged, in that they enjoy more options, for example in regard to their visa status, travel between home and host society and access to health care. Instead, my goal has been to demonstrate that *despite* their generally better position in society, their mobility has costs and constraints. I believe that future research on those costs and constraints for a wide range of immigrants will in turn highlight persisting barriers that affect *all* newcomers to the US health care system, regardless of socioeconomic background, race, gender or ethnicity, and will be able to help address the question of how to make health care more accessible for all those unfamiliar with the system – local first-time users, foreign students, immigrants, refugees, highly skilled migrants and so on.

Although the group of highly skilled migrants makes up a substantial number of the total immigrants in the United States, they have largely been unexplored by medical anthropological research. This has presumably been due to the fact that highly skilled migrants tend to be seen as politically, socially and economically acceptable as well as being seen to smoothly and effortlessly integrate into society and the local health care system (cf. Beaverstock 2005). While this might be true to some extent, this does not mean we should dismiss the experiences of this group in the health care context. On the contrary, it is my firm belief that excluding middling transnationals, such as the highly skilled migrants I spoke with for this research, from health care research leaves a crucial gap in our overall understanding of immigrant health care needs. With this research project I thus hope to have sufficiently demonstrated the importance of highly skilled migrants for future medical anthropological as well as health policy research. In particular:

(1) As this project has shown, the short duration of immigrants' stays in the host society often affected their desire and/or ability to integrate into the local medical system. For example, while establishing a first point of contact with a physician did not have high priority due to their limited time in the United States, this decision can nevertheless increase the likelihood of adverse health outcomes, despite my informants' generally higher socioeconomic background. For others, keeping closely aligned with their home country's health care providers in light of their pending return, rather than fully integrating into the US system, might be the more sensible decision, despite experiencing dissatisfactory health care in the meantime. It remains to be seen whether and to what extent the short-term duration being a key factor for health care decisions holds true also for other, less privileged groups of immigrants. Further research and health policy alike need to take into consideration what other specific difficulties short-term migrants may face, particularly in the medical context.

(2) Additionally, my informants' experiences have shown that insurance coverage of individuals alone is not sufficient to guarantee health care satisfaction and better health outcomes. While there has only recently been a more active interest in health insurance culture in medical anthropological research (Ahlin, Nichter and Pillai 2016; Dao and Mulligan 2016; Dao and Nichter 2016), I would argue that additional research on transmigrants' struggles with health insurance culture is needed in order to provide us with a deeper understanding of immigrants' health care needs in general, and is imperative in order to assist newcomers to the system with their

successful integration into US health care. While further research on highly skilled migrants would presumably require additional lobbying efforts, as they are not seen as an obvious target group for such research by health insurance companies or employers, I hope that this study has shown that much can be gained by a better understanding of *all* immigrants' experiences.

(3) As discussed throughout this research, the differences in health care culture and medications available not only represent a barrier for some immigrants but can also undermine their trust in the host society's health care system, again, regardless of immigrants' socioeconomic and educational backgrounds. The different biomedical settings transnationals find themselves in can even impact their sense of belonging in the host society (cf. Horton 2004; Calvo, Jablonska-Bayro and Waters 2017), making their study a crucial aspect of integrating immigrants into the host society. Excluding a subset of transmigrants from this research thus seems not only problematic, but also unwise, both because this creates an incomplete picture of immigrants' health care needs and because underlying causes of barriers affecting all newcomers to the system tend to get overlooked if research only focuses on those in the most vulnerable positions. Future research should therefore focus on a multitude of diverse groups of immigrants, with different gender, race and ethnicity as well as socioeconomic and educational backgrounds, in order to determine the impact of different health care cultures, and to ultimately guide newcomers' integration into the US health care system more effectively.

(4) The results of this research project have also highlighted several broader issues regarding immigrant health care affecting all groups of transmigrants within the United States. Many of these have remained largely unexamined by previous studies, as most research focuses on the many other pressing barriers more disadvantaged groups of immigrants' experience. However, as the experiences of my informants indicated, many of the typical barriers associated with less privileged immigrant groups, such as medical costs, cultural and linguistic issues as well as insufficient insurance coverage, also affect highly skilled immigrants. Thus, the assumed underlying causes of many barriers do not necessarily lie exclusively in the socioeconomic and educational background of immigrants, but also in the cultural, structural and functional differences in health care systems. I have therefore argued that the lack of a 'common sense' understanding of US health care, and the assumptions of what good health care should look like, brought by

immigrants based on their home health care setups present a significant barrier, one which needs to be examined further. Additionally, not only barriers to immigrant health care but also their underlying causes need to be further scrutinized for our overall understanding of transnational health care needs. In turn, our understanding of how, when and for what reasons immigrants access health care in the host society, and when they access health care back home instead, can inform health policies attempting to increase immigrant health care utilization and improve health outcomes.

(5) Another key finding of this research that has important implications, for both future research and health policy, is the extent to which highly skilled migrants engage in transnational health care seeking and the substantial difference in their motivations for doing so. In particular, are transnational health care strategies, such as insurance juggling, exclusive to highly skilled or other more privileged groups of immigrants? To what extent do the transnational setup and the planned durations of immigrants' stays in the host society determine their transnational health care seeking? I believe that a more detailed analysis of these strategies and practices across diverse groups of immigrants is necessary to gain a fuller understanding of transnational health care seeking. Of particular interest here is also how their transnational setup influences the health care decisions taken by patients, as well as how engaging in these strategies and practices impacts the physician–patient relationship (cf. Gonzalez-Vazquez, Pelcastre-Villafuerte and Taboada 2016).

While I have based my research on the considerable body of medical anthropological scholarship on differences in biomedicine and transnational health care, research in migration studies, including a growing body of work on skilled migrants and transnational elites, as well as studies on cross-cultural health policy research, to my knowledge a comparable project has not been carried out before. This research has accordingly delivered new empirical and theoretical results bridging the gap between research on highly skilled migrants and the study of biomedical culture in the age of globalization. In sum, although the results I have presented in this book are community-specific (i.e. in the first instance pertaining only to highly skilled migrants from Germany, India and Japan in Washington, DC), my findings can generalize to different settings involving migrants in medical environments from both theoretical and applied viewpoints. To achieve this, I propose further research that integrates medical anthropological scholarship with studies on highly skilled transnationals as well as health policy research, which can provide us with a detailed understanding of transnational health care needs. These results can then not only guide medical service providers in their encounters with their transnational patients, but also inform health policy in order to improve immigrants' access to health services, patient satisfaction and health care delivery outcomes.

Notes

1. As discussed in Chapter 1, I refer to 'culture' or 'cultural difference' as 'a set of practices and behaviours defined by customs, habits, language, and geography that groups of individuals share', as suggested by Napier et al. (2014: 3).
2. (Krish, Indian male, US citizen, in the US since 2000).
3. (Irrfan, Indian male, Green Card holder, in the US since 2002).
4. (Dr Stein, Family Medicine).
5. (Dr Silva, Oncologist).
6. (Dr Kowalski, Dentist).
7. (Dr Griffith, Family Medicine).
8. (Priya, Indian female, G2 visa, in the US since 1995).
9. (Salman, Indian male, H-1B visa, in the US since 2007).
10. (Anna, German female, A1 visa, in the US since 2014).
11. (Saki, Japanese female, J1 visa, in the US since 2016).
12. (Markus, German male, G4 visa, in the US since 2012).
13. (Nitya, Indian female, Green Card holder, in the US since 1998).
14. (Sonam, Indian female, G4 visa, in the US since 2001).
15. (Ayami, Japanese female, Green Card holder, in the US since 2010).
16. (Julia, German female, A1 visa, in the US since 2012).
17. (Dr Thomas, Paediatrics).
18. (Dr Costas, Paediatrics).
19. (Krish, Indian male, US citizen, in the US since 2000).
20. (Hitoshi, Japanese male, J1 visa, in the US since 2014).
21. (Vihaan, Indian male, waiting for Green Card approval, in the US since 2002).
22. Since my informants from India did not seem to come from less well-off families than informants from Germany or Japan, I have ruled out their financial background as the key driver for their fear of overwhelming medical costs; see also the discussion in Chapter 3, 'Health insurance in India'.
23. (Anna, German female, A1 visa, in the US since 2014).
24. (Alia, Indian female, J2 visa, in the US since 2016).
25. (Dr Wang, Family Medicine).
26. (Vihaan, Indian male, waiting for Green Card approval, in the US since 2002).
27. (Ichiko, Japanese female, K1 visa, in the US since 2016).
28. (Jonas, German male, A1 visa, in the US since 2014).
29. (Dr Das, Paediatrics and Medical Genetics).
30. (Priya, Indian female, G2 visa, in the US since 1995).
31. (Vihaan, Indian male, waiting for Green Card approval, in the US since 2002).
32. (Tobias, German male, J1 visa, in the US since 2017).
33. (Jonas, German male, A1 visa, in the US since 2014).
34. https://www.healthsystemtracker.org/chart-collection/health-spending-u-s-compare-countries-2/#GDP%20per%20capita%20and%20health%20consumption%20spending%20per%20capita,%202020%20(U.S.%20dollars,%20PPP%20adjusted) (accessed 3 September 2022).
35. http://www.vox.com/cards/health-prices/america-is-getting-gouged-on-health-care-prices (accessed 12 February 2022).

References

Agustin, Laura. 2003. 'Forget victimization: Granting agency to migrants', *Development* 46 (3): 30–6.
Agustin, Laura. 2006. 'The disappearing of a migration category: Migrants who sell sex', *Journal of Ethnic and Migration Studies* 32 (1): 29–47.
Ahlin, Tanja, Mark Nichter & Gopukrishnan Pillai. 2016. 'Health insurance in India: What do we know and why is ethnographic research needed', *Anthropology and Medicine* 23 (1): 102–24.
American Immigration Council. 2015. *New Americans in Washington, DC: The political and economic power of immigrants, Latinos, and Asians in our nation's capital*. Technical report. American Immigration Council, Washington, DC.
American Immigration Council. 2017. *Immigrants in the District of Columbia*. Technical report. American Immigration Council, Washington, DC.
Anderson, Ben. 2011. 'Affect and biopower: Towards a politics of life', *Transactions of the Institute of British Geographers* 37 (1): 28–43.
Anderson, Warwick. 2014. 'Making global health history: The postcolonial worldliness of biomedicine', *Social History of Medicine* 27 (2): 372–84.
Aneesh, A. 2000. *Rethinking Migration: High-skilled labor flows from India to the United States* (Working Paper). Center for Comparative Immigration Studies.
Anthias, Floya. 2012. 'Transnational mobilities, migration research and intersectionality: Towards a translocational frame', *Nordic Journal of Migration Research* 2 (2): 102–10.
Arai, Yumiko & Naoki Ikegami. 1998. 'Health care systems in transition: An overview of the Japanese health care systems', *Journal of Public Health Medicine* 20 (1): 29–33.
Bailey, Ajay & Clara Mulder. 2017. 'Highly skilled migration between the Global North and South: Gender, life courses and institutions', *Journal of Ethnic and Migration Studies* 43 (16): 2689–703.
Baker, Kelly & Brenda Beagan. 2014. 'Making assumptions, making space: An anthropological critique of cultural competency and its relevance to queer patients', *Medical Anthropology Quarterly* 28 (4): 578–98.
Baker, Paul, Costas Gabrielatos, Majid Khosravinik, Michal Krzyzanowski, Tony McEnery & Ruth Wodak. 2008. 'A useful methodological synergy? Combining critical discourse analysis and corpus linguistics to examine discourses of refugees and asylum seekers in the UK press', *Discourse & Society* 19 (3): 273–306.
Baker, Paul & Tony McEnery. 2005. 'A corpus-based approach to discourses of refugees and asylum seekers in UN and newspaper texts', *Journal of Language and Politics* 4 (2): 197–226.
Baldassar, Loretta. 2014. 'Too sick to move: Distant "crisis" care in transnational families', *International Review of Sociology* 24 (3): 391–405.
Bärnighausen, Till & Rainer Sauerborn. 2002. 'One hundred and eighteen years of the German health insurance system: Are there any lessons for middle- and low-income countries?' *Social Science and Medicine* 54: 1559–87.
Basch, Linda, Nina Glick Schiller & Cristina Szanton Blanc. 1994. *Nations Unbound*. Langhorne, PA: Gordon and Breach.
Batalova, Jeanne. 2006. *Skilled Immigrants and Native Workers in the United States*. New York: LFB Scholarly Publishing.
Batalova, Jeanne & Lindsay Lowell. 2006. '"The best and the brightest": Immigrant professionals in the US'. In *The Human Face of Global Mobility: International highly skilled migration in Europe,*

North America and the Asia-Pacific, edited by Michael Smith & Adrian Favell, 81–101. New Brunswick, NJ: Transaction Publishers.

Beaverstock, Jonathan. 2005. 'Transnational elites in the city: British highly-skilled inter-company transferees in New York City's financial district', *Journal of Ethnic and Migration Studies* 31 (2): 245–68.

Beider, Perry & Stuard Hagen. 2004. *Limiting Tort Liability for Medical Malpractice*. Economic and Budget Issue Brief. Congressional Budget Office, Washington, DC.

Berger, David. 2014. 'Corruption ruins the doctor–patient relationship in India', *British Medical Journal* 348: g3169.

Bergmark, Regan, Donald Barr & Ronald Garcia. 2010. 'Mexican immigrants in the US living far from the border may return to Mexico for health services', *Journal of Immigrant and Minority Health* 12: 610–14.

Betancourt, Joseph, Alexander Green, Emilio Carrillo & Owusu Ananeh-Firempong. 2003. 'Defining cultural competence: A practical framework for addressing racial/ethnic disparities in health and health care', *Public Health Reports* 118: 293–302.

Betancourt, Joseph R, Alexander Green, Emilio Carrillo & Elyse R. Park. 2005. 'Cultural competence and health care disparities: key perspectives and trends', *Health Affairs* 24 (2): 499–505.

Bilecen, Basak, Gül Çatir & Ash Orhon. 2015. 'Turkish–German transnational social space: Stitching across borders', *Population, Space and Place* 21: 244–56.

Blank, Robert. 2012. 'Transformation of the US healthcare system: Why is change so difficult?' *Current Sociology* 60 (4): 415–26.

Blendon, Robert, John Benson, Michael Botta, Deborah Zeldow & Minah Kang Kim. 2012. 'A four-country survey of public attitudes towards restricting health costs by limiting the use of high-cost medical interventions', *BMI Open* 2 (e001087): 1–6.

Blendon, Robert, John Benson, Karen Donelan, Robert Leitman, Humphrey Taylor, Christian Koeck & Daniel Gitterman. 1995. 'Who has the best health care system? A second look', *Health Affairs* 14 (4): 220–30.

Blendon, Robert, Mollyann Brodie, John Benson, Drew Altman & Tami Buhr. 2006. 'Americans' views of health care costs, access and quality', *The Milbank Quarterly* 84 (4): 623–57.

van Bochove, Marianne & Godfried Engbersen. 2015. 'Beyond cosmopolitanism and expat bubbles: Challenging dominant representations of knowledge workers and trailing spouses', *Population, Space and Place* 21: 295–309.

Borovoy, Amy. 2005. *The Too-Good Wife: Alcohol, codependency, and the politics of nurturance in postwar Japan*. Berkeley, CA: University of California Press.

Borovoy, Amy & Christina Roberto. 2015. 'Japanese and American public health approaches to preventing population weight gain: A role for paternalism?' *Social Science and Medicine* 143: 62–70.

Brown, Henry. 2008. 'Do Mexican immigrants substitute health care in Mexico for health insurance in the United States? The role of distance', *Social Science and Medicine* 67: 2036–42.

Bump, Jesse. 2015. 'The long road to universal health coverage: Historical analysis of early decisions in Germany, the United Kingdom and the United States', *Health Systems and Reform* 1 (1): 28–38.

Butcher, Melissa. 2010. 'From "fish out of water" to "fitting in": The challenge of re-placing home in a mobile world', *Population, Space and Place* 16: 23–36.

Calvasina, Paola, Carles Muntaner & Carlos Quiñonez. 2015. 'Transnational dental care among Canadian immigrants', *Community Dentistry and Oral Epidemiology* 43: 444–51.

Calvo, Rocío, Joanna Jablonska-Bayro & Mary Waters. 2017. 'Obamacare in action: How access to the health care system contributes to immigrants' sense of belonging', *Journal of Ethnic and Migration Studies* 43 (12): 2020–36.

Cangia, Flavia. 2018. 'Precarity, imagination, and the mobile life of the "trailing spouse"', *Ethos* 46 (1): 8–26.

Carpenter-Song, Elizabeth, Megan Nordquest Schwallie & Jeffrey Longhofer. 2007. 'Cultural competence reexamined: Critique and directions for the future', *Psychiatric Services* 58 (10): 1362–5.

Castells, Manuel. 2000. 'Materials for an exploratory theory of the network society', *British Journal of Sociology* 51 (1): 5–25.

Castles, Stephen. 2000. *Ethnicity and Globalization*. London: Sage Publications.

De Certeau, Michel. 1980. 'On the oppositional practices of everyday life', *Social Text* 3: 3–43.

Charmaz, Kathy. 1996. 'Grounded theory'. In *Rethinking Methods in Psychology*, edited by Jonathan Smith, Rom Harré & Luk Van Langenhove, 27–49. London: Sage Publications.
Cheng, Tsung-Mei. 2003. 'Taiwan's new national health insurance program: Genesis and experience so far', *Health Affairs* 22 (3): 61–76.
Chiswick, Barry. 2005. *High Skilled Immigration in the International Arena* (IZA Discussion Papers 1782). Bonn: Institute for the Study of Labor (IZA).
Chiswick, Barry & Timothy Hatton. 2003. 'International migration and the integration of labor markets'. In *Globalization in Historical Perspective*, edited by Michael Bordo, Alan Taylor & Jeffrey Williamson, 65–120. Chicago: University of Chicago Press.
Choi, Jin Young. 2013. 'Negotiating old and new ways: Contextualizing adapted health care-seeking behaviors of Korean immigrants in Hawaii', *Ethnicity & Health* 18 (4): 350–66.
Clark, Brietta. 2008. 'The immigrant health care narrative and what it tells us about the US health care system', *Annals of Health Law* 17 (2): 229–78.
Cleary, Paul, Susan Edgman-Levitan, Marc Roberts, Thomas Moloney, William McMullen, Janice Walker & Thomas Delbanco. 1991. 'Patients evaluate their hospital care: A national survey', *Health Affairs* 10 (4): 254–67.
Clinton, Bill. 1992. 'The Clinton Health Care Plan', *The New England Journal of Medicine* 327 (11): 804–7.
Congressional Budget Office. 2017. *How Repealing Portions of the Affordable Care Act Would Affect Health Insurance Coverage and Premiums*. Washington, DC: Congressional Budget Office.
Conradson, David & Alan Latham. 2005a. 'Friendship, networks and transnationality in a world city: Antipodean transmigrants in London', *Journal of Ethnic and Migration Studies* 31 (2): 287–305.
Conradson, David & Alan Latham. 2005b. 'Transnational urbanism: Attending to everyday practices and mobilities', *Journal of Ethnic and Migration Studies* (31) 2: 227–33.
Constant, Amelie, Teresa García-Muñoz, Shoshana Neuman & Tzahi Neuman. 2015. *A 'Healthy Immigrant Effect' or a 'Sick Immigrant Effect'? Selection and policies matter* (IZA Discussion Papers 9338). Bonn: Institute for the Study of Labor (IZA).
Consumer Science & Analytics (CSA). 2013. *Health & Society Barometer – Europ Assistance/CSA: 7th wave of the barometer*. Consumer Science & Analytics.
Cooke, Thomas. 2008. 'Gender role beliefs and family migration', *Population, Space and Place* 14: 163–75.
Cotlear, Daniel, Somil Nagpal, Owen Smith, Ajay Tandon & Rafael Cortez. 2015. *Going Universal* (99455). World Bank Group.
Cranston, Sophie. 2017. 'Expatriate as a "good" migrant: Thinking through skilled international migrant categories', *Population, Space and Place* 23: e2058.
Crawley, Heaven & Dimitris Skleparis. 2018. 'Refugees, migrants, neither, both: Categorical fetishism and the politics of bounding in Europe's "migration crisis"', *Journal of Ethnic and Migration Studies* 44 (1): 48–64.
Crosby, Alison. 2006. *The Boundaries of Belonging: Reflections on migration policies into the 21st century* (Inter Pares Occasional Paper 7). Ottawa: Inter Pares.
Crosby, Alison. 2007. 'People on the move: Challenging migration on NGOs, migrant and sex work categorization', *Development* 50 (4): 44–9.
Dao, Amy & Jessica Mulligan. 2016. 'Toward an anthropology of insurance and health reform: An introduction to the special issue', *Medical Anthropology Quarterly* 30 (1): 5–17.
Dao, Amy & Mark Nichter. 2016. 'The social life of health insurance in low- to middle-income countries: An anthropological research agenda', *Medical Anthropology Quarterly* 30 (1): 122–43.
Davies, Mark. 2008–. *The Corpus of Contemporary American English: 450 million words, 1990–Present (COCA)*. Accessed 22 November 2022. http://corpus.byu.edu/coca.
Davies, Mark. 2010. *The Corpus of Historical American English: 400 million words, 1810s–2000s (COHA)*. Accessed 22 November 2022. https://corpus.byu.edu/coha.
Davies, Mark. 2013. *Corpus of Global Web-Based English: 1.9 billion words from speakers in 20 countries (GloWbE)*. Accessed 22 November 2022. http://corpus.byu.edu/glowbe.
Dean, Jennifer & Kathi Wilson. 2009. '"Education? It is irrelevant to my job now. It makes me very depressed . . .": Exploring the health impacts of under/unemployment among highly skilled recent immigrants in Canada', *Ethnicity and Health* 14 (2): 185–204.
Deaton, Angus. 2008. 'Income, health and wellbeing around the world: Evidence from the Gallup World Poll', *Journal of Economic Perspectives* 22 (2): 53–72.

Debas, Haile, Ramanan Laxminarayan & Stephen Straus. 2006. 'Complementary and alternative medicine'. In *Disease Control Priorities in Developing Countries*, edited by Dean Jamison, Joel Breman, Anthony Measham, George Alleyne, Mariam Claeson, David Evans, Prabhat Jha, Anne Mills & Philip Musgrove, 1281–91. Washington, DC: World Bank.

Derose, Kathryn Pitkin, José Escarce & Nicole Lurie. 2007. 'Immigrants and health care: sources of vulnerability', *Health Affairs* 26 (5): 1258–68.

Dickman, Samuel, David Himmelstein & Steffie Woolhandler. 2017. 'Inequality and the health-care system in the USA', *The Lancet* 389 (10077): 1431–41.

Dilger, Hansjörg, Susann Huschke & Dominik Mattes. 2015. 'Ethics, epistemology, and engagement: Encountering values in medical anthropology', *Medical Anthropology: Cross-cultural studies in health and illness* 34 (1): 1–10.

Dilger, Hansjörg, Abdoulaye Kane & Stacey Langwick (eds). 2012. *Medicine, Mobility, and Power in Global Africa*. Bloomington and Indianapolis: Indiana University Press.

Dilger, Hansjörg & Dominik Mattes. 2018. 'Im/mobilities and dis/connectivities in medical globalisation: How global is global health?' *Global Public Health* 13 (3): 265–75.

Dixon-Woods, Mary, Deborah Kirk, Shona Agarwal, Ellen Annandale, Tony Arthur, Janet Harvey, Ronald Hsu, Savita Katbamna, Richard Olsen, Lucy Smith, Richard Riley & Alex Sutton. 2005. *Vulnerable Groups and Access to Health Care: A critical interpretive review*. Report for the National Co-ordinating Centre for NHS Service Delivery and Organisation R&D.

Dyck, Isabel. 2006. 'Travelling tales and migratory meanings: South Asian migrant women talk of place, health and healing', *Social and Cultural Geography* 7 (1): 1–18.

Dyck, Isabel & Parin Dossa. 2007. 'Place, health and home: Gender and migration in the constitution of healthy space', *Health and Place* 13: 691–701.

Ecks, Stefan. 2006. 'Pharmaceutical citizenship: Antidepressant marketing and the promise of demarginalization in India', *Anthropology and Medicine* 12 (3): 239–54.

Elleuch, Amira. 2008. 'Healthcare service quality perception in Japan', *International Journal of Health Care Quality Assurance* 24 (6): 417–29.

Ellis, Randall, Moneer Alam & Indrani Gupta. 2000. 'Health insurance in India', *Economic and Political Weekly* 35 (4): 207–17.

Escobar, Arturo. 2001. 'Culture sits in places: Reflections on globalism and subaltern strategies of localization', *Political Geography* 20: 139–74.

Fadiman, Anne. 1997. *The Spirit Catches You and You Fall Down*. New York: Farrar, Straus and Giroux.

Faist, Thomas, Basak Bilecen, Karolina Barglowski & Joanna Sienkiewicz. 2015. 'Transnational social protection: Migrants' strategies and patterns of inequalities', *Population, Space and Place* 21: 193–202.

Falk, Isidore. 1977. 'Proposals for national health insurance in the USA: Origins and evolution, and some perceptions for the future', *The Milbank Memorial Fund Quarterly* 55 (2): 161–91.

Favell, Adrian, Miriam Feldblum & Michael Smith. 2006. 'The human face of global mobility: A research agenda'. In *The Human Face of Global Mobility: International highly skilled migration in Europe, North America and the Asia-Pacific*, edited by Michael Smith & Adrian Favell, 1–25. New Brunswick: Transaction Publishers.

Favell, Adrian, Miriam Feldblum & Michael Smith. 2007. 'The human face of global mobility: A research agenda', *Society* 44 (2): 15–25.

Fechter, Anne-Meike & Katie Walsh. 2010. 'Examining "expatriate" continuities: Postcolonial approaches to mobile professionals', *Journal of Ethnic and Migration Studies* 36 (8): 1197–210.

Findlay, Allan & Sophie Cranston. 2015. 'What's in a research agenda? An evaluation of research developments in the area of skilled international migration', *International Development Planning Review* 37 (1): 17–31.

Findlay, Allan, F. Li, Amanda Jowett & Ronald Skeldon. 1996. 'Skilled international migration and the global city: A study of expatriates in Hong Kong', *Transactions of the Institute of British Geographers* 21 (1): 49–61.

Fletcher, Rebecca. 2016. 'Keeping up with the Cadillacs: What health insurance disparities, moral hazard, and the Cadillac tax mean to the Patient Protection and Affordable Care Act', *Medical Anthropology Quarterly* 30 (1): 18–36.

Flintrop, Jens. 2003. 'Gesetzliche Krankenversicherung: Eine Jahrhundertentscheidung', *Deutsches Ärzteblatt* 12: 540–3.

Flores, Glenn, Milagros Abreu, Mary Olivar & Beth Kastner. 1998. 'Access barriers to health care for Latino children', *Archives of Pediatrics and Adolescent Medicine* 152: 1119–25.

Foucault, Michel. 1978. *The History of Sexuality: An introduction*. Volume I, trans. Robert Hurley. London: Penguin.

Foucault, Michel. 2002 [1963]. *The Birth of the Clinic*. Trans. A. M. Sheridan-Smith. London: Routledge.

Fox, Reneé. 2005. 'Cultural competence and the culture of medicine', *The New England Journal of Medicine* 353 (13): 1316–19.

Frank, Robert. 2002. 'Integrating homeopathy and biomedicine: Medical practice and knowledge production among German homeopathic physicians', *Sociology of Health and Illness* 24 (6): 796–819.

Frankenberg, Ronald. 1981. 'Allopathic medicine, profession, and capitalist ideology in India', *Social Science and Medicine* 15A: 115–25.

Galea, Sandro. 2017. 'How the Trump administration's policies may harm the public's health', *The Milbank Quarterly* 95 (2): 229–32.

Geertz, Clifford. 1975. 'Common sense as a cultural system', *The Antioch Review* 33 (1): 5–26.

van der Geest, Sjaak. 1997. 'Is there a role for traditional medicine in basic health services in Africa? A plea for a community perspective', *Tropical Medicine and International Health* 2 (9): 903–11.

Gideon, Jasmine. 2011. 'Exploring migrants' health seeking strategies: The case of Latin American migrants in London', *International Journal of Migration, Health and Social Care* 7 (4): 197–208.

Giordano, James. 2013. 'Ethical considerations in the globalization of medicine: An interview with James Giordano', *BMC medicine* 11(1): 69.

Glick Schiller, Nina, Linda Basch & Cristina Szanton Blanc. 1992. 'Transnationalism: A new analytic framework for understanding migration', *Annals of New York Academy of Sciences* 645: 1–24.

Glick Schiller, Nina, Linda Basch & Cristina Szanton Blanc. 1995. 'From immigrant to transmigrant: Theorizing transnational migration', *Anthropological Quarterly* 68 (1): 48–63.

Glick Schiller, Nina & Noel Salazar. 2013. 'Regimes of mobility across the globe', *Journal of Ethnic and Migration Studies* 39 (2): 183–200.

Gonzalez-Vazquez, Tonatiuh, Blanca Pelcastre-Villafuerte & Arianna Taboada. 2016. 'Surviving the distance: The transnational utilization of traditional medicine among Oaxacan migrants in the US', *Journal of Immigrant and Minority Health* 18 (1): 190–8.

Good, Byron. 1994. *Medicine, Rationality and Experience: An anthropological perspective*. Cambridge, New York, Melbourne: Cambridge University Press.

Good, Mary-Jo DelVecchio. 1995. 'Cultural studies of biomedicine: An agenda for research', *Social Science and Medicine* 41 (4): 461–73.

Good, Mary-Jo DelVecchio, Cara James, Byron Good & Anne Becker. 2002. *The Culture of Medicine and Racial, Ethnic, and Class Disparities in Healthcare* (Russell Sage Working Papers 109). New York: Russell Sage Foundation.

Grimmer-Solem, Erik. 2005. 'German social science, Meiji conservatism, and the peculiarities of Japanese history', *Journal of World History* 16 (2): 187–222.

Grineski, Sara. 2011. 'Why parents cross for children's health care: Transnational cultural capital in the United States–Mexico border region', *Social Theory & Health* 9: 256–74.

Hahn, Robert & Arthur Kleinman. 1983. 'Biomedical practice and anthropological theory: Frameworks and directions', *Annual Review of Anthropology* 12: 305–33.

Hamdy, Sherine. 2013. 'Political challenges to biomedical universalism: Kidney failure among Egypt's poor', *Medical Anthropology* 32 (4): 374–92.

Hardie, Andrew. 2012. 'CQPweb – Combining power, flexibility and usability in a corpus analysis tool', *International Journal of Corpus Linguistics* 17 (3): 380–409.

Hercog, Metka. 2017. *The Privileged and Useful Migrant: An evaluation of changing policy and scholarly approaches towards high-skilled migration*. National Center of Competence in Research for Migration and Mobility Studies.

Hirsch, Jennifer. 2003. 'Anthropologists, migrants, and health research', *American Arrivals: Anthropology Engages the New Immigration* 1: 229–57.

Holmes, Seth M., Ernesto Castañeda, Jeremy Geeraert, Heide Castaneda, Ursula Probst, Nina Zeldes, Sarah S. Willen, Yusupha Dibba, Raphael Frankfurter, Anne Kveim Lie, John Fredrik Askjer and Heidi Fjeld. 2021. 'Deservingness: Migration and health in social context', *BMJ Global Health* 6 (Suppl. 1): p.e005107.

Horton, Richard & Pam Das. 2011. 'Indian health: The path from crisis to progress', *The Lancet* 377: 181–3.
Horton, Sarah. 2004. 'Different subjects: The health care system's participation in the differential construction of the cultural citizenship of Cuban refugees and Mexican immigrants', *Medical Anthropology Quarterly* 18 (4): 472–89.
Horton, Sarah. 2013. 'Medical returns as class transformation: Situating migrants' medical returns within a framework of transnationalism', *Medical Anthropology* 32 (5): 417–32.
Horton, Sarah, Cesar Abadía, Jessica Mulligan & Jennifer Thompson. 2014. 'Critical anthropology of global health "takes a stand" statement: A critical medical anthropological approach to the US's Affordable Care Act', *Medical Anthropology Quarterly* 28 (1): 1–22.
Horton, Sarah & Stephanie Cole. 2011. 'Medical returns: seeking health care in Mexico', *Social Science & Medicine* 72 (11): 1846–52.
Horton, Sarah & Louise Lamphere. 2006. 'A call to an anthropology of health policy', *Anthropology News* 47 (1): 33–6.
Iglehart, John. 1988. 'Japan's medical care system', *The New England Journal of Medicine* 319 (12): 807–12.
Iglehart, John. 1991. 'Germany's health care system', *The New England Journal of Medicine* 324 (24): 1750–6.
Ikegami, Naoki & John Campbell. 1999. 'Health care reform in Japan: The virtues of muddling through', *Health Affairs* 18 (3): 56–75.
Ikegami, Naoki, Byung-Kwang Yoa, Hideki Hashimoto, Masotoshi Matsumoto, Hiroya Ogata, Akira Babazono, Ryo Watanabe, Kenji Shibuya, Bong-Min Yang, Michael Reich & Yasuki Kobayashi. 2011. 'Japanese universal health coverage: Evolution, achievement, and challenges', *The Lancet* 378: 1106–15.
Iredale, Robyn. 2001. 'The migration of professionals: Theories and typologies', *International Migration* 39 (5): 7–26.
Iredale, Robyn. 2005. 'Gender, immigration policies and accreditation: Valuing the skills of professional women migrants', *Geoforum* 36: 155–66.
Jain, Ankit, Selva Swetha, Zeena Johar & Ramesh Raghavan. 2014. 'Acceptability of, and willingness to pay for, community health insurance in rural India', *Journal of Epidemiology and Global Health* 4: 159–67.
Johnson, Rachel, Somnath Saha, Jose Arbelaez, Mary Beach & Lisa Cooper. 2004. 'Racial and ethnic differences in patient perceptions of bias and cultural competence in health care', *Journal of General Internal Medicine* 19: 101–10.
Johnston, Meghan & Rebecca Herzig. 2006. 'The interpretation of "culture": Diverging perspectives on medical provision in rural Montana', *Social Science and Medicine* 63: 2500–11.
Jones, Stephen. 2000. 'Medical aspects of expatriate health: Health threats', *Occupational Medicine* 50 (8): 572–8.
Journal of Ethnic and Migration Studies (2005). *Ordinary and Middling Transnationalisms.* Special Issue of *Journal of Ethnic and Migration Studies* 31 (2).
Jütte, Robert. 1999. 'The historiography of nonconventional medicine in Germany: A concise overview', *Medical History* 43: 342–58.
Kane, Abdoulaye. 2012. 'Flows of medicine, healers, health professionals, and patients between home and host countries'. In *Medicine, Mobility, and Power in Global Africa*, edited by Hansjörg Dilger, Abdoulaye Kane & Stacey Langwick, 190–212. Bloomington and Indianapolis: Indiana University Press.
Khan, Shamshad. 2006. 'Systems of medicine and nationalist discourse in India: Towards "new horizons" in medical anthropology and history', *Social Science and Medicine* 62: 2786–97.
Khare, Ravindra. 1996. 'Dava, Daktar and Dua: Anthropology of practiced medicine in India', *Social Science and Medicine* 43 (5): 837–48.
Kibele, Eva, Rembrandt Scholz & Vladimir Shkolnikov. 2008. 'Low migrant mortality in Germany for men aged 65 and older: Fact or artifact?' *European Journal for Epidemiology* 23: 389–93.
Kickbusch, Ilona S. 2001. 'Health literacy: Addressing the health and education divide', *Health Promotion International* 16 (3): 289–97.
Kleinman, Arthur. 1997. *Writing at the Margin: Discourse between anthropology and medicine.* Berkeley, CA: University of California Press.
Kleinman, Arthur & Peter Benson. 2006. 'Anthropology in the clinic: The problem of cultural competency and how to fix it', *PLoS Medicine* 3 (10): 1673–6.

Knipper, Michael, Conny Seeleman & Marie-Luise Essink-Bot. 2010. 'How should ethnic diversity be represented in medical curricula? A plea for systematic training in cultural competence', *Tijdschrift voor Medisch Onderwijs* 29 (1): 54–60.

Kofman, Eleonore. 2000. 'The invisibility of skilled female migrants and gender relations in studies of skilled migration in Europe', *International Journal of Population Geography* 6: 45–59.

Kofman, Eleonore. 2014. 'Towards a gendered evaluation of (highly) skilled immigration policies in Europe', *International Migration* 52 (3): 116–28.

Kohut, Andrew & Michael Remez. 2009. 'Media less influential in views on health care, economy than on other issues'. News Release. Washington, DC: Pew Research Center.

Koser, Khalid & John Salt. 1997. 'The geography of highly skilled international migration', *International Journal of Population Geography* 3: 285–303.

Koskela, Kaisu. 2013. 'Boundaries of belonging: Highly skilled migrants and the migrant hierarchy in Finland', *Journal of Finnish Studies* 17 (1 and 2): 19–41.

Kou, Anu & Ajay Bailey. 2017. '"Some people expect women should always be dependent": Indian women's experiences as highly skilled migrants', *Geoforum* 85: 178–86.

Koutonin, Mawuna Remarque. 2015. 'Why are white people expats when the rest of us are immigrants?' *The Guardian*. 13 March.

Krause, Kristine. 2008. 'Transnational Therapy Networks among Ghanaians in London', *Journal of Ethnic and Migration Studies* 34 (2): 235–51.

Ku, Leighton. 2009. 'Health insurance coverage and medical expenditures of immigrants and native-born citizens in the United States', *American Journal of Public Health* 99 (7): 1322–8.

Ku, Leighton & Sheetal Matani. 2001. 'Left out: Immigrants' access to health care and insurance', *Health Affairs* 20 (1): 247–56.

Kumar, Shiva, Lincoln Chen, Mita Choudhury, Shiban Ganju, Vijay Mahajan, Amarjeet Sinha & Abhijit Sen. 2011. 'Financing health care for all: Challenges and opportunities', *The Lancet* 377: 668–79.

Kunz, Sarah. 2016. 'Privileged mobilities: Locating the expatriate in migration scholarship', *Geography Compass* 10 (3): 89–101.

Kurata, John, Yoshiyuki Watanabe, Christine McBride, Keiichi Kawai & Ronald Andersen. 1994. 'A comparative study of patient satisfaction with health care in Japan and the United States', *Social Science and Medicine* 39 (8): 1069–76.

Langwick, Stacey, Hansjörg Dilger & Abdoulaye Kane. 2012. 'Transnational medicine, mobile experts'. In *Medicine, Mobility, and Power in Global Africa*, edited by Hansjörg Dilger, Abdoulaye Kane & Stacey Langwick, 1–27. Bloomington and Indianapolis: Indiana University Press.

Lee, Jane Yeonjae, Robin A. Kearns & Wardlow Friesen. 2010. 'Seeking affective health care: Korean immigrants' use of homeland medical services', *Health & Place* 16 (1): 108–15.

Leung, Maggi. 2017. 'Social mobility via academic mobility: Reconfigurations in class and gender identities among Asian scholars in the Global North', *Journal of Ethnic and Migration Studies* 43 (16): 2704–19.

Levitt, Larry. 2015. 'Why health insurance literacy matters', *Jama* 313 (6): 555–6.

Lidola, Maria & Fabiano Borges. 2017. 'Negotiating horizontality in medical South–South cooperation: The Cuban mission in Rio de Janeiro's urban peripheries', *Global Public Health* 13 (3): 355–68.

Lock, Margaret. 2013. 'The epigenome and nature/nurture reunification: A challenge for anthropology', *Medical Anthropology* 32 (4): 291–308.

Lock, Margaret & Vinh-Kim Nguyen. 2010. *An Anthropology of Biomedicine*. Chichester: Wiley-Blackwell.

Loh, Chung-Ping, Katrin Nihalani & Oliver Schnusenberg. 2012. 'Measuring attitude toward social health insurance', *The European Journal of Health Economics* 13: 707–22.

Lopez-Class, Maria, Felipe Castro & Amelie Ramirez. 2011. 'Conceptions of acculturation: A review and statement of critical issues', *Social Science and Medicine* 72: 1555–62.

Lowell, Lindsay. 2007. *Trends in International Migration Flows and Stocks, 1975–2005* (Working Paper 58). Paris: OECD Publishing.

McDonald, James & Steven Kennedy. 2004. 'Insights into the "healthy immigrant effect": Health status and health service use of immigrants to Canada', *Social Science and Medicine* 59: 1613–27.

Mahroum, Sami. 2001. 'Europe and the immigration of highly skilled labour', *International Migration* 39 (5): 27–43.

Malmusi, Davide, Carme Borrell & Joan Benach. 2010. 'Migration-related health inequalities: Showing the complex interactions between gender, social class and place of origin', *Social Science and Medicine* 71: 1610–19.

Maretzki, Thomas & Eduard Seidler. 1985. 'Biomedicine and naturopathic healing in West Germany: A historical and ethnomedical view of a stormy relationship', *Culture, Medicine and Psychiatry* 9: 383–421.

Marks, Shula. 1997. 'What is colonial about colonial medicine? And what has happened to imperialism and health?' *Social History of Medicine* 10 (2): 205–19.

Mayda, Anna & Giovanni Peri. 2017. 'The economic impact of US immigration policies in the Age of Trump'. In *Economics and Policy in the Age of Trump*, edited by Chad Bown, 69–78. London: CERP Press.

Mayhew, Les. 2001. *Japan's Longevity Revolution and the Implications for Health Care Finance and Long-Term Care* (Discussion Paper PI-0108). Laxenburg, Austria: International Institute for Applied Systems Analysis.

Mays, Nicholas & Catherine Pope. 2000. 'Assessing quality in qualitative research', *British Journal of Medicine* 320: 50–2.

Messias, Deanne. 2002. 'Transnational health resources, practices, and perspectives: Brazilian immigrant women's narratives', *Journal of Immigrant Health* 4 (4): 183–200.

Morley, Michael, Noreen Heraty & David Collings (eds). 2006. *New Directions in Expatriate Research*. Basingstoke: Palgrave Macmillan.

Mossialos, Elias, Martin Wenzl, Robin Osborn & Dana Samak. 2016. *2015 International Profiles of Health Care Systems*. New York: Commonwealth Fund.

Napier, David, Clyde Ancarno, Beverley Butler, Joseph Calabrese, Angel Chater, Helen Chatterjee, François Guesnet, Robert Horne, Stephen Jacyna, Sushrut Jadhav, Alison Macdonald, Ulrike Neuendorf, Aaron Parkhurst, Rodney Reynolds, Graham Scambler, Sonu Shamdasani, Sonia Smith, Jakob Stougaard-Nielsen, Linda Thomson, Nick Tyler, Anna-Maria Volkmann, Trinley Walker, Jessica Watson, Amanda de C. Williams, Chris Willott, James Wilson & Katherine Woolf. 2014. 'Culture and health', *The Lancet* 384 (9954): 1607–39.

New York Times. 1917. 'Urge more study of health insurance'. *New York Times*, 8 March.

Numbers, Ronald. 1978. 'Almost persuaded: American physicians and compulsory health insurance, 1912–1920', *The Henry E. Sigerist Supplements to the Bulletin of the History of Medicine* 1–158.

Oberlander, Jonathan. 2010. 'Long time coming: Why health reform finally passed', *Health Affairs* 29 (6): 1112–16.

O'Connor, Bonnie Blair. 1995. *Healing Traditions: Alternative medicine and the health professions*. Philadelphia, PA: University of Pennsylvania Press.

OECD & UNDESA. 2013. *World Migration in Figures*. United Nations and OECD.

Ohnuki-Tierney, Emiko. 1994. *Rice as Self: Japanese identities through time*. Princeton, NJ: Princeton University Press.

Ong, Aihwa. 1995. 'Making the biopolitical subject: Cambodian immigrants, refugee medicine and cultural citizenship in California', *Social Science and Medicine* 40 (9): 1243–57.

Ormond, Meghann. 2014. 'Harnessing diasporic medical mobilities'. In *Migration, Health and Inequality*, edited by Felicity Thomas & Jasmine Gideon, 150–62. London: Zed Books.

Paez, Kathryn, Jerilyn Allen, Mary Beach, Kathryn Carson & Lisa Cooper. 2009. 'Physician cultural competence and patient ratings of the patient–physician relationship', *Journal of General Internal Medicine* 24 (4): 495–8.

Papademetriou, Demetrios & Stephen Yale-Loehr. 1996. *Balancing Interests: Rethinking US selection of skilled immigrants* (International Migration Policy Program 4). Washington, DC: Carnegie Endowment for International Peace.

Papanicolas, Irene, Jonathan Cylus & Peter Smith. 2013. 'An analysis of survey data from eleven countries finds that "satisfaction" with health system performance means many things', *Health Affairs* 32 (4): 734–42.

Partington, Alan. 2013. 'Corpus analysis of political language'. In *The Encyclopedia of Applied Linguistics*, edited by Carol Chapelle, 1–8. Oxford: Blackwell Publishing.

Parutis, Violetta. 2011. '"Economic migrants" or "middling transnationals"? East European migrants' experiences of work in the UK', *International Migration* 52 (1): 36–55.

Patel, Vikram, Shiva Kumar, Vinod Paul, Krishna Rao & Srinath Reddy. 2011. 'Universal health care in India: The time is right', *The Lancet* 377: 505.

Payer, Lynn. 1996. *Medicine & Culture*. New York: Holt.

Pearce, Michael. 2008. 'Investigating the collocational behaviour of MAN and WOMAN in the BNC using Sketch Engine', *Corpora* 3 (11): 1–29.
Portes, Alejandro, Luis Guarnizo & Patricia Landolt. 1999. 'The study of transnationalism: Pitfalls and promise of an emergent research field', *Ethnic and Racial Studies* 22 (2): 217–37.
Prasad, Purendra. 2007. 'Medicine, power and social legitimacy: A socio-historical appraisal of health systems in contemporary India', *Economic and Political Weekly* 42 (34): 3491–8.
Price, Marie, Ivan Cheung, Samantha Friedman & Audrey Singer. 2005. 'The world settles in: Washington, DC, as an immigrant gateway', *Urban Geography* 26 (1): 61–83.
Quirke, Viviane & Jean-Paul Gaudilliere. 2008. 'The era of biomedicine: Science, medicine and public health in Britain and France after the Second World War', *Medical History* 52: 441–52.
Rabinow, Paul & Nikolas Rose. 2006. 'Biopower today', *BioSocieties* 1: 195–217.
Rajeev, A. & Sanam Latif. 2009. 'Study of the knowledge, attitude and experience of medical tourism among target groups with special emphasis on South India', *Online Journal of Health and Allied Sciences* 8 (2): 6.
Ramakrishna, Jayashree & Mitchell Weiss. 1992. 'Health, illness, and immigration: East Indians in the United States', *The Western Journal of Medicine* 157: 265–70.
Ramani, K. & Dileep Mavalankar. 2006. 'Health system in India: Opportunities and challenges for improvements', *Journal of Health Organization and Management* 20 (6): 560–72.
Reddy, Srinath, Vikram Patel, Prabhat Jha, Vinod Paul, Shiva Kumar & Lalit Dandona. 2011. 'Towards achievement of universal health care in India by 2020: A call to action', *The Lancet* 377: 760–8.
Regets, Mark. 2001. *Research and Policy Issues in High-Skilled International Migration: A perspective with data from the United States* (IZA Discussion Paper 366). Forschungsinstitut zur Zukunft der Arbeit (IZA).
Reich, Michael, Naoki Ikegami, Kenji Shibuya & Keizo Takemi. 2011. '50 years of pursuing a healthy society in Japan', *The Lancet* 378: 1051–3.
Reid, T. R. 2009. *The Healing of America*. New York: Penguin Press.
Rose, Nikolas. 2007. 'Molecular biopolitics, somatic ethics and the spirit of biocapital', *Social Theory and Health* 5: 3–29.
Rothman, David. 1991. 'The public presentation of Blue Cross, 1935–1965', *Journal of Health Politics, Policy and Law* 16 (4): 671–93.
Rothman, David. 1993. 'A century of failure: Health care reform in America', *Journal of Health Politics, Policy and Law* 18 (2): 271–86.
Rudmik, Luke, Dominika Wranik & Caroline Rudisill-Michaelsen. 2014. 'Physician payment methods: A focus on quality and cost control', *Journal of Otolaryngology – Head and Neck Surgery* 43 (34): 1–5.
Rutten, Mario & Sanderien Verstappen. 2014. 'Middling migration: Contradictory mobility experiences of Indian youth in London', *Journal of Ethnic and Migration Studies* 40 (8): 1217–35.
Ryan, Louise, Rosemary Sales, Mary Tilki & Bernadetta Siara. 2009. 'Family strategies and transnational migration: Recent polish migrants in London', *Journal of Ethnic and Migration Studies* 35 (1): 61–77.
Salazar, Noel & Alan Smart. 2011. 'Anthropological takes on (im)mobility', *Identities* 18 (6): i–ix.
Sandoz, Laure. 2016. 'Understanding migration policies from migrants' perspective'. In *24th World Congress of Political Science*. Poznań, Poland.
Scheppers, Emmanuel, Els van Dongen, Jos Dekker, Jan Geertzen & Joost Dekker. 2006. 'Potential barriers to the use of health services among ethnic minorities: A review', *Family Practice* 23: 325–48.
Schnusenberg, Oliver, Chung-Ping Loh & Katrin Nihalani. 2013. 'The role of financial wellbeing, sociopolitical attitude, self-interest, and lifestyle in one's attitude toward social health insurance'. *Applied Health Economics and Health Policy* 11: 369–81.
Schoen, Cathy, Robin Osborn, Michelle Doty, Megan Bishop, Jordon Peugh & Nandita Murukutla. 2007. 'Toward higher-performance health systems: Adults' health care experiences in seven countries, 2007', *Health Affairs* 26 (7): w717–w734.
Schoen, Cathy, Robin Osborn, Phuong Huynh, Michelle Doty, Kinga Zapert, Jordon Peugh & Karen Davis. 2005. 'Taking the pulse of health care systems: Experiences of patients with health problems in six countries', *Health Affairs Web Exclusive* (W5): 509–25.

Schoen, Cathy, Robin Osborn, David Squires, Michelle Doty, Roz Pierson & Sandra Applebaum. 2010. 'How health insurance design affects access to care and costs, by income, in eleven countries', *Health Affairs* 29 (12): 2323–34.

Schoen, Cathy, Robin Osborn, David Squires, & Michelle Doty. 2013. 'Access, affordability, and insurance complexity are often worse in the United States compared to ten other countries', *Health Affairs* 32 (12): 2205–15.

Schühle, Judith. 2018. 'State-of-the-art or the art of medicine? Transnational mobility and perceptions of multiple biomedicines among Nigerian physicians in the US', *Global Public Health* 13 (3): 298–309.

Schulte, Margaret. 2013. *Healthcare Delivery in the USA: An introduction*. Boca Raton, FL: CRC Press.

Shetterly, Susan, Judith Baxter, Lynn Mason & Richard Hamman. 1996. 'Self-rated health among Hispanic vs. non-Hispanic white adults: The San Luis Valley health and aging study', *American Journal of Public Health* 86 (12): 1798–1801.

Shim, Janet. 2010. 'Cultural health capital: A theoretical approach to understanding health care interactions and the dynamics of unequal treatment', *Journal of Health and Social Behavior* 51 (1): 1–15.

Shore, Cris & Stephen Nugent (eds). 2002. *Elite Cultures: Anthropological perspectives*. London: Routledge.

Siddiqui, Zakaria & Gabriela Tejada. 2014. 'Development and highly skilled migrants: Perspectives from the Indian diaspora and returnees', *International Development Policy* 5: 5.2.

Sime, Daniela. 2014. '"I think that Polish doctors are better": Newly arrived migrant children and their parents' experiences and views of health services in Scotland', *Health & Place* 30: 86–93.

Singer, Audrey, Jill Wilson & Brooke DeRenzis. 2009. *Immigrants, Politics, and Local Response in Suburban Washington*. Washington, DC: Brookings Institution.

Singer, Merrill. 1995. 'Beyond the ivory tower: Critical praxis in medical anthropology', *Medical Anthropology Quarterly* 9 (1): 80–106.

Sklair, Leslie. 2002. 'Democracy and the transnational capitalist class', *The Annals of the American Academy of Political and Social Science* 581: 144–57.

Smith, Michael. 2005. 'Transnational urbanism revisited', *Journal of Ethnic and Migration Studies* 31 (2): 235–44.

Starr, Paul. 1982. *The Social Transformation of American Medicine*. New York: Basic Books.

Starr, Paul. 2011. *Remedy and Reaction*. New Haven, CT: Yale University Press.

Stodulka, Thomas. 2015. 'Emotion work, ethnography, and survival strategies on the streets of Yogyakarta', *Medical Anthropology* 34 (1): 84–97.

Stodulka, Thomas. 2017. 'Yogyakarta street careers: Feelings of belonging and dealing with sticky stigma', *Anthropologia* 4 (2): 145–63.

Strauss, Anselm & Juliet Corbin. 2008. *Basics of Qualitative Research: Procedures and techniques for developing grounded theory*. Los Angeles: Sage Publications.

Stülb, Magdalena & Yvonne Adam. 2009. 'Die Sicht der Patient/-innen–medizinethnologische Ansätze in der interkulturellen Kommunikation im Gesundheitswesen'. In *Interkulturelle Öffnung des Gesundheitssystems*, edited by Christiane Falge & Gudrun Zimmermann, 41–57. Baden-Baden: Nomos.

Sun, Ken. 2014. 'Transnational healthcare seeking: How aging Taiwanese return migrants view homeland public benefits', *Global Networks* 14 (4): 533–50.

Swami, Balu. 2002. 'The German health care system'. In *Handbook of International Health Care Systems*, edited by Khi Thai, Edward Wimberley & Sharon McManus, 333–58. New York, Basel: Marcel Dekker.

Taylor, Janelle. 2003. 'Confronting "culture" in medicine's "culture of no culture"', *Academic Medicine* 78 (6): 555–9.

Thomas, Felicity. 2010. 'Transnational health and treatment networks: Meaning, value and place in health seeking among Southern African migrants in London', *Health & Place* 16: 606–12.

Thomson, Sarah, Robin Osborn, David Squires & Miraya Jun (eds). 2012. *International Profiles of Health Care Systems, 2012*. New York: Commonwealth Fund.

Tiilikainen, Marja. 2012. 'It's just like the internet: Transnational healing practices between Somaliland and the Somali diaspora'. In *Medicine, Mobility, and Power in Global Africa*, edited by Hansjörg Dilger, Abdoulaye Kane & Stacey Langwick, 271–94. Bloomington and Indianapolis: Indiana University Press.

Tsianos, Vassilis & Serhar Karakayali. 2010. 'Transnational migration and the emergence of the European border regime: An ethnographic analysis', *European Journal of Social Theory* 13 (3): 373–87.
Turner, Leigh. 2005. 'From the local to the global: Bioethics and the concept of culture', *Journal of Medicine and Philosophy* 30 (3): 305–20.
Vertovec, Steven. 1999. 'Conceiving and researching transnationalism', *Ethnic and Racial Studies* 22 (2): 447–62.
Vertovec, Steven. 2007. 'Super-diversity and its implications', *Ethnic and Racial Studies* 30 (6): 1024–54.
Villa-Torres, Laura, Tonatiuh Gonzalez-Vazquez, Paul Fleming, Edgar Gonzalez-Gonzalez, Cesar Infante-Xibille, Rebecca Chavez & Clare Barrington. 2017. 'Transnationalism and health: A systematic literature review on the use of transnationalism in the study of the health practices and behaviors of migrants', *Social Science and Medicine* 183: 70–9.
Virk, Amrit & Rifat Atun. 2015. 'Towards universal health coverage in India: A historical examination of the genesis of Rashtriya Swasthya Bima Yojana – the health insurance scheme for low-income groups', *Public Health* 129: 810–17.
Viruell-Fuentes, Edna. 2007. 'Beyond acculturation: Immigration, discrimination, and health research among Mexicans in the United States', *Social Science and Medicine* 65: 1524–35.
Viruell-Fuentes, Edna, Patricia Miranda & Sawsan Abdulrahim. 2012. 'More than culture: Structural racism, intersectionality theory, and immigrant health', *Social Science and Medicine* 75: 2099–106.
Voigt-Graf, Carmen. 2005. 'The constitution of transnational spaces by Indian migrants in Australia', *Journal of Ethnic and Migration Studies* 31 (2): 365–84.
Wang, Lu & Ming-Jung Kwak. 2015. 'Immigration, barriers to healthcare and transnational ties: A case study of South Korean immigrants in Toronto, Canada', *Social Science and Medicine* 133: 340–8.
Watanabe, Satoko, Jiro Imanishi, Masako Satoh & Kotaro Ozasa. 2001. 'Unique place of Kampo (Japanese Traditional Medicine) in complementary and alternative medicine: A survey of doctors belonging to the Regional Medical Association in Japan', *The Journal of Experimental Medicine* 194: 55–63.
Wear, Delese. 2003. 'Insurgent multiculturalism: Rethinking how and why we teach culture in medical education', *Academic Medicine* 78 (6): 549–54.
Weil, Alan. 2017. 'Coverage expansion, accountable care, and more', *Health Affairs* 36 (1).
Wendt, Claus & Rubin Minhas. 2010. 'The power of ideas: Can Obama's healthcare reforms change the US health system?' *The International Journal of Clinical Practice* 64 (4): 423–5.
Wetzel, Miriam. 2011. 'The US health care system'. In *The Health Care Dilemma: A comparison of health care systems in three European countries and the US*, edited by Elizabeth Armstrong, Martin Fischer, Ramin Parsa-Parsi & Miriam Wetzel, 383–407. Hackensack, NJ: World Scientific.
White, Chapin & Stuart Hagen. 2006. *Medical Malpractice Tort Limits and Health Care Spending*. Background Paper. Washington, DC: Congressional Budget Office.
WHO. 2001. *Legal Status of Traditional Medicine and Complementary/Alternative Medicine: A worldwide review*. Geneva: World Health Organization.
WHO. 2010. *The World Health Report: Health Systems Financing: The path to universal coverage*. Geneva: World Health Organization.
Whyte, Susan Reynolds. 2009. 'Health identities and subjectivities: The ethnographic challenge', *Medical Anthropology Quarterly* 23 (1): 6–15.
Wilding, Raelene. 2007. 'Transnational ethnographies and anthropological imaginings of migrancy', *Journal of Ethnic and Migration Studies* 33 (2): 331–48.
Willis, Katie & Brenda Yeoh. 2002. 'Gendering transnational communities: A comparison of Singaporean and British migrants in China', *Geoforum* 33: 553–65.
Wilson, David. 2014. 'Information, partisanship, and public support for health insurance requirements in the United States', *Political Sciences and Public Affairs* 2 (4): 1–4.
Wolf, Angelika. 2012. 'Health security on the move: Biobureaucracy, solidarity, and the transfer of health insurance to Senegal'. In *Medicine, Mobility, and Power in Global Africa*, edited by Hansjörg Dilger, Abdoulaye Kane & Stacey Langwick, 92–114. Bloomington and Indianapolis: Indiana University Press.
Wörtz, Markus & Reinhard Busse. 2005. 'Analysing the impact of health care system change in the EU member states – Germany', *Health Economics* 14: 133–49.

Yamada, Tadashi, Tetsuji Yamada, Chia-Ching Chen & Weihong Zeng. 2014. 'Determinants of health insurance and hospitalization', *Cogent Economics and Finance* 2: 920271.

Yamashita, Hitoshi. 2004. 'Complementary and alternative medicine in Japan: Imitation and originality', *Focus on Alternative and Complementary Therapies* 9: 3–4.

Yang, Joshua. 2010. 'Contextualizing immigrant access to health resources', *Journal of Immigrant Minority Health* 12 (3): 340–53.

Yeoh, Brenda & Katie Willis. 2005. 'Singaporean and British transmigrants in China and the cultural politics of "Contact Zones"', *Journal of Ethnic and Migration Studies* 31 (2): 269–85.

Yu, F., T. Takahashi, J. Moriya, K. Kawaura, J. Yamakawa, K. Kusaka, T. Itoh, S. Morimoto, N. Yamaguchi & T. Kanda. 2006. 'Traditional Chinese Medicine and Kampo: A review from the distant past for the future', *The Journal of International Medical Research* 34: 231–9.

Yuval-Davis, Nira, Floya Anthias & Eleonore Kofman. 2005. 'Secure borders and safe haven and the gendered politics of belonging: Beyond social cohesion', *Ethnic and Racial Studies* 28 (3): 513–35.

Zinner, Michael & Kevin Loughlin. 2009. 'The evolution of health care in America', *Urologic Clinics of North America* 36: 1–10.

Index

acculturation 20, 38
Affordable Care Act 32, 43–4, 46, 49–51, 70, 74, 76, 142, 183
    repeal 32, 50, 70, 74
allopathic (*see* biomedicine)
alternative medicine 33, 35–6, 104–9, 114–15, 117, 164, 176, 180
    acupuncture 105, 107–8, 117, 164
    Ayurveda 33, 36, 104–8, 117, 164
    chiropractor 106–8, 164
    herbal remedies 33, 36, 104, 107–8, 117, 164, 170
    homeopathy 33, 36, 104–8, 117, 153, 164
    hydrotherapy 105
    Kampo 33, 105–8, 117
    moxibustion 105, 117
    naturopathy 105, 107–8
    osteopath 107–8
    Siddha 105
    Unani-Tibb 105
    Yoga 105
antibiotics 77, 101–3, 153, 159

barriers
    cultural barriers 124, 140, 144, 146, 158, 183
    financial barriers 134, 156, 158, 165
    linguistic barriers 100, 123–5, 145–6, 156, 159, 162, 172
belonging 7, 123, 137, 146, 186
biomedicine 10, 75, 78, 81, 95–8, 101, 104–5, 114, 116–17, 187
biopower 95, 97, 116

common sense 95, 134–5, 137–9, 143, 186
complementary medicine (*see* alternative medicine)
corpora
    COCA 34, 70
    COHA 34, 71
    GloWbE 34, 50, 74
cost of health care
    fee-for-service 47, 73, 129
    out-of-pocket 45, 52, 58–9, 64–5, 75, 81, 158, 160, 165
    point-fee system 57, 85, 90
    reimbursement 35, 59, 61, 63, 65–6, 75, 85, 131, 137
    spending 5, 14, 45, 49, 52, 58–9, 75, 89, 93, 99, 118, 183

cultural competence 3, 7, 79, 103, 109–15, 117–18
culture
    health care culture 79, 160, 181, 186
    health insurance culture 40–1, 46, 69, 72, 148, 179–80, 185

dentist 22, 24, 26, 56–7, 61, 75, 112–13, 118, 123, 139, 158, 160–2, 165–6, 168–70, 182, 188
deservingness 120, 127
diagnostics 90, 92–4, 96, 114, 180
discrimination 12, 18, 20, 38, 127–8, 132, 157, 178

elite 2–3, 11, 14, 17, 19, 54, 178, 187
embassy 22–3, 28, 54, 61–2, 65, 67, 84, 124, 131, 133–4, 155, 157, 162
employment 18, 21, 25, 38, 43, 48, 53–4, 58, 61–2, 75
expat bubbles 21, 29, 133

gender 10, 12–13, 18, 21, 30, 37–8, 53, 112, 115–16, 149, 178, 184, 186

health belief 41, 109, 114
health care strategies
    alternative insurance coverage 133, 151, 165–6
    delaying health care seeking 7, 72, 148, 150, 160–2, 166, 168–9, 171, 173–4
    insurance juggling 166–7, 182, 187
    medical tourism 156, 176
    planned treatments 156–7
    pre-emigration health care 149–50, 160–1, 168–9, 176
    returning home 38, 122, 150, 155–6, 159, 162, 164, 169, 172–3, 175, 182
    self-diagnosis 150, 153
    self-medication 60, 75, 107, 153–5, 166–7, 170–1, 182
health decision 100, 141
holistic medicine (*see* alternative medicine)

inequality 12–13, 20–1, 38, 43, 69, 116, 120
intersectional approach 12, 18, 30–1

litigation 83, 94, 116

INDEX   201

medical devices 78–80, 90, 92–3, 180
  computerized tomography (CT) scan 80, 90–3, 114, 180
  magnetic resonance imaging (MRI) 63, 80, 90–3, 114, 180
  ultrasound 92, 172
  x-ray 92, 95
medical home 157, 171
Medicare and Medicaid 12, 49–50, 71, 74, 122, 137
misunderstanding 95, 113, 123–4, 146
mobility 11–14, 17, 19, 21, 37–8, 150, 179, 184

nostalgia (*see* preferred style of care)

Obamacare (*see* Affordable Care Act)

physician visits
  appointments 5, 25, 84, 87–8, 154
  check-up 57, 90, 149, 156–8, 160–1, 167, 170, 172, 174, 180, 182
  free choice of physician 53, 55, 57, 79, 87, 90, 130
  primary care 62, 86, 88–9, 114, 116
  specialization 83, 88, 94
  waiting times 87–8, 104, 153–5, 161
postcolonialism 8, 73, 98, 116
preferred style of care 8, 148, 157, 182
prescription 7, 10, 43, 50, 55–6, 59, 74–5, 77, 94, 98–9, 101–3, 114–15, 142, 153–5, 158, 172–3, 180
private health insurance 47–8, 50, 53–4, 58, 60, 65, 131, 133–4, 165
privilege 6–7, 13–15, 19, 21, 37, 40–1, 68, 79, 127, 142, 145, 149, 151, 165, 170, 174–5, 177–81, 184–7
public health insurance 52–4, 135, 165

race and ethnicity 3, 9–13, 17–20, 27, 29–30, 37–8, 98, 109, 111, 115, 122, 175, 178, 181, 184, 186

short-term immigration 20, 140, 174, 185
Social Security 48–9, 71–2
solidarity, principle of 53, 75
stereotype 110, 112, 123, 127–8, 178
surgery 5, 77, 81, 83, 86, 91, 99, 116, 132, 170

traditional medicine (*see* alternative medicine)
trailing spouse 11, 21–3, 25, 31, 37–9, 54, 65, 68, 89, 124–5, 129, 137
transnational categories
  asylum seeker 12, 17, 178
  displaced person 12
  expatriate 2, 8, 11–13, 21, 28, 31, 36, 39, 81, 133, 169
  immigrant 1–3, 5–8, 10–21, 24–9, 36–41, 57, 60–2, 72, 77–8, 83, 95, 111–13, 117, 120–4, 126–9, 131, 134–7, 139–40, 142–6, 148–51, 153, 156–7, 159–65, 167–8, 170, 173–7, 179–82, 184–8
  middling transnationals 14, 37, 54, 179, 185

migrant 1–8, 10–24, 26–7, 29–30, 32, 36–9, 41–2, 46, 50, 61–2, 69, 73, 77, 79, 100–1, 113, 115, 119, 121–5, 127–9, 134–6, 138–41, 143–5, 148–51, 156, 158–9, 164, 167, 170, 172–3, 175–82, 184–7
refugee 12, 178
tourist 12
trafficked person 12
traveler 12, 14
transnationalism 2, 11, 31
  Transnational Cultural Capital 151, 153, 159, 165, 170–1
  transnational health care seeking 8, 73, 149, 152, 170, 172–6, 181–2, 187
  transnational setup 167, 182, 187
  Transnational Therapy Network 151, 153, 159, 164–5, 170–1
trust 38, 43, 45, 58, 86, 94, 123, 125, 130–1, 137, 140, 150, 156, 158–9, 162–3, 171, 182, 186

unfamiliarity 7, 10, 113, 123, 126, 133, 150, 163, 167, 184
uninsured 20, 44, 50, 74, 128, 150, 153, 158, 175
US health insurance
  co-pay 51, 55–6, 60, 65, 68, 128, 139, 144, 162
  deductible 45, 51, 55, 68, 129, 139, 162, 181
  in-network/out-of-network 50, 121, 137
  insured 19, 42, 44, 49, 51–6, 58–62, 64–5, 68, 128–9, 131, 133, 139, 142, 162, 179, 183–4
  premium 50–1, 54, 57–9, 70, 74, 135
  underinsurance 40, 50, 69, 128, 158, 179
utilization 3, 5, 46, 52, 95, 119, 121, 129, 150, 181, 183, 187

vaccine 99, 101–2, 141, 160
visa category 16, 24–5, 38
  A1 25, 28, 39, 55, 65, 75, 84, 116, 132–4, 146, 155, 159, 175–6, 188
  E1 25, 147
  F1 25, 69, 75, 146, 175
  G2 25, 45, 73, 116, 146–7, 176, 188
  G4 25, 39, 51, 60, 62, 64, 75–7, 89, 91–2, 116–17, 136, 146–7, 165, 171, 175, 188
  Green Card 25, 29, 39–40, 66, 68–9, 74, 76, 83, 93, 115–17, 130, 142, 146–7, 175–6, 188
  H1B 4, 16, 18, 25, 39, 45, 69, 75, 91, 98, 102, 116, 146–7, 154, 188
  H4 25, 117, 175
  J1 25, 39, 63, 75–6, 88, 102, 116–17, 119, 147, 160, 162, 166, 175–6, 188
  J2 25, 46, 117, 129, 148, 176, 188
  L2 25, 116
visa status 46, 68, 157, 178, 184

Washington, DC 1, 6, 11, 22–4, 26–9, 38–9, 57, 60–1, 83, 94, 111–13, 115, 125, 127, 132, 137, 142, 163–5, 171–2, 187

Milton Keynes UK
Ingram Content Group UK Ltd.
UKHW011721070224
437437UK00007B/104